ASTROLOGY
IN ANCIENT
MESOPOTAMIA

"Michael Baigent was one of the most studious yet open-minded historians of modern times. *Astrology in Ancient Mesopotamia* stands the test of time and remains essential for every bookshelf."

ANDREW COLLINS, AUTHOR OF
GÖBEKLI TEPE: GENESIS OF THE GODS

ASTROLOGY
IN ANCIENT
MESOPOTAMIA

The Science of Omens and
the Knowledge of the Heavens

MICHAEL BAIGENT

Bear & Company
Rochester, Vermont • Toronto, Canada

Bear & Company
One Park Street
Rochester, Vermont 05767
www.BearandCompanyBooks.com

Text stock is SFI certified

Bear & Company is a division of Inner Traditions International

Originally published in 1994 by Arkana under the title *From the Omens of Babylon*

Library of Congress Cataloging-in-Publication Data
Baigent, Michael.
  Astrology in ancient Mesopotamia : the science of omens and the knowledge of
the heavens / Michael Baigent.
      pages cm
  Originally published: From the omens of Babylon. London ; New York :
Arkana, 1994.
  Includes bibliographical references and index.
  Summary: "A detailed study of the earliest forms of astrology in Mesopotamia
and their far-reaching hermetic influences from the Renaissance to the present
day" — Provided by publisher.
  ISBN 978-1-59143-221-0 (pbk.) — ISBN 978-1-59143-222-7 (e-book)
  1. Astrology, Iraqi. 2. Astrology—Iraq—History to 634. I. Baigent, Michael.
From the omens of Babylon. II. Title.
  BF1714.I73B35 2015
  133.50935—dc23
                                                                    2014048277

Printed and bound in the United States by Lake Book Manufacturing, Inc.
The text stock is SFI certified. The Sustainable Forestry Initiative® program
promotes sustainable forest management.

10 9 8 7 6 5 4 3 2 1

Text design by Priscilla H. Baker and layout by Virginia Scott Bowman
This book was typeset in Garamond Premier Pro with Blondi Sans and
Herculanium used as display typefaces

CONTENTS

✳

PART 1

THE DISCOVERIES

PART 2

THE MYTHS AND THE PLANETS

PART 3

THE AFTERMATH

ACKNOWLEDGMENTS

My gratitude must first go to my wife, Jane, who constantly encouraged me to pursue this project.

Next I should like to thank my colleagues, Dianne Binnington, Nicholas Campion, Charles Harvey, and Richard Leigh, for their ideas, for their criticism, and for their support. I owe, too, a particular debt to Erin Sullivan for finding a place for this book.

I must thank Dr. Christopher Walker of the Western Asiatic Department in the British Museum and Dr. Francesca Rochberg-Halton of Notre Dame University, Indiana, who gave freely of their advice and information in order to illuminate certain dark areas in my understanding.

I should also like to thank Sabine Bauch for her translations from German and Caroline Wingent for easing my recalcitrant prose and punctuation back into acceptable bounds. Finally, of course, I owe much to the efficient staff of the British Library Reading Room, Bloomsbury.

But, above all else, I am in debt to those ancient astrologers who, seduced by the night, gazed in wonder at the endless dark sky, which stretched far beyond the temple towers of Mesopotamia.

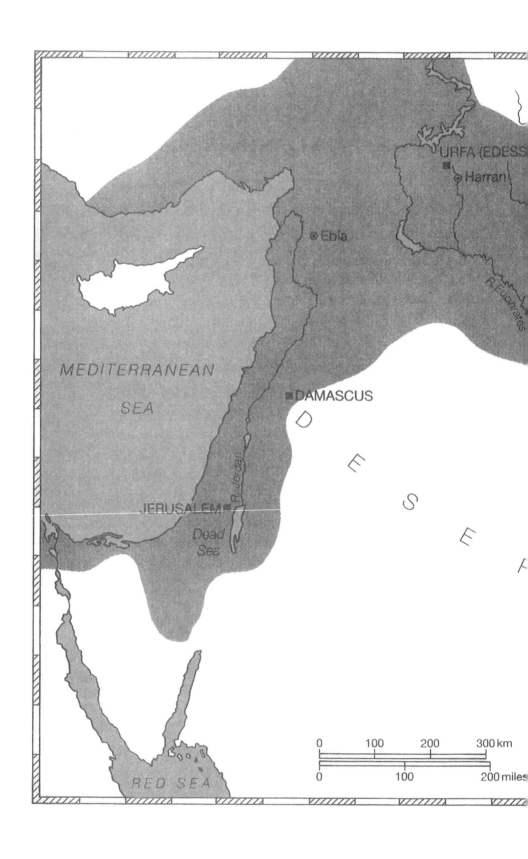

URFA (EDESS...
Harran

Ebla

R. Euphrates

MEDITERRANEAN

SEA

DAMASCUS

D

E

S

E

R. Jordan

JERUSALEM

Dead
Sea

RED SEA

| 0 | 100 | 200 | 300 km |

| 0 | 100 | 200 miles |

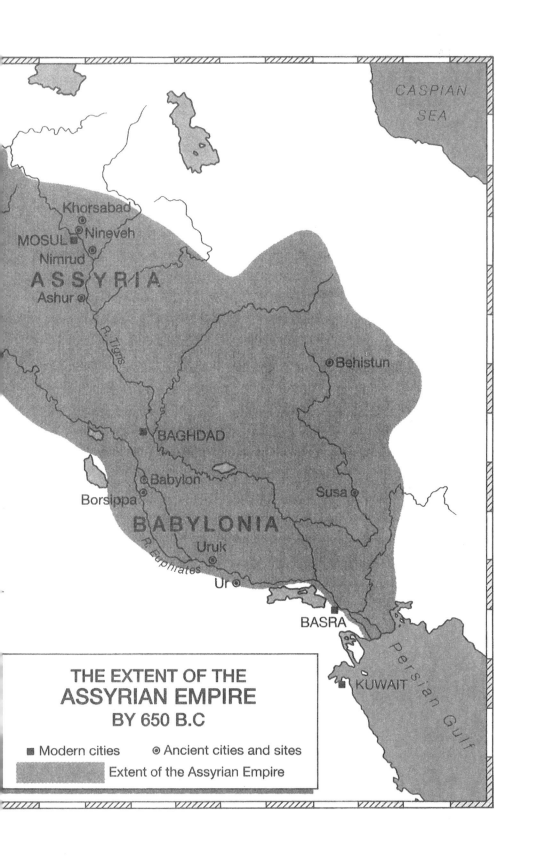

THE EXTENT OF THE
ASSYRIAN EMPIRE
BY 650 B.C

■ Modern cities   ◉ Ancient cities and sites
Extent of the Assyrian Empire

INTRODUCTION

The type of astrology that involves human affairs en masse is termed *mundane.* Its area of concern embraces kingdoms and nation-states together with their rulers. It is to be distinguished from the more familiar modern practice, that of natal astrology. This, proceeding from the basis of a birth chart—a symbolic representation of a particular individual—seeks a greater understanding of an individual's life, talents, and psychological dynamics. Mundane astrology, on the other hand, seeks a greater understanding of the dynamics of the mass of individuals who are gathered together in the "body politic."

The earliest astrology known was discovered inscribed upon the ancient clay tablets excavated in Mesopotamia over the last century and a half. So far as the extant texts allow us to form any judgment, this astrology from the past appears to be exclusively mundane in its orientation. Indeed, the individual birth chart does not appear in the historical record until some twelve hundred years later than the first known codified mundane astrological text—this latter dating from the period of the Babylonian king Ammisaduqa, who reigned during the first half of the second millennium BCE.

The initial object of this book is twofold: first, to explore the state of astrology in the Babylonian and Assyrian empires and, second, to investigate the extent to which, if at all, modern astrological practice has inherited those ancient interpretations and techniques.

However, during the course of these inquiries a third line of exploration will emerge that concerns a particular important religious and magical
aspect of early Babylonian cosmological speculation. This aspect survived
the triple onslaught of Aristotelian philosophy, Christianity, and Islam to
cross over to the West, where it played a significant role in the greatest
European cultural change over the last millennium: the Renaissance. It
will be argued that the residues of Babylonian magic helped to midwife
the birth of the artistic explosion that marked this extraordinary period.

Astrological symbolism depends upon mythology; this book then will
explore the complicated realms of Mesopotamian mythology—a mythology,
incidentally, almost devoid of consistency, unlike that of Greece or Rome.
Because this ancient Mesopotamian mythology was in a continuous state of
change—for the mythology served the state and thus changed as the state
changed—no easy delineation of the pantheon can be devised. However,
despite the impossibility of definitive answers, this investigation cannot be
circumvented, for the mythology of such a nation is entwined with its magic
and astrology; all are reflections of the nation's psychological reality.

Astrology is to be taken seriously. It is important to any exploration of
the inhabitants of history. Despite the self-evidence of this statement,
few historians have been prepared to take the study into account, both
for its own sake and for the insight it reveals into the intellectual traditions of the past. One of the few who have taken the time to investigate
the area, the late Professor Leo Oppenheim of the Oriental Institute of
the University of Chicago, repeatedly stressed the importance of astrology in understanding the Mesopotamian cultures of the past.

Yet, regardless of his insight, many scholars still seem content to dis-
miss astrology as "superstition" or "creative idiocy," thus consciously or
unconsciously depriving this aspect of history of the professional attention needed to reveal its contents. Typical of the hostile attitude so often
adopted is that of the archaeologist Georges Roux, in all other respects
sensitive to the flavor of the ancient Middle East. He seems almost personally outraged at the ancient priests when he writes "while the most

objectionable end-product of the Mesopotamian belief in destiny, astrology, permeated and corrupted the religions of the West."[1]

Commonly, historians, while fully prepared to range widely over most aspects of ancient life, however bizarre they might seem to us today, quite clearly retain a marked personal disdain for astrology. A good example is evinced in an otherwise excellent work on ancient Babylon by Professor H. W. F. Saggs. His book is comprehensive: it fills some 504 pages of text, yet only three pages describe Babylonian astrology—and this in the face of the assertion by a fellow historian and author of a book on ancient Babylon, Joan Oates, that not only was divination one of the most basic features of Babylonian life, but the omen texts form the greatest number of surviving examples of ancient Mesopotamian literature. Clearly something is wrong.

Part of the reason for Saggs's attitude is revealed when he allows his prejudice to emerge: he speaks of astrology as "a folly which, to judge by the space devoted to it in certain daily newspapers and women's magazines, is still far from eradicated from our civilizations."[2] Apart from his assumption that astrology should be eradicated, one wonders about the source of his aversion to women's magazines.

Such personal hostility on the part of respected scholars working and teaching in the field has placed numerous obstacles in the way of other professionals, who have thus tended to avoid it. This has led to many of the astrological tablets being accorded a low priority and thus never being translated and published. Consequently, any study of the subject must necessarily remain limited because it has available as its source material only a part of what might potentially be provided. Fortunately, recent decades have seen a serious attempt on the part of certain Assyriologists to rectify the situation.

Despite the present limitations, an attempt will be made to understand the field, utilizing tablets that have been translated into English, French, or German by such experts as the late professor Ernst Weidner in Germany, Reginald Campbell-Thompson in England, Emmanuel Laroche in France, Dr. Christopher Walker at the British Museum, Professor

Sima Parpola in Finland, and Herman Hunger and Erica Reiner at the University of Chicago Oriental Institute. The latter, who studied under Leo Oppenheim, is continuing the important work of translating the codified astrological series, the Enuma Anu Enlil, a task first begun in the 1930s by the late Ernst Weidner. The most recent work on this series is that of a former student of Erica Reiner, Dr. Francesca Rochberg-Halton, whose doctoral dissertation concerning the Babylonian moon omens from the Enuma Anu Enlil has been published in an augmented form.

A more complete understanding of how astrology developed over the centuries is useful not only to historians but also to those concerned with the wider task of comprehending the growth of ancient Mesopotamian intellectual ability and expression. The last word on this could perhaps go to Professor Parpola, who, in the introduction to his massive translation of astrological and other divinatory reports, writes: "Considering the fact that the roots of modern science are largely to be sought in ancient Mesopotamia, the value of the corpus [of letters from the diviners] for the history of sciences hardly needs stressing."[3]

While some of the ancient Mesopotamian inscriptions and ruins had been cursorily examined by European explorers in the eighteenth century, the true time of discovery was the mid to late nineteenth century, when adventurers who combined bravery, obsession, and intellectual skill began to uncover the treasures that lay buried beneath remote sandy hills. These gifted amateurs had no guidelines to operate by, no precedents to help them with their techniques of excavation and preservation. Inevitably they made mistakes and through ignorance destroyed much that would now be of value.

Nevertheless, these amateurs did, through their excitement and their enthusiasm, bring the process of archaeology to the attention of an increasingly intrigued public, who, in turn, grew eager for more discoveries and provided some funding—however meager those funds seemed at the time to those in the field. Indeed, from such courageous obsession, a great era of discovery was born.

PART 1

✳

THE DISCOVERIES

1

THE AMATEUR
ARCHAEOLOGISTS

Buried beneath the Iraqi deserts that straddle the muddy waters of the twin rivers Tigris and Euphrates lie the scattered remnants of ancient cities, temples, and palaces. For the observer looking across the plains, lying flat to the far horizon where the desert meets the sky, these ruins are reduced now to immense weathered mounds that rise above the barren landscape like giant sand dunes blown up by the wind of a thousand years.

Only occasionally a recognizable fragment of the past remains: perhaps a crumbling tower standing like a wind-torn skeleton, its baked mud bricks shed like scales, year by year, to fall abandoned upon the surrounding sand. Other imperious residues, their lower stages meticulously restored by archaeologists, have regained a semblance of their former power and grandeur.

With a few exceptions, and however enthusiastically they might be presented, the ruins of Mesopotamia are not as immediately impressive as those of many other ancient cultures—for example, Egypt or Mexico. Rather, they appear as forlorn and sad monuments to ancient pride, which, as year follows upon year, slowly, irrevocably dissolve back into the earth from which they arose. The demise of these great cities is in dramatic contrast with the pure arrogance that radiates from the statues of their ancient rulers, which now stand staring blindly across the galleries of our museums, forgotten kings of wasteland and broken bricks.

The overriding reason for the decay of these vast structures is simply that they were mainly constructed of highly perishable mud bricks, which, without constant maintenance, soon disintegrated under the extremes of climate endemic to the area. Yet, despite the inherent limitations of this building material, the ancient inhabitants of the area frequently built structures that were dramatic and awesome by any standard, then or now. Some of the staged temple towers—ziggurats— reached heights approaching those of modern tower blocks. The temple at the ancient city of Ur, for example, exceeded three hundred feet in height, that is, over thirty stories, the elevation of an average skyscraper, but built of mud bricks. To the ancient desert nomads who herded their sheep and goats across the dry plains, these immense towers in the distance must truly have marked the power centers—the earthly home of the gods—or, as the Old Testament prophets never seem tired of proclaiming, the site of all earthly evil, the home of those who competed with the gods.

Today, even though the deserts rule rather than great dynasties, remnants of the ancient culture persist with a surprising tenacity; from these ancient peoples comes, for example, our division of time. Why, we might ask, do we divide our hours and minutes into divisions of sixty? It is not because of any mathematical or astronomical necessity. The answer is simply that the ancient Mesopotamians did so, and we have continued the practice—several thousand years later—presumably because there has never been any great reason to change the habit.

Yet more has come to us across the thousands of years and miles that separate us from our past in the land between the twin rivers. Our children hear the tales of Abraham and Sarah, Isaac and Rebecca, of a man who worked without payment for seven years only to gain the wrong woman in marriage, of Nimrod the hunter, of kings, of warriors with shining swords and burnished armor, and of diviners who lived in the temples of Babylon and Ur, cities of the desert plains.

The symbolism of Western religions, too, reveals much that has been transported to us from ancient Mesopotamia. The symbol of the equal-armed cross—the "Greek" or perhaps "Templar" cross—was common in the past, it is thought, as a symbol of the sun god Shamash, although, as we shall see, this cross may rather symbolize the Babylonian god Nabu, now Mercury. The statues of the ancient kings show them wearing crosses of this shape around their necks rather like one would wear a modern chivalric decoration.

Western mythology, as depicted in the Old Testament, also has its roots firmly embedded in the sandy plains and cities of Mesopotamia. Both the creation story and the record of the great flood have been found preserved in very early literature discovered by archaeologists. These predate, by a millennium or more, the records of the Hebrew scribes whose romanticized and garbled history forms so much of our sacred literature.

The traveler in the region today might have difficulty believing that any great cities could ever have survived in these regions—the site of the city of Nippur, for instance, is now but drifting sands, looking for all the world like part of the more desolate quarters of the great Arabian Desert. Nevertheless, it is clear that in the past these lands were very fertile and well husbanded, for they produced sufficient food and materials for the sustenance of thousands of communities in villages, towns, and cities whose remains are still scattered all over Mesopotamia; archaeologists have recorded the sites of more than six thousand city mounds, called *tells,* and they estimate that the original population of the area would have numbered in the millions. These remains, only a small number of which have been investigated, are testimony that there are many treasures awaiting future generations of excavators.

Amateur pioneering archaeologists risked their health and often their lives to uncover the buried empires of Sumer (or Shumer), Akkad, and Babylon, empires that once stretched from Oman on the Persian Gulf across southern Turkey, then down the Mediterranean coast to Egypt. Four of these pioneers stand out: the Englishmen Henry Creswicke Rawlinson and Austen Henry Layard, the Frenchman Paul-Émile Botta—to whom falls the honor of having uncovered the first Assyrian sculpture—and the native Kurd Hormuzd Rassam. During the mid to late nineteenth century, these men laid the foundations of Mesopotamian archaeology.

The political base for expeditions into the interior was Baghdad, during the nineteenth century merely a sleepy provincial capital of the indolent and decaying Turkish Empire. Early British diplomatic representatives based there had shown a dilettante's desultory interest in those ancient sites that were readily accessible, but little more. It was to take a later successor to this post to begin the systematic work required to reveal the impressive remains that served to fuel British aspirations in the field of archaeology. This later diplomat was Henry Creswicke Rawlinson, who was destined to become the first to decipher the Assyrian language, now correctly called Akkadian. Rawlinson was appointed British resident (a government official) in Baghdad in 1843. However, it was not just chance that took him to this post; in fact, Rawlinson had turned down a lucrative Indian posting specifically to reside in Baghdad. He wished to continue a project that had already assumed a dominant position in his life: the task of deciphering ancient inscriptions he had found on the borders of Iraq and Iran. For archaeology, Rawlinson's presence in Baghdad was to prove vital.

In 1827, as a young man, Rawlinson left England for India and the army. He had already discovered a fascination with languages during his Latin and Greek studies at school, so while serving in India, he took every opportunity to pursue his interest, learning Persian, Arabic, and Hindustani. Following a period of service as an army officer, in 1833 he joined the Intelligence Corps and was quickly sent to Persia as a member of a deputation to the shah. Within two years he was appointed military adviser to the shah's brother. This post required him to reside in the southern Iranian town of Kermanshah. Some twenty-two miles to the east of Kermanshah in the mountain of Behistun, as Rawlinson was soon to discover, was a huge and enigmatic inscription carved far up a sheer cliff face. This inscription was a lasting monument to the hollowness of ancient imperial arrogance, for, despite the fact that it was carved in three ancient languages, it remained totally unintelligible because none of the languages could be translated; all three were unknown. Yet, to the ancient king who had ordered the inscription carved, these languages would have been the three greatest of his world—languages of such lineage, stability, and omnipotence that he could not have thought possible a time when they might be forgotten. Sadly, inevitably, that time was not more than one thousand years ahead.

Rawlinson recognized the importance of the texts and, beginning in 1835, began to visit the site regularly to obtain an exact copy of all three so that he could attempt a decipherment.

Much later, Rawlinson was to learn that the inscription had been carved by order of the Persian king Darius, who ruled in the fifth century BCE. His stonemasons had carved the text into a carefully prepared surface, which, after the work was complete, had been covered with a waterproof clear varnish. The inscription was trilingual, being written in ancient Persian, Elamite, and Akkadian. In the same way that the Rosetta Stone provided the key to the decipherment of Egyptian hieroglyphs, this inscription at Behistun was eventually to enable the ancient writing of Assyria and Babylon to be translated. The script used for all three was the attractive yet curious triangular characters now called cuneiform—from the Latin *cuneus,* or wedge.

The task of copying the inscriptions was not without considerable personal risk. The ancient masons had, upon the completion of their work, cut away much of the surrounding stone, presumably in an attempt to prevent the inscription ever being defaced. As a result, of the three texts, only the Persian could immediately be reached. Rawlinson himself climbed high up on the rock face and, standing on the very

small ledge, which was all that remained below it, laboriously tran-
scribed the lines of cuneiform characters.

It was a task entailing considerable effort and no small amount of
courage on the part of Rawlinson. The ledge he had to stand upon was
only eighteen inches wide. Above him burned the summer sun, and
below stretched a precipitous drop of four hundred feet to the ground.

While not a man to readily admit to fear, Rawlinson confessed in
his journal that this task involved "considerable risk"—a conclusion that
would appear to have been somewhat understated, "terrifying" being
an adjective that comes more quickly to mind. Complicating matters
further was the problem of how he should reach the upper portions of
the text, which clearly could be approached only by means of a ladder.
Unfortunately, a ladder of length sufficient to reach these upper characters proved highly unstable upon the narrow ledge, so Rawlinson was
forced to resort to the frightening expedient of standing upon the very
uppermost rung of a short ladder balanced precariously upon the very
outside of the small rock ledge, steadying himself against the rock with
one hand while copying the text with the other: "In this position," he
wrote in his journal, "I copied all the upper inscriptions and the interest
of the occupation entirely did away with any sense of danger."[1]

Thus occupied, Rawlinson continued visiting the mountain to add
to his text from 1835 until 1837. By this date, when he was posted
away from the area, he had succeeded in copying some two hundred
lines of the Persian text. However, his departure from Persia meant
that his studies on this inscription would have to wait for a number
of years, until he could arrange his return to the area. His chance to
return did not present itself until 1842, when he left the army and took
up employment as the British resident in Baghdad, arriving there in
December 1843. Early the next summer Rawlinson was again at the
rock of Behistun. This time he was determined to complete a copy of
all three inscriptions, whatever the personal risk.

Rawlinson began completing and revising his copy of the Persian
inscription by again climbing on the narrow ledge and, as he had done

before, transcribing the text into his notebooks, which, filled with such precariously and dangerously obtained copies, can be seen today in the British Museum. The short description appended to the exhibit fails to mention the sangfroid entailed in their production. When, however, Rawlinson came to attempt the Elamite portion of the text, a much greater difficulty presented itself, for only on the far side of this section of the inscription was there any form of ledge that might provide some semblance of support. But to reach this, a sheer precipice had to be crossed. Rawlinson's first attempt to cross almost proved fatal. He had purchased a ladder with which to try to bridge the gap, and as the two upright shafts were of differing lengths—an oddity that would appear to render this ladder useless for normal work—he placed the longest shaft across the gap with the intention of making his way across upon the lower.

Unfortunately, this scheme was very nearly the cause of his death. The ladder, a product of some indigenous tradesman, differed from those of Rawlinson's previous experience in not having its rungs firmly secured in their sockets. In fact, they were simply jammed in with no further attempt at nailing or binding, and consequently the moment Rawlinson stepped out into the middle of the precipice, the ladder fell apart, its pieces tumbling down the rocky side of the cliff to the desert far below. To the horror of his friends, who were watching from below, Rawlinson desperately clung to the single remaining shaft of timber before managing to clamber to safety. It is a tribute to his personal bravery that he did not let this narrow escape deter his efforts and persevered until he had managed to copy all of this section of text. He then turned his attention to the third and last section, the Akkadian.

If copying the other texts had seemed difficult, this one appeared impossible. It was above a sheer rock face with no apparent gaps or ledges that might give even a minimum of support. To all observers Rawlinson appeared defeated at last. He decided to seek advice. In the area lived a number of local tribesmen who spent their lives around the mountain, hunting the wild goats that roamed the region. These tribesmen were used to running nimbly from crag to crag in pursuit of game and so were well experienced in making their way about apparently impossible slopes. Rawlinson sought their opinion; they looked at the last section of text and unanimously proclaimed it impossible to reach.

Three years were to pass before Rawlinson managed to obtain his copy of the Akkadian text. A young Kurdish boy was to be the agent of his success. Having heard of the Englishman's interest, in 1847 this young boy appeared at Rawlinson's camp and offered to make an attempt to reach the Akkadian section of text. Rawlinson immediately offered him a substantial reward should he be successful. The next day, carrying a rope and pegs, the boy clambered by his fingers and toes across some twenty feet of apparently smooth rock at the very top of the precipice. Once across, he used the rope and pegs to build himself a swinging seat, from which he made a paper "squeeze" of the entire inscription.

By this time Rawlinson had gained a greater confidence in his decipherments of the Persian and Elamite scripts. He had begun publishing the texts, accompanied by translations, in the London-based *Journal of the Royal Asiatic Society*. The first part of the Persian inscriptions appeared in 1846, the last in 1849. Shortly thereafter, following upon the successful attempt on the Akkadian inscription by the young Kurdish boy, Rawlinson was able to attempt a decipherment of this too, publishing his report in the same journal, beginning in 1851. Although we now know that this work contained many errors, the fact remains that the way had been opened. The Akkadian language could now be read with a satisfactory degree of comprehension.

And what of the vital paper squeeze? It was stored for some years behind a statue in the Assyrian gallery of the British Museum, where, it seems, it was largely eaten by mice.

Interest in these ancient sites was not limited to obsessive and eccentric Englishmen alone. In 1842, while Rawlinson was still serving in India, a Frenchman, Paul-Émile Botta, arrived in the northern Mesopotamian town of Mosul, where he had been posted as French consul. Because he had a keen interest in antiquities, he was, by December of that year, digging into the large mound of Kuyunjik, which lay across the Tigris River from Mosul. This huge mound, more than one mile in circumference and reaching almost one hundred feet in height, quite obviously hid some ruined site of importance.

It is now known that it covered the remains of ancient Nineveh—once the royal capital of Assyria—and contained the royal palace of King Ashurbanipal, who reigned from 668 to 627 BCE, and his father, Esarhaddon, 680 to 669 BCE. However, at the beginning, while Botta pursued his digging into the mound with some enthusiasm, he found nothing worthy of his efforts, nothing that would lead him to suspect the existence of the treasures that were eventually to be uncovered there. He continued unsuccessfully until, increasingly frustrated, he finally despaired of the site and decided, in early 1843, to act upon the advice of a villager from the north, who had insisted that many complete bricks bearing strange inscriptions could be easily picked up at his home village, Khorsabad. In consequence, Botta brought his digging at Kuyunjik to a halt and in March of that year transferred his attention to his informant's village.

Almost immediately, even before Botta himself arrived on the site, his workmen found walls covered with the remains of reliefs and inscriptions. Botta, by now very short of time, rushed to the site and quickly sketched all the figures that the excavations had revealed. Then, upon his return to Mosul, he wrote the first of his detailed letters back to the authorities in France. These letters created a sensation. Botta had, in a very real sense, discovered an unknown civilization. The result was that the French government quickly advanced sufficient funds to enable Botta to continue with the excavation of the site.

As conscientious and dedicated as these early archaeologists were, their efforts were hardly scientific by today's exacting standards. In fact, some critics of their methods claim that archaeology would have been better

THE AMATEUR ARCHAEOLOGISTS   15

served had these amateurs never gained access to the field at all. The feeling of these critics is that it would have been better to have waited another quarter century or more until the science of archaeology had progressed sufficiently to cope with the variety of problems that became apparent during the early Mesopotamian excavations.

This kind of criticism is exaggerated and unfair. It was because of the early mistakes and the desire to do better that the science of archaeology grew. However, the anguish from which these criticisms arise is most understandable. It is certainly true that these early investigators destroyed more than they revealed, despite the early recognition of the major problems that confronted them. Botta, especially, was beset by them. Under the mound of Khorsabad lay the Assyrian palace of Dur Sharrukin, home of King Esarhaddon, father of Ashurbanipal. This palace had been destroyed by fire 2,500 or more years earlier. As a result, many of the sculptures and reliefs had been reduced to lime, and once they were exposed to the air, they rapidly began to crumble. Time after time a dramatic sculpture was exposed, but barely had Botta begun to draw a copy than it crumbled into dust, vanishing forever. For a time almost everything he discovered was destroyed in this way.

Botta, too, constantly faced other difficulties—disease, disputes with local landowners, and constant obstruction by the regional governor, who imagined, erroneously, that the archaeologist was seeking buried treasure. This pressure from the governor eventually forced Botta's excavations to cease until he had finally received his vital *firman* from the imperial authorities in Istanbul. This was his official permit to dig anywhere he liked upon government land, without hindrance. His permit arrived, and in May 1844 Botta resumed work. His excavations continued until the end of the year, when he gathered together a large number of sculptures he had found and shipped them down the Tigris to the port of Basra, where, in 1846, a French naval ship carried them to France. They were placed on display in the Louvre, where they caused a sensation as the first objects from this "lost civilization" to be displayed anywhere in Europe. The other competitor in the field, the British Museum, was not to acquire such works until the following year.

In the summer of 1842, shortly after Botta had arrived in Mosul for the first time, he was visited by a young English traveler who shared the consul's passion for antiquities (if not his opium), and Botta was happy to show him around several local sites where antiquities were to be found. This traveler, Austen Henry Layard, then continued his journey to Istanbul, where he served for some years as secretary to the British ambassador. While carrying out his official duties, Layard attempted to raise sufficient interest and money to begin his own archaeological research. He was fortunate in that Botta had retained a liking for him, so much so that, following the dramatic initial discoveries at Khorsabad leading to the dispatch to Paris that was to galvanize French official-dom into supporting his excavations, Botta forwarded instructions that Layard was to be allowed to read the dispatch as it was carried through Istanbul on its way to France. Quite naturally, reading this report of Botta's discoveries served to fuel Layard's enthusiasm for his own archaeological ambitions and increased his growing impatience and frustration; he still could not obtain the necessary financial support.

It was later that same year, December 1843, that Rawlinson arrived in Baghdad to take up his official post. While pursuing his own research he had familiarized himself with Botta's discoveries and became increasingly concerned lest the French should gain a monop-oly in the area. Accordingly, early in 1845 he contacted Layard, who was still in Istanbul, regarding the possibility of his initiating a sea-son of archaeology. The result was that the English ambassador to the Ottoman Empire, about to depart on leave to the United Kingdom, decided to subsidize personally a short excavation by Layard.

Greatly excited by this prospect, Layard could barely wait, and as soon as the funds came into his hands he left immediately for Mosul, where he began digging at a site that he had long thought promising. This was at Nimrud, beside the Tigris, some five hours travel downriver. His excavations began in November 1845 and were almost immediately successful.

Layard uncovered several rooms containing inscribed marble slabs, as well as dramatic statues of two huge winged bulls, each over twice the height of a man. At this point, unfortunately, the pasha of Mosul intervened, forcing Layard, like Botta before him, to abandon the site temporarily. Unable to continue, Layard took the opportunity to travel south to Baghdad, where he spent Christmas with Rawlinson. Upon his return to Mosul in January 1846, Layard brought with him as an assistant Hormuzd Rassam, the brother of the British vice consul in Mosul. Rassam was to prove important to Layard. Not only did he demonstrate an ability to manage the often cantankerous teams of local laborers employed to dig into the mound, but he also had numerous local contacts upon whom he could call for assistance if necessary.

Layard's official permission, his firman, eventually arrived from Istanbul, thus regularizing his situation in the face of the pasha's obstruction. Additionally, he was granted the right to send all antiquities that he found back to the United Kingdom. Within a short time he had also been appointed the official agent for the British Museum and allocated funds to help toward the costs of excavation. Unfortunately, then and afterward, the amount sent was simply too little to allow excavation on the scale that the sites needed. Layard was thus, by virtue of this miserly financial support, encouraged to plunder rather than to excavate carefully, for, despite their very parsimonious outlay, the British authorities demanded dramatic discoveries at least on the scale of those produced by Botta. In acceding to this demand Layard was to draw to himself considerable criticism from later archaeologists.

Layard was bedeviled by the same problems as Botta: initially much that he found was destroyed by its exposure to the air. Time and time again in his writings he describes the sculptures and artifacts that he unearthed only to see them literally crumble to dust before his eyes. He writes of one incident that "a perfect helmet . . . was discovered. When the rubbish was cleared away it was perfect, but immediately fell to pieces. . . . Several helmets of other shapes, some with the arched crest, were also uncovered; but they fell to pieces as soon as exposed."[2]

The excavation of the mound of Nimrud itself often proved difficult. Local conditions were harsh: some nights it rained so violently that water poured through Layard's quarters, forcing him to spend the night huddled uncomfortably in a corner. In summer his huts became impossible to live in, swarming with insects, particularly sandflies, along with scorpions. Violent whirlwinds swept over the surrounding land, often causing great damage to his camp. On at least one occasion Layard returned from his excavation site to find that no trace of his quarters remained. A whirlwind had littered the wooden frames over hundreds of yards. All the tents had vanished, and his furniture lay scattered over the surrounding plains. These violent storms also occasionally struck the mound while excavation was in progress. In these cases, Layard writes, his only place of refuge was found by crawling under a large sculpture nearby. His workmen, though, having no such shelter, were forced to crouch down in their trenches, almost suffocated by the swirling clouds of dust and sand.

Work at Nimrud continued into 1847, by which time Layard had become keen to return to the United Kingdom. Before he departed, though, he staked a claim—by conducting a short excavation—to the huge mound of Kuyunjik, that "stern shapeless mound," as he described it, "rising like a hill from the scorched plain," and following this brief investigation, in June 1847 Layard and Hormuzd Rassam departed west.

In August 1847 the first of Layard's discoveries, the carved slabs from Nimrud, were placed on display in the British Museum, where, like the Paris sculptures the year before, they created considerable public excitement and enthusiasm. Popular interest in ancient Mesopotamia ran high; it was fueled first by these displayed treasures and, two years later, by the publication of Layard's book, *Nineveh and Its Remains*. This work caught the imagination of the British public and went through four editions in five months. As a result of this publicity, further funds were made available by the authorities of the British Museum, although, as before, they were barely sufficient for the task of excavation.

Despite his public success Layard was reluctant to return to the Middle East. Nevertheless, by the end of 1849, he and Rassam were again in Mosul preparing for another season's excavation. By a chance encounter during his passage through Istanbul, Layard had managed to consolidate his concession at Kuyunjik, which site, being privately owned, was not in fact covered by the rights allocated in his official permit. The owner of the mound happened to be in Istanbul in the throes of some severe financial difficulties and was grateful when Layard offered assistance. In return Layard was given all rights of excavation on the mound.

Layard's second expedition saw a shift away from an emphasis on dramatic sculptures and toward a greater concern with inscriptions. This reorientation had come about through the increased confidence with which these ancient texts could be read, a confidence that owed much to the work of Rawlinson, who had begun publishing his translations three years earlier, in 1846. In addition Rawlinson, armed with £3,000 of the British Museum's money, in 1849 returned to Iraq, where he conducted excavations until 1855.

The result of this increased effort was that, with an increasing accuracy, the ancient history of Mesopotamia was being pieced together. This was to have important consequences not only in the field of history but also in that of religion. Much was being discovered that appeared to offer parallels to certain Old Testament stories, and this began to excite biblical scholars; simultaneously, a number of very strange texts were being unearthed, texts that spoke of magic, of astrology, and of other, often bizarre, forms of divination.

A sense that mystery and hidden occult practices were contained in these ancient texts began to seep out from the world of scholarship into the receptive minds of a public already intrigued by the strange world of the occult, as promulgated in the nineteenth century by such figures as Éliphas Lévi, Paul Christian, Papus, and Joséphin Péladan in France, along with Edward Bulwer-Lytton and later Madame Blavatsky with her Theosophical Society in Britain.

✳

On his second expedition of 1849, Layard began excavating the mound of Kuyunjik and discovered beneath it one of the palaces used by a king mentioned in the Old Testament, Sennacherib, who invaded Israel around 700 BCE.[3] This discovery of evidence establishing the existence of a biblical figure, together with relics and chronicles of his time, drew religious criticism firmly into the field of archaeology and was to entice into it those who sought above all to "prove" the truth of the Bible. In this palace was the first of the libraries that were to be discovered in the mound. Layard removed many thousands of inscribed cuneiform tablets, which were forwarded to the British Museum for translation.

As well as his concerns with Kuyunjik, Layard was simultaneously maintaining an excavation at Nimrud, farther south. Yet, despite his growing success in archaeology, he was becoming increasingly dissatisfied with life in the East. In April of 1851 he left again for the United Kingdom, vowing never to return to the deserts of Mesopotamia. He had had enough of the poor conditions and the constant problems.

Upon his return to the United Kingdom, Layard began a new career as a member of Parliament. In 1852 he was appointed undersecretary of state for foreign affairs. He also later served as ambassador to Madrid and then to Istanbul. In 1878, during his service in the latter post, he was knighted. Yet, true to his vow, he never returned to Mesopotamia.

2

THE SCRAMBLE FOR ANTIQUITIES

The latter half of the nineteenth century was unfortunately character-
ized by an undignified scramble for antiquities, a scramble in which
the representatives of all the countries in the field were involved. It
is a period that no one country can truly be proud of. Their teams of
archaeologists vied with each other for the antiquities, and their workers at times came near to open warfare in disputes over digging rights
or ownership of discoveries.

These problems emerged from the very beginning. They were an
inevitable and predictable consequence of both the British and the
French archaeologists holding Ottoman firmans granting the right
of excavation "in any ground belonging to the state." These permits,
simultaneously comprehensive and vague, formed the basis of continual
conflict between the opposing interests.

The beginning of this period was marked by the greatest debacle
in the history of Assyrian archaeology—the disaster on the Tigris in
1855. In the spring of that year most of the antiquities found by Botta
at Khorsabad, filling around 120 cases, together with some sixty-eight
cases of reliefs from Kuyunjik donated by Rawlinson, eighty cases of

antiquities for the Prussian government, and all the results of a French expedition to Babylon, were being shipped on rafts to the port of Basra, where they were to be transported to France. Near the head of the Shatt al-Arab waterway these rafts were attacked by local tribesmen, who were convinced that the archaeologists were transporting great treasures. Having boarded the rafts and broken open the packing cases, the tribesmen, finding merely stone statues and reliefs, became infuriated. In great anger they tossed all the antiquities overboard. Only two rafts managed to escape and reach Basra with their cargoes intact. Despite considerable effort, the recovery of the objects from the riverbed proved unsuccessful; the antiquities were lost. It was a galling end for the efforts of the French team.

The man who lost most was the French archaeologist Victor Place. Since 1851 he had led the renewed expeditions to Khorsabad, but unfortunately he had never managed to achieve any form of cordial relationship with the local people, with the consequence that the French team rapidly earned themselves a reputation for deviousness in their transactions, despite the fact that the wages they paid were more liberal than those offered by the British. The French position was additionally complicated by their propensity for displaying a certain flamboyant temperament, an attitude that did little to advance their cause. At one stage, for example, a member of the French team, overexcited by some discoveries he had made, shot and killed the local sheikh. The archaeologist supposed, apparently, that the sheikh was intending to murder him for the antiquities that had been discovered. One writer records sarcastically: "the natives, who had always regarded it as a species of insanity that the Europeans should spend their time and money in digging up and carrying off old stones and bricks, were confirmed in their impression."[1]

Hormuzd Rassam reappeared in Mosul in 1852, having been appointed by the British Museum as its official agent. It was his teams of unruly workmen who so often ran foul of those employed by Victor Place. At one particular site the mutual competition erupted into open hostility, and the opposing teams came to blows, scuffling with each other in the excavation trenches.

A major dilemma soon confronted Rassam over the rights to Kuyunjik: he had become increasingly certain that much more of value lay beneath the mound. Unfortunately, the part of the site that he considered most likely to prove rich in finds was already being excavated by Place. The latter had, upon his arrival in Mosul, sought permission from Rawlinson to dig at Kuyunjik—hitherto a specifically British privilege, following Layard's groundwork. Rawlinson generously conceded to Place a large part of the mound. However, once Rassam returned to the site and began to dig, it became, in a real sense, divided by national boundaries. At first both teams managed to keep to their respective areas, and any potential disputes were averted. However, Rassam began working his men as close as possible to the boundary of the French sector, and so the possibility of friction seemed unavoidable.

Rassam's methods were always an extension of his strong sense of independence. He operated in the field almost as a roving warlord. He seldom sought the protection of local chiefs as did the other archaeologists, who constantly found themselves in danger from groups of bandits or wild tribesmen. In contrast, Rassam always traveled with a sizable band of armed men, who generally proved effective at keeping trouble away. On one occasion, though, even the presence of this formidable group was not sufficient to prevent a fight from erupting. It was calmed only by the fortuitous arrival of a detachment of Ottoman cavalry, which just happened to be under the command of a friend of Rassam.

Early December 1853 saw Place's trenches slowly creeping toward an area on the mound of Kuyunjik that the local residents, invariably quietly knowledgeable in such matters, had always regarded as potentially valuable. Rassam was determined to be the first to dig in this area, but forbidden as he was by the "gentlemen's agreement" between Rawlinson and Place, he decided to operate clandestinely by digging at night. Thus, on the evening of December 20, Rassam's team secretly set to work. By the third night of excavation, they had uncovered a large and exquisitely executed stone relief, which depicted a king standing in his chariot, about to leave for a hunting expedition. Further excavation revealed that Rassam's workers had broken into one of the galleries of a royal palace, a gallery that had walls lined with intricately carved reliefs showing scenes of a royal lion hunt. The artistic achievement that these represented was astounding and of extraordinary quality. Today they can be admired in a special section of the Assyrian Gallery in the British Museum, where they have been reerected in their original order. Rassam's men had discovered the palace of King Ashurbanipal, who had reigned over Assyria during the seventh century BCE from his capital, Nineveh—the remains of which lay beneath the mound of Kuyunjik. Having made this discovery Rassam relaxed, for he knew that he could now operate openly by day. It had become an established convention that whenever a new palace was discovered, other archaeologists would not interfere.

It was not long before word of his discovery reached the local populace. It rapidly caused considerable excitement in Mosul, and hundreds of curious onlookers flocked to Kuyunjik to watch the digging. Place, who had been supervising his other excavation at Khorsabad, rushed immediately back to Kuyunjik the moment he heard the news. He could be forgiven a certain amount of anger over what had happened, but he showed considerable good grace by accepting the fait accompli and, indeed, congratulated Rassam upon his good fortune.

There can be no doubt that Place felt cheated out of a discovery that, in time, would surely have been his. Later, in 1867, when he published his lavish three-volume work on Nineveh, Place chose to ignore the role of Hormuzd Rassam completely. The latter too seems to have retained a certain unease about the questionable tactics he had employed to obtain this discovery. In his autobiography, published near the end of the century, Rassam had as a frontispiece a photograph of himself not, as might be expected, by the ruins of Nineveh, but rather holding an illustration of the Balawat gates—today also on display in the British

Museum. The discovery of these gates, at least, had indisputably been the result of his own initiative and expertise.

The ancient gallery that was broken into by Rassam's workers was found to contain something of even greater value than the lion hunt reliefs, something that was to add flesh to the worn and broken bones from the past so far discovered.

The gallery was rectangular—some fifty feet long—and, as Rassam's workers cleared it of rubble, they saw piled down the center of the gallery tens of thousands of small clay tablets, most of which bore the miniature cuneiform script of the period. They had uncovered the complete royal library of King Ashurbanipal, with written records dating from Old Testament times in a repository whose destruction took place during the teaching of the prophet Jeremiah.

All these tablets were subsequently shipped back to the United Kingdom, where they all too often arrived in very bad condition, partly due to the haphazard packing of them and partly as a result of Rassam's rough methods of retrieval. His men would simply shovel the delicate clay tablets into buckets, which were, in turn, emptied into boxes for shipping. Nevertheless, despite this lack of care, many of the tablets did arrive complete, and many more, broken into pieces, were later fitted together so that they could be read. The scholars soon discovered that they had been supplied with a treasure trove. To great excitement it was discovered, for example, that among the wealth of information contained in this library were tablets giving ancient prebiblical accounts of the creation and the flood.

These discoveries, appearing at the same time that Charles Darwin was propagating his ideas on evolution and the Church was having its foundations rocked by the critical approach to scripture of Modernist theological scholars, who were calling into question the literal truth of biblical texts, caused a frisson of panic to move through the conservative Church. As a result, orthodoxy moved to shore up its position. In 1870 the Pope had himself voted "infallible," thus investing his pronouncements with divine sanction and enabling him to ignore actual history when mythologized Church history was involved.

In 1875 George Smith published his revelations of the Babylonian creation myth, which first appeared in a British newspaper. This, along with other discoveries of early Babylonian myths that were so clearly similar to, or identical with, those recorded in the Old Testament, created an intense interest on the part of both scholars and the lay public.

Some saw these discoveries as supporting the critical Modernist approach, while, conversely, others saw them offering a means of proving the Bible to be true, lending support to a literal interpretation of scripture. Vested interests, far beyond the concerns of history or linguistic scholarship, then conspired to create a huge and impatient public demand for ever more information about ancient Mesopotamia. The field grew controversial and, for some, glamorous and exciting.

Adding to the sense that great mysteries were yet to be revealed, the year before, in 1874, Professor Archibald Sayce had published the first study of the astrology of the ancient Babylonians and Assyrians.* Sayce, an expert in translating Akkadian—indeed, an author of a book on the subject—then collaborated with Smith on a new edition of the creation epic, which appeared to an eager public in 1880. During the subsequent two decades, works regularly appeared with translations of the more controversial religious and cultic texts that had been revealed by the excavations: works on Assyrian and Babylonian magic, divination, and astrology. The floodgates were opened upon those very ancient ideas that, it was now realized, had given birth to so many "modern" religious and philosophical concepts.

---

*Sayce, "Astronomy and Astrology of the Babylonians." The earliest publication of an astrological report was a translation by Dr. J. Oppert in 1871 in *Journal Asiatique* 18, pages 443–49.

3

THE LAND OF
THE TWIN RIVERS

As the large number of ancient sites testifies, Mesopotamia was not always as barren as it appears today. In the past, the region, bounded and watered by the twin rivers Tigris and Euphrates, was as productive as any modern agricultural area. It was a region of intensive farming and breeding, truly a garden of plenty, as the Old Testament records: "And a river went out of Eden to water the garden; and from thence it was parted, and became into four heads. . . . And the fourth river is Euphrates."[1] The ancient Sumerian word for the open pastureland of the lower Mesopotamian plains was *eden,* and it is probable that these ever-fertile lands formed the basis of the early legend of human origins.

Modern research indicates that the weather conditions of the area have not altered significantly over the last few thousand years; the rainfall and the river flow seem very similar to that of the past. What has changed is the fertility of the soil: it has greatly deteriorated.

In the past these lands not only produced vast quantities of grain but also supported a great number of animals, both wild and domesticated. Yet the resulting wealth remained vulnerable, for it was dependent upon the steady flow of the rivers. Unfortunately, despite their size, these rivers could not always be relied upon to produce regular and sufficient irrigation. In addition to this, over the years, the water courses of the rivers changed. In many cases this has caused the modern-day rivers to move many miles from those cities that once lay upon their banks. Unlike the Nile, for instance, with its regular flooding of the Egyptian farmlands with rich mud from the upper regions, the twin rivers of Mesopotamia were highly unpredictable. One year they might flood disastrously, causing immense damage to both crops and water-control mechanisms; the next year there might be an equally destructive drought. It has been observed that Mesopotamia seems to hang forever in the balance between a desert and a swamp.

It was always important, then, from very early times, to seek some reliable method of controlling the supply of water for the needs of irrigation. Although some rain did fall in the south—about ten inches per year, the same as in modern times—this was insufficient for the needs of agriculture. Early cultures quickly discovered that efficient control of water by means of terraces and channels could produce the net effect of a far higher precipitation. Crops could be grown that, in an uncontrolled region, would need a rainfall perhaps five times greater.

Of necessity then, from at least the fifth millennium BCE, canals and reservoirs were developed. This eventually gave rise to a widespread and elaborate irrigation system covering the entire region. Some of the canals that were constructed in the past were so large that small ships could sail upon them. The ever observant Greek historian Herodotus, writing in the fifth century BCE, records that the largest of these canals, one that joined the Tigris to the Euphrates, was so wide that it had to be crossed by boats.[2]

The result of this highly efficient irrigation system, when in good repair, was the facilitation of an agricultural yield sufficient to support several million people living in an increasingly centralized manner. The waterways tended to silt up regularly, and a large bureaucratic administration evolved to ensure that they were kept in good working order and to construct new facilities when necessary. Unfortunately, like all such national enterprises then and now, the system never operated at maximum efficiency. The thousands of canals still to be seen in ruins were never all in use at any one time, despite the high priority accorded to their repair by successive Mesopotamian kings.

An unfortunate result of this extensive irrigation, coupled with a lack of adequate drainage, which was carried out over so many thousands of years, has been the gradual increase in the salt content of the soil. In a freely running river this salt is swept into the sea; when a river is controlled, dammed, and pushed through canals, the salt remains in the earth, slowly destroying its ability to bear crops. The effects of this process were first noticed during the first dynasty of Babylon. Today, four thousand years later, because of this increased salinity, much of the once-prosperous land has become sterile, its ruined topsoil scattered by the winds.

One of the crucial social changes in the history of humankind was from nomadic hunter to settled farmer, from being a food collector to being a food producer. This latter settled stage in human history is termed the Neolithic and is considered to last until the discovery of the use of metal. Evidence of the Neolithic period is found generally in the remains of permanent communities, of huts or houses, for these farmers, both male and female, had to live a stable life in order to tend their animals or crops. The cultivation of plants and the domestication of animals led to the growth of permanent communities, which typifies this period in history. In addition, by remaining stable, farmers began to understand their land, to learn the rudiments of irrigation and soil fertility and to demand regular delineation of ownership—property boundaries needed to be arranged, marked, and recorded in some manner. The development of ritual aimed at appeasing those divine rulers whose task it was to ensure the continued fertility of the soil can be seen as very probably originating in this period. All the evidence points to this worship being centered upon some unknown and ancient mother goddess.

The concept outlined above is exemplified in the Neolithic

community of Jarmo, which developed in the foothills of the Zagros Mountains on the border of Iraq and Iran. Remains found there have been carbon dated to sometime around 6750 BCE. Even at this very early time, long before the development of writing, the inhabitants of this community apparently had a well-developed religion. Small clay statuettes of a pregnant woman—assumed to be a mother goddess—have been found in large numbers, suggesting that each household contained at least one example. Unfortunately, nothing further can be said about the organization or cultic practices of this religion—if this is indeed what it was. We do not know whether they had linked their goddess to any planet, perhaps to Venus, or perhaps to the moon, and neither do we know whether they had developed any associated mythology. That they had would seem probable, but without written records there is no way of telling. One thing is virtually certain, though: that all the later cults of Mesopotamia, in which the mother goddess took a prominent role, would have had their roots somewhere in the preliterate period, in some Neolithic cult such as that seen at Jarmo.

Written history begins about 3,500 years later, in the south of Mesopotamia. On the flat alluvial plains through which the twin rivers meander in their final descent to the sea, a highly complex and sophisticated culture arose. With this marked increase of complexity arose the concurrent necessity for a method of recording—initially commercial—activity.

The earliest traces of this culture are seen in the crumbled cities of Ur, Uruk, Babylon, and others that date from around 3000 BCE. By this time there were already kings and priests who ruled over a highly stratified society comprising skilled workers, artists, merchants, civil servants, scribes, and all the other occupations found in a cosmopolitan city. Writing had been developed, apparently with considerable enthusiasm, for some 250,000 tablets have so far been found. On these, in addition to records of commercial transactions, was recorded the mythology of a highly complicated religion utilizing many different gods. This southern civilization, distinguished primarily by its lan-

guage, which bears no resemblance to any other known speech, was that
of the Sumerians. It is with them that recorded history begins.

The process by which this culture developed out of the much less
complex Neolithic communities is unknown, for the evidence is sparse.
However, archaeology, despite its limitations, can demonstrate that such
a development did undoubtedly take place. It has been found that every
major Sumerian city arose out of a small town or village built during a
much earlier period, called, in academic circles, the Ubaid. This period
can be dated to around 4000 BCE. Traces of these early communities
are discovered when archaeologists excavate to the very lowest levels, far
below the remaining Sumerian cities—themselves often many meters
below the ground.

One remarkable feature of these very ancient communities is that
they were all, so far as archaeology can tell us, apparently built around
a central temple, which was, without exception, the grandest building
in the town. This reveals a degree of cultural centralization that may
also reflect a religious centralization. And if this is so, then it may be
a demonstration of a process that will be explored later: the process by
which certain of the many gods became dominant, thus creating a "centralized" mythology.

In the late 1940s, excavations at the Sumerian city of Eridu revealed
that beneath the ziggurat, which itself dates to 2100 BCE, lay the
remains of seventeen earlier temples, all built one on top of another.
The fourteen upper levels revealed varying traces of the Ubaid and the
later Uruk cultures. The three lowest temples date from a culture even
earlier than the Ubaid. This indicates that the same site had been used
for religious practices from as early as 5000 BCE. It is certainly possible,
if not indeed probable, that the same religion continued in essentially
the same form during this period, but without any written records it is
impossible to draw firm conclusions. Unfortunately, it is just as possible
that invaders may have taken the city and imposed their own imported
cultic practices upon the area, utilizing preexisting sacred buildings.
Yet, despite this uncertainty, an important aspect of this early culture

has been revealed: it is evidence of the very early beginning of a religion as a prominent, potentially wealthy, and organized city cult necessitating a centrally situated sacred building, thus, of course, also providing evidence of its social and cultural prominence.

Archaeology, then, does not support the belief, popular in the twentieth century, that the Sumerian civilization appeared suddenly and mysteriously, fully developed, upon the Mesopotamian plains, having been transported in its entirety from another, as yet unknown, land. While it is true that there remain many enigmas surrounding this early civilization, no evidence has yet been found that could lend support to such a romantic view of Sumerian origins. Yet, while dispelling this myth, it is fair to point to at least one area of mystery that remains.

The Sumerians wrote about their past; these stories are an uncertain blend of fact and mythology, but they all agree upon certain themes. The Sumerians themselves wrote that they came from the island of Dilmun, where resided the descendants of the kings who lived "before the flood." Today, following upon considerable archaeological investigation, it is certain that this island of legend is in fact modern-day Bahrain Island.

In April 1954 the Danish archaeologist Geoffroy Bibby, having set out to excavate some of the large number of grave mounds on the island, unearthed a Sumerian-period temple beneath a sandy mound. Two years later, having returned for a third season of excavations, he investigated a tell covering about forty acres—roughly the same size as the city of Ur. Almost immediately he came upon the remains of a large city wall. Over the next six years he excavated, discovering it to be a well-planned symmetrical city with an effective public water supply. He unearthed seals and other commercial objects similar to those that had been found both in Ur and in Mohenjo-Daro on the west bank of the Indus River in Pakistan.[3]

Thus Bibby's findings suggest that Bahrain had been a large trading center between Ur and Mohenjo-Daro, with a city as large as any in Sumer. Widening his view, he found associated remains as far afield as

Kuwait, Qatar, Abu Dhabi, and a site two hundred miles into the deserts of Saudi Arabia. This was proof that the state of Dilmun, perhaps centered upon the island of Bahrain, was large, wealthy, and important.

In addition, beneath the surface of the desert, perhaps twenty feet below the sand, Bibby discovered an extraordinary construction. The ancient engineers had built hidden water channels underground. These were walled and roofed and ran for many miles under the sand.[4] Similar water channels have also been found in the deserts of Oman, along with a small Sumerian-type temple.[5]

It is clear, then, that the Sumerian civilization extended across the sea, not only to Oman but farther. Excavations in the Indus Valley civilization in Pakistan have proved contact between the latter and Mesopotamia. Perhaps the Sumerian kings of the historical dynasties did indeed come from elsewhere "before the flood." But from where? The Indus Valley or farther afield? Or could these legends reflect not an influx of new people but rather an influx of a new ruling dynasty or class that carried with it the writing and technology?

In the literature of the Sumerians we find a more recognizable point of contact, the origins of Western mythology as it is recorded in the opening chapters of the Old Testament. The Sumerians, it seems, first wrote the story of the creation of the earth together with humankind in a poem of seven tablets called the *Enuma Elish* (*When on High*). It appears too that elements of the Adam and Eve story similarly existed, but they have unfortunately not yet been found by the archaeologists. Perhaps, though, this story is extremely old. From the area of Lake Van in Turkey come small statuettes of a woman and a snake looking at each other, all one body in the shape of a crescent moon. Is this not a representation of the heart of the story of Eve—that both she and the snake were aspects of the feminine? The esoteric teachings of the Gnostics maintained a legend to this effect.[6]

The kingdom of Sumer was essentially a confederation of powerful city-states each under its own particular king and god, the former being the terrestrial representative of the latter. Interestingly, early Sumer had thirteen city-states—could this relate to the thirteen lunar months? Could this be the origin of the later significance of this number thirteen—often recorded as a group of twelve plus one? Could unity have been perceived as the sum of thirteen parts?

Each of these cities was large, holding with its associated villages and suburbs perhaps thirty thousand people. The city god was considered to own the state as well as having control over its population. This naturally gave the temple and its priests great powers over the available finance and workforce.

The Sumerians were extremely precise in their bureaucratic methods, recording every detail and transaction upon their sun-dried clay tablets. It is from these tens of thousands of tablets that it has been possible to build a rich portrait of daily life in a Sumerian city, for these tablets record details of business contracts, accounts, wages, lists of products to be sold or shipped, and types and numbers of animals being traded in the markets.

To judge from these tablets, all the workers in each of these city-states were organized into various trade guilds, each apparently having a leader. Indeed, the picture that emerges is one of a highly organized, rigidly structured society. This is perhaps the explanation for the success of the great public works programs that built the temples and canals.

The first known royal inscription is that of the king of Kish around 2700 BCE. There can be no suggestion, though, that this was the first royal dynasty; surviving documents are able only to record a cultural pattern already in existence, not its beginning. We can merely conclude from this first regal inscription that by this stage in history, the king of Kish had been recognized as the dominant personality in Sumer, ruling over the entire territory of the thirteen cities.

This dominance of Kish did not last, however, for in about 2400 BCE a distinct change occurred. For centuries another group of people linguistically distinct from the Sumerians had gradually been moving into Mesopotamia from the south and west; they now produced a great leader and, under his command, overthrew the Sumerian civilization. These people were the Semites, and their great leader was King Sargon.

In 2400 BCE Sargon, king of Akkad, built the first great Mesopotamian empire. For the first time Sumer in the south and Akkad in the north were unified under the same crown. This established the political pattern for the next two thousand years. The kingdom of Akkad, in northern Iraq, now dominated Mesopotamia, and for this reason the Semitic language of this newly emergent people was known as Akkadian. But even though Akkadian was a totally different tongue from Sumerian, the Akkadians continued to use the Sumerian cuneiform script to write their language. This is perhaps evidence that there had been a long period of intermixture between the cultures before Sargon's dominance. The later languages, Babylonian and Assyrian, are variant dialects of Akkadian, using a modified version of the Sumerian pattern of cuneiform.

After this initial coalescence, empire followed empire as the different regions of Mesopotamia assumed, then lost, prominence over the region. The period during the great empires of Babylon and subsequently Assyria, from about 1800 BCE until about 800 BCE, saw the methodical development and codification of science, mathematics, and astrology. The result was an established corpus of technical literature for each of the various disciplines, much of which was to find its way into the library uncovered by Hormuzd Rassam in the 1800s, the royal library of Ashurbanipal in his capital, Nineveh.

The destruction of the region began in the seventh century BCE. In 612 BCE the Assyrian capital, Nineveh, was destroyed, and once again Babylon became the imperial capital. This was during the neo-Babylonian dynasty. Then, in 539 BCE, Babylon itself was captured by the Persians under King Cyrus, thus ending forever the great Semitic empires of Mesopotamia. However, despite the devastation wrought by constant warfare and invasion, the region continued to remain fertile and productive well into classical times.

The Greek historian Herodotus visited Babylon following its

capture by Cyrus and wrote an account of the city's fertility and wealth. He claimed a huge size for the city—it was square, he said, with sides almost fourteen miles long, giving a circumference of nearly fifty-six miles. To him it was the most impressive city in the world. Archaeology has proved that the city itself was much smaller than Herodotus suggested, the circuit of the walls being about ten miles—still, nonetheless, very impressive, and if all the suburbs of Babylon were to be included, then Herodotus's account may have been close to the truth.

Time was running out for the declining Babylonian culture. Following Alexander the Great's invasion in the fourth century BCE, the center of the ancient world was to shift gradually from Mesopotamia to the Mediterranean. This process was hastened by Alexander and his successors, who founded a series of Greek cities in the conquered lands. In time these new cities replaced the once important cities of the old empires. Although Babylonia continued to be heavily populated, its power was broken forever, and with the formation of the Greek Seleucid Empire, the administrative capital was moved to a new city, Antioch, founded in 300 BCE near the Mediterranean coast. Subsequently, renewed waves of invasion ravaged the land, breaking down every attempt to maintain a stable central government and adding to the increasing ruin of the old cities.

For Babylon in particular, the beginning of the decline came in the third century BCE with the transfer of administrative power to Antioch and trade to Seleucia on the Tigris, both newly founded Greek cities. The latter soon became the largest city in Mesopotamia, reaching an eventual population of around six hundred thousand.

Babylon's decline further intensified when, in 126 BCE, after yet another invasion—this time by the Parthians—the city fell and was yet again occupied by a foreign race bringing their new gods and customs. But this time Babylon's day was over; it no longer had a population of sufficient resilience, or a position of sufficient importance, to regain its former dynamism and recover. From this point the city began a rapid slide into obscurity and ruin. When in 199 CE the Roman emperor

Septimus Severus entered the city, he found it deserted—the mammoth walls were still standing, but they enclosed only ruins. Later still, in the fourth century CE, the historian Zosimus mentions the existence of a huge "king's park" in the area, describing walls surrounding it and a huge palace with lands standing in the center. This park was said to be well stocked with wild animals for the hunting pleasure of the Persian kings. Historians consider that Zosimus is here speaking of the remnants of Babylon, its walls now enclosing a game park.

By the seventh century CE, wars and infertile soil had virtually ruined all of Mesopotamia, and the administration that for so long maintained the all-important irrigation canals had finally collapsed. As the water vanished from the towns and cities, the population rapidly dispersed. Within a comparatively short period of time, both the cities and the farmland became covered by desert sand, and the world all but forgot the existence of the great ancient empires.

4

THE ROYAL LIBRARY
OF NINEVEH

"The rare tablets on your route that are not found in Assyria," commanded King Ashurbanipal, "seek out and bring to me."[1] Ashurbanipal, king of Assyria from 668 BCE, was well aware of the treasures preserved within the clay tablets held in the temple and palace libraries throughout Assyria and Babylonia. He was surprisingly learned; he was a competent mathematician and was himself able to read the cuneiform tablets—those in both Akkadian and ancient Sumerian—and carried on an active daily correspondence with informants resident in many different cities. Indeed, Ashurbanipal himself may have been competent in astrology because as a child he had received his education from a famous contemporary astrologer, Balasi. A letter survives from the latter thanking King Esarhaddon for the honor of teaching the crown prince, Ashurbanipal.[2]

Ashurbanipal had organized a wide-ranging and systematic search for rare tablets in order, we presume, that he might compile a library that contained the full wealth of learning available at the time. Interestingly, his search was particularly thorough in the southernmost cities of the empire—those that had formerly belonged to the ancient kingdom of

Sumer and thus could be expected to contain ancient collections of long-forgotten texts.

> You shall put these tablets in your strong box. No one shall with-
> hold tablets from you; and if there be any tablet or spell which I
> have failed to mention to you, and you perceive that it is good for my
> palace, search for it and get it and bring it to me.*

Ashurbanipal knew that much of the intellectual tradition of his predecessors had been hidden, destroyed, or simply mislaid. But now legend, history, divination, rituals, dreams, and magical spells, indeed all the literature of the ancient intellectual world, began arriving at his palace at Nineveh. There is no reason for us to think that his search was anything other than comprehensive and successful. Thus, so far as we know, his library was a "time capsule" of the ancient intellectual traditions, and its discovery by the archaeologists was an event of incalculable consequence. Unfortunately, as we shall see, not all of its contents survived, and so we cannot be certain of the exact percentage of the whole these recovered texts represent.

Subsequent analysis by modern scholars of the contents of his library has revealed that his dominant concern was to seek out all "scientific" texts, that is, the ritual and omen writings that certainly predominate—the pure literary or mythological works form only a very small part of the surviving collection.

Nevertheless, by means of such an intensive effort, Ashurbanipal gathered together an impressive library that even included tablets of such antiquity that they date from "before the flood."[3] Certainly scholars in Mesopotamia were aware of this learning from such ancient

---

*See Waterman, *Royal Correspondence of the Assyrian Empire,* volume 4, page 213. Some copies of the Enuma Anu Enlil tablets found in Nineveh originally came from the south and may have been picked up under these orders. See Rochberg-Halton, *Aspects of Baby-lonian Celestial Divination,* page 174, referring to one tablet of *EAE* 20. Identified tablets have come from Uruk, Babylon, and Borsippa.

times, and one writes: "I have studied the antediluvian stone inscriptions which were sealed, abstruse, confused."[4]

Of course, by the eighth century BCE, writing was not only to be found carved in stone or pressed into clay tablets. During the excavations of Nimrud, which lasted from 1949 to 1963, a curious "book" was uncovered. This unique artifact, today on display in the British Museum, consists of a series of ivory "pages" that are hinged together. Each of the "pages" had a slightly raised edge so that they could hold a flat surface of wax. The cuneiform signs were then pressed into the wax. Amazingly, the example discovered contains a section of the astrological series Enuma Anu Enlil, but, as most of the wax has disappeared, it is not possible to state with any certainty how much of the series this "book" originally contained. Proof that this method of recording the astrological series was in use concurrently with the clay tablets is provided in a passing mention in a report from the astrologer Balasi, who states that the quote he was recording came from a tablet of wax.[5]

Wood was similarly used for the recording of information: in the signatures on the tablets from Nimrud it is stated that they were written "according to the wording of a tablet made of tamarisk wood."[6] Presumably, then, some at least of the standard texts were of cuneiform painted or carved upon wood. That their use was early is established by a line in tablet twenty of the Enuma Anu Enlil. We find reference to "a writing board of the 11th year of Adad-apla-iddina, king of Babylon."[7] This year was 1058 BCE. It is hardly surprising that none of these boards have apparently survived the last three millennia.

Among the tablets found in the Nineveh palace library were parts of four, or possibly five, that recorded a set of acquisitions made in Babylonia for Ashurbanipal. These were added, according to the two dates mentioned in the texts, early in 647 BCE.[8] This was a few months after the end of a civil war that had erupted between Ashurbanipal and his brother, the ruler over the southern empire from its capital of Babylon. It is likely that these acquisitions were, at least in part, spoils of war, even though quite a number seem to have been donated by the original owners. Perhaps pressure was brought to bear upon them.

Of interest to historians is, first, that these acquisitions came from private libraries and, second, that not just clay tablets were listed but also the valuable multipaged wax-covered writing boards. In addition, mention was made of single writing boards, and it is these that were probably painted rather than covered with wax. The multipaged texts are known to have had up to sixteen "pages" and could thus hold considerably more information than a clay tablet.[9]

Like modern libraries, this catalog lists the texts acquired by title and by subject. What is surprising is the great number of texts thus acquired: although many of the catalog tablets are damaged, it is estimated that the original total comprised around two thousand clay tablets and about three hundred multipaged writing boards. The names of fifteen former owners are recorded along with, in nine cases, their professions: two were exorcists, three were diviners, three were astrologers or sons of astrologers (*tupsharru*), and one was the son of a priest, which type was unspecified.[10] Of the contents of the texts, the most common was omen literature, in particular astrology and entrail divination. The catalog also records a variety of other texts received in smaller numbers: the Gilgamesh epic, "esoteric" writings, ritual texts, lamentations, medical recipes, dream books, texts to counter witchcraft, lists of auspicious days, unknown literary works, and part of the astronomical book mul.Apin.

One owner donated 435 clay tablets, and another gave 342; yet even this amount did not apparently make up the full extent of their personal libraries because none of the professionals gave up any texts that related to their particular specialist field. Rather, they gave up those they held relating to others, the implication being that they retained those that were of immediate relevance to their work.

The existence, however, of such specialized literature outside the area of the owners' professional concern is testimony to the breadth of their education and learning. In fact, the simple existence itself of private libraries—evidently a widespread phenomenon—is testimony to the depth of the intellectual world in ancient Mesopotamia.

A large number of the ancient tablets that Ashurbanipal's agents collected were kept as they were found, even though they were written in the old Sumerian script. Others were recopied, not always accurately, into Ashurbanipal's Akkadian. In some cases both the antique and the recopied versions of the same text have survived, and it is possible to see the quality of the translation, thus allowing modern scholars to demonstrate that in certain cases they understand Sumerian better today than did some of the scribes working 2,500 years ago in Nineveh.

It is difficult to determine with any confidence how many scholars and officials were allowed access to Ashurbanipal's palace library or to what extent its contents routinely provided a source of commercial and political data. It is important to bear in mind that this library was a royal collection aimed primarily at the needs of the royal administration. It has to be considered most unlikely that any but court officials were ever allowed access. Whether, through such royal intermediaries, others such as city officials or commercial traders could check laws, reports, or standard editions of texts is not known.

Hormuzd Rassam's excavations in the nineteenth century revealed the true size and elegance of Ashurbanipal's library, with its walls holding the spectacular lion hunt frieze; one conclusion that can be drawn as a result is that this long gallery was a room in which it would have been both an honor and a pleasure to study. Its splendor is evidence of the value that Ashurbanipal placed upon it and, by extension, upon the intellectual tradition that he inherited and perhaps revitalized.

As he grew up Ashurbanipal would have become aware of the constant stream of information sent to his father from all the larger cities of the empire. King Esarhaddon not only had his scholarly informants in many of the cities of Assyria and Babylonia but also had a special representative, his "eye and ear" in the south, Mar-Ishtar, from whom twenty-four letters survive speaking of astrology and magic. He served the king well, playing a key role in the rebuilding of destroyed temples in Babylonian cities and in the subsequent "reorganization" of the religious cults.[11]

King Ashurbanipal similarly had a well-organized network of specialized scholars reporting to him regularly. Not only were the various commercial and political events noted, but every astronomical observation of significance was recorded. It is evident that part of the duty of the astrologers was to keep a daily watch upon the heavens.

These reports of astrological phenomena were almost always accompanied by an interpretation that gave a brief prediction of the effect upon the kingdom. These predictions and interpretations of celestial events were, in the main, drawn from their great series of astrological texts, the Enuma Anu Enlil, named from its opening line, "When the Gods Anu and Enlil . . ."—thus, incidentally, informing us that astrology was the concern of these two gods: Anu, the god of heaven, and Enlil, the god of earth, implying the interrelationship of the two realms.

The texts of this canonical series continued over many tablets, and for ease of identification each tablet carried in a special section at the end both the title of the complete work and the first line of text from the next tablet in the series. This was the Akkadian equivalent of a modern book's title page.

We cannot be clear about the exact arrangement of the tablets in the library, as Rassam's archaeological methods were primitive and little was made in the way of plans or records. All we know is that down the middle of the gallery stood long wooden tables or shelves that had originally held the thousands of baked clay tablets, each one within a protective wooden or clay case. Every case was filed for ease of retrieval by means of a small triangular clay tag listing its contents. This was attached to the case by a short length of cord.

The number of cuneiform tablets held today in the world's libraries and museums is immense. Of all types of tablets—commercial, literary, scientific—dating from Sumerian to neo-Babylonian, more than 500,000 presently exist. The British Museum alone holds 130,000 tablets, as well as a number of crates filled with more in the basement that "no one likes to even think about"; the Istanbul museum has about 85,000; Paris and Berlin each hold some 25,000; and the North American universities—

Yale, Philadelphia, and Chicago—together hold some 75,000 more, and this does not include those held in various private collections.

In addition to these there is a large collection held in Baghdad, the true size of which is unknown to outside scholars. Thousands of artifacts were looted during the course of wars in the region. It is hoped that they will eventually turn up on the antique market.

The tablets that concern astrology are primarily those from the palace libraries of Sennacherib and Ashurbanipal found in the ancient city of Nineveh, buried beneath the mound of Kuyunjik. Large collections of these exist, but it is impossible to be sure of their original location in the ruin. The British Museum's Kuyunjik collection of more than 25,000 tablets and fragments is made up of those found by Layard, Rassam, and later excavators, all of whom dug through the trenches and spoil heaps of earlier expeditions. Their excavation was thus very haphazard and the recording of their provenance virtually nonexistent. Indeed, some tablets from Layard's first excavation at Nimrud are known to have been cataloged through error or perhaps convenience with those from Kuyunjik.

In consequence, unless the tablet itself specifically states that it was owned by one or another king, we cannot be certain which of the two (or perhaps three, if we include Nimrud) libraries it might have come from.

Within the Kuyunjik collection are about 3,500 reports and fragments of reports that emanate from the scholars and "scientific" advisers to Kings Esarhaddon and Ashurbanipal. As tablet fragments are joined together this number will reduce, perhaps leaving about 3,000 tablets representing the total of known reports.

Until relatively recently the great majority of these tablets had not been published, let alone translated. Some 1,500, which include astrological reports, were published as hand-drawn facsimiles by R. F. Harper between 1892 and 1914, while the first 277 astrological translations of Babylonian texts were published by Professor Reginald Campbell Thompson in 1900. Harper's 1,500 facsimiles were translated and published in 1930 by Professor Leroy Waterman, but modern research has indicated that his work is very unreliable and should be used "only with great reservations."[12]

After many years of working under these limitations, a beginning was made upon the task of publishing the entire Assyrian State Archives, including a retranslation of the work of Campbell Thompson and Waterman. In 1970 Professor Simo Parpola of the Academy of Finland published the 370 astrological reports that had been identified from the "scientific" neo-Assyrian advisers, and in 1983 he published his extensive and detailed commentary upon them. In addition to this, starting in 1964 he worked with other scholars on translating those letters, which fall into other categories—religious, military, and political—including all the later neo-Babylonian reports also held in the archives.

Of the 370 reports from the astrologers and other diviners published by Parpola in 1970, only eighty-one concerned astrology, astronomy, or calendar calculation. However, of the total number, only four carried dates. Furthermore, the kings to whom they were addressed remained unidentified. Initially, then, their use to historians seemed very limited because without a date they could not be placed in any particular historical context in order to extend our knowledge of any particular period. However, Parpola realized that the astronomical events observed by the writers and described, often in detail, within the texts could potentially be used to date them. Eventually, after much careful and difficult analysis, 231 were successfully assigned to a specific date.

Once these had been dated and thus assigned to the reign of a particular king, a curiosity immediately presented itself: almost half the letters were written in just four years—from 672 to 669 BCE—the last years of the reign of Esarhaddon. Additionally, they were not evenly distributed over this period but were written in "clusters," demonstrating the existence of periods of greater and lesser intellectual activity. The maximum number of letters from any one astrologer during such a short period was the eleven received from Adad-shumu-usur during a two-month period in mid 669 BCE.[13]

Parpola's conclusion about this apparent imbalance was that the reports sent during this four-year period probably represented the normal extent of correspondence between the king and his scholars; in this case very little has subsequently been lost.[14] The much fewer reports attested for other years before and after this period reflect not a lesser amount of intellectual activity but rather that these particular tablets have been either destroyed in the past or not yet found. A rather similar situation is observed in the recording of important astronomical events such as eclipses. These are well recorded, as would be expected, but only for the years 675 to 666 BCE.

The contents of the libraries of Esarhaddon and Ashurbanipal, perhaps numbering, as we have noted, some twenty-five thousand tablets, were discovered in several distinct sections. One section comprised the royal administrative reports—up to three thousand letters to the king from his advisers, including astrologers—which give a wealth of information on Assyrian religious, medical, political, and military life. A second section contained the official histories detailing the political events during the king's reign; here were found not only the relatively durable clay tablets but also a substantial number of clay cylinders containing historical texts. A great number of these simply fell to pieces upon being brought into contact with the air, and thus their information was lost.

Another section of the library held a collection, perhaps definitive, of Assyrian mythology and literature; there were also some two hundred tablets devoted to the Sumerian and Akkadian languages, composing a type of dictionary, and a large section of some three hundred tablets added a remarkable collection of specialized omen texts that were arranged in a canonical series. Finally, there was a group of commercial texts, contracts, no doubt retained for the same archival reasons as would pertain today.

Archaeologists soon discovered that the Assyrians, and the Babylonians before them, were devoted to the various arts of divination. The basis of this devotion lay in their ancient cosmological beliefs regarding the nature of the universe and the task of humankind.

For the Mesopotamians, earth and the heavens above were not separate domains but were two parts of one realm. Earth and heaven were complementary; one depended upon the other, and both were equally important. There was no concept, for example, of earth being in any way "lesser" than heaven. Indeed, while they believed that the omens studied by their specialist diviners were messages sent from the gods, these messages, these omens, could just as easily be drawn from events upon the earth as events witnessed in the skies. This point is made very clearly in a manual for diviners that was recovered by archaeologists: "The signs in the sky, just as those on the earth, give us signals."[15]

The second key point to understanding the attitude of the Mesopotamians is the discovery that, from the very earliest times, they viewed humankind as being, in part, divine, born of the very substance of the gods, created of their divine "flesh and blood." The story of the Babylonian Noah, Atra-Hasis, dating from the early second millennium BCE, explains:

> *Let one god be slaughtered*
> *So that all the gods may be cleansed in a dipping*
> *From his flesh and blood*
> *Let Nintu mix clay,*
> *That god and man*
> *May be thoroughly mixed in the clay,*
> *So that we may hear the drum for the rest of time*
> *Let there be a spirit from the god's flesh.*[16]

The third factor in understanding this view of the universe is the ancient belief that the task of humankind was to serve the gods:

> *Let the birth-goddess create offspring*
> *And let man bear the toil of the gods.*
> *You are the birth-goddess, creatress of mankind*

Create Lullu [man] that he may bear the yoke.
Let him bear the yoke assigned by Enlil,
Let man carry the toil of the gods.[17]

Thus it was vitally important to know precisely what the gods required. This is no doubt why they saw the night sky with its constellations as the Shitir Shame, the Book of Heaven, upon which was written the commands of the gods.

The Mesopotamians saw all anomalous phenomena as omens, as divine communications that might be read by the trained diviner. In consequence, these diviners, members of a specialist intellectual fraternity (called generally a "priesthood," though with no suggestion of celibacy) attached to the palace or temple, devoted their time to the interpretation of such omens drawn from a vast range of natural phenomena. For these experts celestial events—the movements of clouds; the direction of winds or shooting stars; the birth of malformed animals or children; the occurrence of lightning, thunder, earthquakes, or floods—were never gratuitous; all had significance, all potentially revealed the desires of the gods, if only they could be read correctly. And to read them correctly was the task of the diviner.

Of course, while we cannot be dogmatic about anything when dealing with these ancient concepts, as we shall see, such omens were evidently conceived as being but signs of a possible future, not portents of some irrevocable coming event. The future—the will of the gods—was negotiable, was malleable, was never, it seems, considered to be *fated* as we understand this term today.

Each of the various techniques for interpreting omens had its standard texts, its own specialized literature. For example, the texts concerning divination from unusual births were compiled into a standard series called the Shumma Izbu, from the opening line of the first text cited, "If a newborn animal . . ." Those diviners who drew omens from the observation of unusual animal behavior had the series Shumma Alu Ina Mele Shakin ("If a city is situated on a hill . . ."); those who divined from autopsies performed upon the entrails (livers, lungs, hearts, intestines, vertebrae, breastbones, stomachs) of ritually slaughtered sheep, usually rams, used the series Shumma Martu ("If the gallbladder . . .");[18] the medical exorcists had their series, Enuma Ana Bit Marsi Ashipu Iffiku ("If the exorcist is going to the house of a patient . . ."); and the astrologers had their great series, the Enuma Anu Enlil ("When the gods Anu and Enlil . . .").

Detailed analysis of the astrological tablets in the library quickly revealed two important facts: first, that astrology developed over a long period of time, the tablets from Nineveh representing the state of the study just prior to the fall of the Assyrian empire and the subsequent influx of foreign philosophies, and second, that the astrology found in these tablets and in the reports made to the king is what is known as mundane astrology, that is, concerned not with the individual but with the king and the state. Nowhere do any individual birth charts appear nor are they referred to in any text. Similarly, the zodiacal signs are absent, as is any concept of the ascendant, even though both have been integral to astrology since classical times. The obvious conclusion is that they were a later development, forming no part of the techniques practiced by the Assyrian and Babylonian astrologers and thus, should it be needed, certain proof of the long development period of the techniques used by modern astrologers.

The astrologers writing to Ashurbanipal and his father were not so specialized that they did not have a competence in many varieties of divination. The sole exception was entrail divination, including hepatoscopy, the examination of the liver of a sacrificial animal, and extispicy, the examination of the lungs, liver, windpipe, gallbladder, and intestines.

The tradition of entrail divination was the jealously guarded preserve of a separate, skilled specialist tradition. Their art entailed the speaking of a question into the ear of a ram. The animal was then slaughtered and its entrails closely examined for any significant bumps or blemishes. While this can be seen to leave room for a certain inaccuracy, the procedure was designed to accommodate such deficiencies: if the first examination did not provide a suitable answer, the tradition allowed for two further attempts in order that a "correct" outcome might be obtained. While it would seem wise on the part of astrologers to distance themselves from such techniques, it can be seen that, in general, considerable creative flexibility was condoned in omen interpretation, a flexibility that is also found in astrology.

Evidence from later times indicates that the kings were well aware of this process and took various steps to eradicate or control it. The Old Testament, for example, preserves a story of this kind that, however embellished, probably contains the memory of some real situation or incident. In the book of Daniel it is recorded that King Nebuchadnezzar of Babylon was troubled by a dream. He wished to understand its meaning and so summoned all the court astrologers and magicians. He not only demanded an interpretation of the dream, but threatened—should they fail him—to execute all his diviners and to destroy their houses. The astrologers asked the king to describe the dream so that they might give an interpretation.

Nebuchadnezzar, evidently cynical in his dealings with advisers, refused. He said simply that, in order to remove the possibility of fraud, the astrologers should not only be able to interpret the dream but should also know, in advance, its contents. Only in this way, he explained, could he have confidence in the interpretation.

The astrologers and diviners again asked to be told the dream. At this point the king became angry and accused them all of simply playing for time, of being unable to comply with his request. Finally, his diviners confessed that his accusations were correct and admitted that the task was beyond them. They added, however, that no other king would ever think of putting such a difficult question to them. Frustrated, the king flew into a rage and ordered them all to be executed—including Daniel, who, under the Babylonian name of Belteshazzar,[19] was an astrologer attached to Nebuchadnezzar's court. This incident allowed Daniel (or whoever this story is based on) a chance to show his abilities.[20]

✳

Modern scholars have attempted to gain some understanding of the structure of the Mesopotamian intellectual tradition: what it meant to be a scholar in those times. While most of the surviving written sources reveal little information about the writers and their milieu, the reports that were sent to Esarhaddon and Ashurbanipal proved to contain fragments of personal information about both the public and the private lives of the writers. By sifting through these reports it is possible to build up some idea of the life of the writers.

The scholars writing the reports fall into five areas of expertise. First there were the scribes, the *tupsharru*: these were the astrologers—the experts in interpreting celestial and meteorological omens. Then there were the haruspices, the *baru,* who were expert in predicting the future through the study of entrails, usually those of rams. Third we find the exorcists, the *ashipu* and the *mashmashu,* who conducted the requisite magic rituals for avoiding evil or illness. Next came the physicians, the *asu,* who treated diseases by physical means, by use of drugs or other therapies. Last we find the singers, the *kalu,* who calmed the anger of the gods with intricate chants.[21]

Among these expert scholars were two social groupings: those who were close to the king, who had access to him on a regular basis, and those, usually operating in provincial cities, who did not. Scholars of the privileged "inner circle," however exalted their social rank, still did not live in the palace but normally owned houses in the residential parts of Nineveh. While they were famous and highly respected members of the court, they clearly lived in constant fear of the king, whom they continually flattered and praised. It is obvious that these high-ranking scholars were, despite the status of their rank and the importance of their information to the king, powerless to influence any state decisions.

They did not form a powerful court cabal of Machiavellian "king-makers," as has been suggested in the past. In contrast, they fulfilled a passive "academic" role: they existed and held their positions simply to answer queries from the king, drawing their answers from the standard scholarly texts. Virtually all the surviving reports were written in response to some specific query from the king. Among these reports there were none that sought to manipulate the king or his political policy. As the natural tendency of such courtiers is to seek even more power through involvement in the affairs of state, we can only conclude that the apparent absence of any evidence suggesting these practices, despite a wealth of data—albeit from a short period of time—is testimony to the kings' strictures against such action.

An analysis of this "inner circle" clustered about Esarhaddon and Ashurbanipal reveals some remarkable family connections: there are at least three cases of father-son relationships, and one of these provides evidence of a long-standing family dynasty. Indeed, one quarter of the recorded "inner circle" belonged to this prominent family dynasty, which had a continuous tradition of intellectual expertise, including astrology, for more than 250 years.[22]

During the reign of Esarhaddon this intellectual dynasty was represented by the two brothers: Nabu-zeru-leshir, chief astrologer, and Adad-shumu-usur, exorcist both to Esarhaddon and Ashurbanipal. Nabu-zeru-leshir's son, Ishtar-shumu-eresh, followed tradition and rose to the position of chief astrologer to Ashurbanipal. He achieved such fame that he earned a mention in the "king list." It is from him that the greatest number of reports has survived—a total of seventy-two. Adad-shumu-usur's son, Urad-gula, was also an exorcist and physician in royal service, but he fell out of favor and was ultimately to lose his position. Two recovered reports show his father pleading on his behalf to the king.[23] All these experts were descendants of the chief astrologer to King Ashurnasirpal II, who had reigned some two hundred years earlier.

This type of dynasty pertained also to the provincial cities; the scholar Tab-silli-marduk, his father, and his uncle all resided in Babylon and all wrote astrological reports to the king.

Professor Parpola comments: "It seems evident . . . that the important court offices of scholarly advisers were in the hands of a few privileged families, a veritable scholarly 'mafia,' which monopolized these offices from generation to generation."[24]

Each of the report writers, for example the astrologers, would have been the head of a well-organized team made up of both experts and trainees. In Assyria, at least, it seems to have been standard practice for this team to comprise ten scholars because the title of the leader, *rabi esherte,* translates as "head of a group of ten."[25] A scribe's training was long and arduous. He had to undertake a deep study of the discipline's "scriptures," the accuracy and validity of which he does not seem to have questioned. Despite this, these scholars were continually adding to the wealth of knowledge. While many of the predictions of eclipses and planetary phases were based upon old and primitive scientific techniques, others have, upon closer inspection, proved to derive from astronomical methods considerably more sophisticated, methods not found in the "canonical" texts. These new techniques resulted from scholarly work upon the mass of data that had accumulated over the preceding millennium from the astrologers' systematic recording of astronomical details. This process was ultimately to give rise to the mathematical astronomy that typified the fifth century BCE and later periods into classical times.

An added complication for the student was that he had to learn not only Akkadian but also ancient Sumerian. He needed to gain competence in both the symbolic and the phonetic use of the same cuneiform signs—this latter a factor that greatly increased the complexity and difficulty of working with ancient texts. Indeed, these difficulties, by themselves, tended to reduce general literacy.

In each city, a team of astrologers would have been needed to maintain an unbroken watch of the heavens. Such teams were attached to the royal court or, at least, supported directly by the king. In several of the cities we have evidence that such astrological organizations were in operation—evidently continuing their existence over hundreds of years.[26]

In classical times, some six hundred years after Ashurbanipal, Babylon and Uruk were still famous for their astrologers. The second-century CE Greek traveler and geographer Pausanias mentioned that the astrologers, the "Chaldeans," were still resident in their quarter near to the temple of Bel in Babylon even though all the other inhabitants had been moved to the new regional capital of Seleucia on the Tigris.[27] Strabo (54 BCE–24 CE), Pliny (23–79 CE), and the astrologer Vettius Valens (second century CE) all mention the Babylonian schools of astrologers lasting until times close to their own. Their assertions receive support from the archaeological record—astronomical texts from Babylon are known, dating until 42/43 CE,[28] and a solar eclipse table written in cuneiform and dated to 75 CE has been found.[29]

The first millennium BCE saw a number of great economic and political changes, which created the conditions whereby intellectuals could function independently of temple and palace, able, it seems, to hire out their talents to all who could afford to pay. The eventual point was reached, under the Persian invaders, at which the diviners were no longer attached to the palaces or temples. This, in some as yet unknown way, helped to provide the grounding for the subsequent inclusion of mathematics in astrology and for the emphasis upon the state to shift toward a concern with the individual. First came the use of the regular zodiac, then individual birth charts, and finally, around the turn of the millennium, the ascendant—the sign rising in the eastern sky at the equator at the moment of birth.

5

LETTERS FROM ASSYRIAN SCHOLARS

As night began to cast its shadow across Mesopotamia, teams of astrologers prepared themselves for their nightly vigil. Under kings Esarhaddon and Ashurbanipal they were enjoined to keep a constant watch upon the heavens. Not only did they keep watch to record the omens commensurate with the celestial events they might witness but also, after the moon had disappeared from sight at the end of the month, they were eager to observe the moment of its reappearance. The first appearance of the new moon was a crucial "peg" for the Babylonian lunar calendar. It denoted the beginning of a new month. Any astrologer who missed it, through negligence or bad visibility, risked the opprobrium of the king, and that could cost an astrologer his post, for the task of the ancient astrologers was not only to read the meaning of the skies but also to control the state calendar.

Almost one thousand years earlier King Hammurabi had put in place a single official calendar within his Babylonian Empire. This demanded that the astrologers master two practical tasks: that of predicting eclipses and that of calculating, in advance, the exact evening upon which the new moon would first become visible. Yet, despite the passing of a millennium and the concurrent advances in mathematics, a truly accurate calendar was still not in operation by Ashurbanipal's day. In fact, this was to require more than another millennium.

Even as late as the seventh century BCE, the observation and measuring of the planetary movements had remained extremely simplistic. For example, an astrologer monitoring the gradual transit of Mars toward a conjunction with Saturn reported on March 13, 669 BCE, to King Esarhaddon: "There is still a distance of about five fingers left; it [the conjunction] is not yet certain. . . . It [Mars] moves about a finger a day."* This letter is an example of one of the major practical tasks of the Mesopotamian astrologers: to observe and record all physical phenomena from which omens could be drawn. These included not only the celestial events to which we have referred but also terrestrial events that modern astrologers would not think to include, such as meteorological phenomena or earthquakes or anomalous events—a mongoose that was run over by the king's chariot became the source of an ominous interpretation. This event was considered sufficiently significant for the king to be advised against a proposed military venture. His defeat seemed likely.[1]

Information gained from such observations was presented to the king in two general manners. The first was bluntly informative, stating simply, for example, that "Mars has emerged from the constellation Scorpio and directed its course towards Sagittarius. The king, my lord,

---

*One finger is equivalent to 5 minutes of a degree. Hence, the movement of Mars—one finger a day—represents a daily motion at variance to the known movement of Mars, which is up to almost 1 degree a day. However, Parpola computes figures that demonstrate that Mars was retrograde at this time and was moving back at the rate of two fingers, while Saturn was moving forward at the rate of one; hence, the relative motion of Mars was one finger, just as the ancient astronomers recorded.

Twenty-four fingers made one cubit, which, in the neo-Babylonian period, was the equivalent of 2 degrees. See Parpola, *Letters from Assyrian Scholars*, 54, volume 1, page 35, and volume 2, page 61. See also Sachs and Hunger, *Astronomical Diaries and Related Texts from Babylonia*, volume 1, page 22.

should know this."[2] Such a report as this served a purely scientific purpose and conveyed no more than a modern planetary ephemeris. More common, however, are reports that not only present the information but also seek an interpretation of the event, to which was added the requisite political advice. "When the planet Mars comes out from the constellation Scorpio, turns and re-enters Scorpio, its interpretation is thus: . . . do not neglect your guard; the king should not go outdoors on an evil day."[3]

Several letters make it clear that the king himself had earlier requested specific information regarding the planetary movements, the anomalous event, or lucky and unlucky days for the coming month from the astrologers or other diviners.[4]

Yet, despite all this intellectual activity, the king, as the following tablet of 669 BCE attests, could still be confused as to the month and even perhaps the day. "What the king, my lord, wrote to me: 'What month do you have now,' the month we have at present is *Addaru,* and the present day is the 27th; the coming month is *Nisannu*."[5]

These reports contain a surprising amount of information on both the intellectual and personal life of the astrologers; the king apparently fulfilled a strongly paternalistic role and was expected to concern himself with details of the astrologers' domestic problems. In one letter the Babylonian astrologer Bel-le'i, having dealt with the official business of the report, adds a plea: could the king arrange to catch a runaway handmaiden?[6]

The king's involvement in such a minor problem reflected the fact that all the astrologers were direct employees of the throne. The king alone, it seems, could authorize their receipt of benefits or changes in the conditions of their lives. "Send me an ass," wrote another Babylonian astrologer, Nergal-itir, to the king, "that it might ease my feet."[7] The granting of medical treatment also appears to have needed authorization from the king: "Bil-ipush, the Babylonian magician, is very ill: let the king command that a physician come and see him."[8]

These personal additions to the reports demonstrate with some clarity that the profession of astrologer was not without its vicissitudes, its errors, and its falls from grace. The astrologers owed their privileged positions and their means of living to the king; if they fell out of favor they could easily lose everything. Their status appears always to have been insecure, and the fear of failure and its consequences emerge from the reports: "We became worried and got scared, and that is why we have now written to the king,"[9] and further: "In deep anxiety, I have nothing to report."[10]

So perhaps we can understand why, when an astrologer had had a success, he was at some pains to ensure that the king was properly aware of the fact. The astrologer Akkullanu, on July 30, 666 BCE, wrote to Ashurbanipal that "If the planet Jupiter is present in the eclipse, all is well with the king; a noble dignitary will die in his stead. Has the king paid attention to this? A full month had not yet passed before his chief judge was dead."* Another, who was perhaps justifiably proud of his success in correctly predicting the moon's movements—which, incidentally, demonstrates how infrequently they must have got it right—saw the need to drive the point home to the king. He wrote stressing that on the first day of the month he had predicted that "On the fourteenth the Moon will be seen with the Sun" and, as he proudly proclaimed, events proved him correct.[11]

All astrologers were not of equal status. Some, such as Ishtar-shumu-eresh, rose to intellectual prominence, in his case to that of chief astrologer, and enjoyed the prestige and benefits of a long relationship with the king. Others were accorded respect for their competence but never rose to high office, remaining based at provincial outposts and never moving closer to the center of power. Yet others, less exalted in rank, were minor but competent members of an astrological team or but students, still dreaming of advancement.

An astrologer's life was always uncertain. The reports detail

---

*This report concerns an incident that began with eighty-seven days of the hundred-day eclipse period having passed before. Following warnings from Akkullanu, a substitute king was hurriedly enthroned in Akkad. See *Letters from Assyrian Scholars,* 298, volume 1, page 255. See also discussion with dating in ibid., volume 2, pages 304–6.

instances of pleas for support or, more specifically, for food and dwelling space. Such entreaties suggest the likelihood that once an astrologer fell out of favor, he was no longer provided for by the court or the temple—perhaps he was even ejected from the latter's precincts.

The astrologer Tabia, following upon some unknown but significant dereliction, fell so far from grace that, following repeated cries to the king for food, he was officially ordered to go out and make bricks for a living.[12] His disgrace was echoed by that of another, Adad-shumu-usur, who was reduced to begging the king: "As a father I am your servant. O king, my lord, may I see your face as those who are acceptable. Alas! I am dying for want of food. I am forced to beg like a dog. Hitherto I have not been negligent."[13]

The practical side of astrology, the physical observations, was beset always by numerous technical problems. On many occasions the astrologers reported that clouds or dust storms had rendered observation impossible. Their mechanical aids were also fallible: one tablet records that accurate observation was negated due to the malfunction of a timing device, an *Abkallu shikla*—probably some form of water clock—which had stopped during the night, making the astrologers lose track of the passing of time.[14]

Even without malfunctioning apparatus, incertitude and error were always present. Despite the advances in Assyrian and Babylonian mathematical procedure, it was still not possible to predict eclipses of the sun consistently, and this was an important deficiency because these events were viewed with considerable apprehension if not fear. An inability to see such an event ahead risked the king's wrath: "In regard to the eclipse of the Sun, of which the king has written, saying, 'Will it take place or will it not take place? Send a definite reply,' the eclipse of the Sun does not occur at my command. The sign is not clear and I am cast down. I do not understand it."[15]

Throughout history one of the distinguishing features of scholarly life has been the highly tuned egotism, arrogance, and self-importance adopted by the majority of those who rise to prominence in their field. Such attitudes have always led to passionate disputes based more upon the friction of egos than upon the clash of doctrines. To bemused onlookers it appears that normally urbane scholars will fight as though their very survival were at stake. The intellectual world of ancient Mesopotamia was not free from such disputes, although we are normally privy only to one end of the argument. The astrologer Akkullanu on one occasion was so contemptuous of an interpretation that he could not bring himself even to argue its faults. Instead, he wrote back to the king, stating bluntly that "This omen is nonsense: the king should disregard it."[16] Whether this subsequently led to an altercation with his wayward colleague we cannot tell, though it would be likely, because the king would almost certainly have reported the error back to its source.

In a number of the reports translated by Professor Parpola we find details of an angry dispute between three astrologers over a point of astronomical identification. In fact, this dispute was founded upon a misunderstanding. The king, Esarhaddon, had been informed by an unspecified astrologer that Mercury was going to rise the next month. He wrote to the astrologer Ishtar-shumu-eresh, asking if this was correct. Modern calculations have shown that at the time of the request Mercury had already risen. Ishtar-shumu-eresh knew this, having undoubtedly observed it himself. In consequence, in a report dated March 24, 669 BCE, he summarily dismissed the error of his unnamed colleague with the Assyrian proverb: "An ignorant one frustrates the judge, an uneducated one makes the mighty worry."[17] Ishtar-shumu-eresh then dropped the subject and proceeded to discuss Venus.

Unfortunately, the king misunderstood this letter and thought that it was Venus that had been observed rising rather than Mercury. With some concern, the king sought a second opinion: he called in two other royal astrologers, Nabu-ahhe-eriba and Balasi, to give their opinions on whether Venus had risen. Correctly, two days later, the astrologer Nabu-ahhe-eriba reported back to the king that Venus was not yet visible and angrily added that "He who wrote to the king . . . is a vile man, a dull-

ard and a cheat. . . . Venus is not yet visible. . . . Who is this person that so deceitfully sends such reports to the king? . . . Tomorrow they should let me glance over them, every single one of them. . . . Why does someone tell lies and boast about these matters? If he does not know, he should keep his mouth shut."[18]

The same day, March 26, 669 BCE, Balasi also wrote a reply to the king, equally dismissive of his colleague: "As regards the planet Venus about which the king, my lord, wrote to me: 'I am told that it has become visible,' the man who wrote this to the king, my lord, does not know what he speaks. . . . Who is the man that writes so to the king my lord? I repeat: he does not understand the difference between Mercury and Venus."[19]

As could be expected, this dispute between proud experts ended with a blazing row, which erupted in the royal palace itself on March 28, 669 BCE. A report has survived from Balasi that reveals the outcome of the affair. On March 29, 669 BCE, he wrote that "As to the planet Mercury . . . yesterday Ishtar-shumu-eresh had an argument with Nabu-ahhe-eriba in the palace. Afterwards, in the evening, both went to make the observation, saw it, and were satisfied."[20]

Aside from such angry clashes, Mesopotamian intellectual life, like that of the modern world, contained its insular experts protecting their positions with an ancient form of jargon—primal astrologese. On one occasion the king asked Ishtar-shumu-eresh to explain precisely what a certain part of an astrological commentary meant. The elderly astrologer wrote back with a very detailed explanation revealing that indeed Assyrian astrology had its confusing linguistic conventions, which outsiders could not readily understand even if they were able to read the tablets: "As regards the planet Venus about which the king, my lord, wrote to me: 'When will you tell me what "Venus is stable in the morning" means?' It is written as follows in the commentary: 'Venus is stable in the morning: the word "morning" here means to be bright, it is shining brightly, and the expression "its position is stable" means it rises in the west.'"[21]

Not every interpretation was drawn from the canonical astrological series found in Ashurbanipal's library, the Enuma Anu Enlil. Astrologers were apparently permitted to add interpretations passed down in some alternative, probably oral, extracanonical tradition that did not form any part of the official teaching, a tradition of which little is known.

One particular report from Ishtar-shumu-eresh explicitly gave an oral provenance for the interpretation offered. He spoke of the omens derived from an observation of Mars, which first left Scorpio but then, turning retrograde, reentered the constellation. This, he stated, indicated an evil day upon which the king should not leave his palace. But, added Ishtar-shumu-eresh, this interpretation came not from the "series" but "from the oral tradition of the masters."[22]

Astrologers seem always to have been under some pressure to produce a prediction from events. However, on occasion a refreshing honesty emerges in the face of textual silence. One of the reports translated by Parpola states of an observation, that there was "no word about it."[23] Of course, if there had been an omen and the astrologer had simply failed to seek it out then he would be in some disrepute as a result. Perhaps something of this sort happened to poor Tabia or Adad-shumu-usur, who, while in disgrace, previously "had not been negligent." Generally, though, astrologers seemed to be quick with an omen, some less comprehensible than others. Professor Parpola provides one example that, with its tortured prose, comes very close to that of a modern bureaucracy: "As regards the rains which were so scanty this year that no harvest was reaped, this is a good omen pertaining to the life and vigour of the king . . . [who] perhaps says: 'Where did you see that? Tell me!' In a report . . . it is written as follows: 'If a sign occurs in the sky and cannot be cancelled, if it happens to you that the rains become scanty, make the king take the road against the enemy: he will conquer whatever country he will go to, and his days of life will become long.'"[24]

The advice is, then, if the rains fail to come then go to war. Perhaps we can see a practical side to this advice, for if the rains fail, so will the crops. This will lead to a famine. Why not, then, take away a large part of the male population to loot some other city, thus gaining food for them and leaving fewer people behind to share the food from the bad harvest at home?

With all the dire consequences of failure—expulsion from the temple, shortage of food, perhaps even execution (the fate of the astrologers in Babylon spoken of in the biblical book of Daniel)—one would expect astrologers to have covered themselves, to have phrased predictions so loosely that they could escape any blame should misfortune result. They were also under such pressure that during at least one documented period an organized exclusion of unwelcome predictions was maintained at court. Evidence of this is found in a letter from an astrologer to King Sennacherib, speaking of the situation that took place during the reign of the latter's father. The writer states that the royal astrologer "made the following arrangement with all the scribes and haruspices, without the knowledge of the king, your father: 'If an untoward sign appears, let's tell the king: "An obscure sign has appeared."' They systematically censored all unfavourable predictions."[25]

An extreme example of this position is found in one report: the astrologer concerned had already stated that he could not see anything bad portended in the particular movement of the planets that had been observed. Nevertheless, to cover his position he stated that it was impossible for him to recommend any action because, he explained, were any misfortune to occur then he would bear the blame: "Whenever it is that the crown prince enters before the king, when Mars is bright, and harm should result, would there not be a measure of blame to us because of it? He should not therefore, at such a time, return."[26]

Of course, in cases of complete uncertainty, there was always the following escape clause: "In regard to that which the king, my lord, has written. . . . On the morrow I shall send. It is not good to think on this matter this day."[27]

6

THE GREAT OMEN SERIES
Enuma Anu Enlil

The world's oldest known astrological text is kept in a drawer in the British Museum. It is a thick clay tablet, tinged red, rounded at the sides. Perfectly preserved, comfortable, almost familiar to hold, it is easy to imagine it forming part of a scholar's daily life. Both the front of the tablet and the reverse, as well as the rounded sides, are covered with line after line of the precise miniature cuneiform characters so distinctive of the neo-Babylonian scribes. And strangely placed in a seemingly random fashion throughout the tablet are a number of curious deep indentations, created, it appears, by the scribe's stylus being plunged into the soft clay at certain points during or after the writing of the text. The function of these "holes"—some arranged in geometric groups, others occurring singly—remains a mystery. Despite their occurrence on other tablets, archaeologists do not yet have any explanation for their occurrence or of their meaning.

   This tablet of astrological predictions was also one of those excavated in the nineteenth century from the king's libraries at Nineveh. It is a systematic compilation of omens drawn from the movements of Venus, and while this example is a late copy, the original text was written during the time of the Babylonian king Ammisaduqa, who reigned in the mid-seventeenth century BCE. This tablet, known to scholars today as the Venus Tablet of Ammisaduqa, was one of the formative texts of the standard astrological series, the Enuma Anu Enlil—the book of the gods of heaven and earth.

That this omen text was indeed written during Ammisaduqa's reign, as is indicated within the text itself,* was accepted in 1975 by two professors at the University of Chicago Oriental Institute, Erica Reiner and David Pingree, both experts in the history of ancient astrology.[1] This investigation and confirmation of its antiquity simultaneously revealed that the text, by the time it had reached the Nineveh library in the seventh century BCE, had undergone considerable expansion and corruption during the hundreds of years of recopying. Although no original version written in Old Babylonian text existed for comparison, the corrupt nature of the text was exposed by virtue of the amount of rearranging that proved necessary in order to return the material to its true astronomical order.

The omens listed on this tablet are derived from the date upon which Venus is first visible above the horizon and the date of its last visibility before it again disappears; thus, these omens relate to Venus's movement around the sun. Venus completes one such cycle (called a synodic period) and returns to its original position in the sky after something approaching 584 days. At the moment of Venus's last visibility in the east it is nearing its greatest distance from the earth. Then, a little over two months later, it will again become visible but this time in the west. It will then stay in sight in the west for about eight months before it disappears once more, this time for a variable period of up to two weeks or so, before again becoming visible in the east and beginning another such cycle.

The tenth omen listed on this tablet gave the key to its dating. In

---

*The end of the first eight-year cycle listed in the text is given the same "year-name" as the eighth year of Ammisaduqa's reign. Hence, they are seen as identical. See Reiner, *The Venus Tablet of Ammisaduqa,* page 9.

fact, this "omen" was not really one at all; rather, it was a record of an ancient observation of the disappearance of Venus on a particular date—the twenty-fifth day of the twelfth month—which, as it states, was in the Year of the Golden Throne. From other records it was already known that this was the eighth year of the reign of King Ammisaduqa. Having thus anchored the omens to true astronomical events, Reiner and Pingree then noticed that the first cycle of omens, one to ten, related to an eight-year cycle of Venus, comprising five synodic periods, or cycles, around the sun, during the first eight years of Ammisaduqa's rule.[2]

The remainder of the tablet is less clear, due to the corrupt nature of the text, but Reiner and Pingree point out that some of the next ten omens may cover the second eight-year period of Ammisaduqa's reign. However, they also suggest that several omens might not date from the time of this king at all. In consequence, little further information regarding the text can be extracted with any confidence.

The basis of the Venus Tablet is a series of omens drawn from nothing more complex than variations observed in the first and last visibilities of Venus. Accordingly, the omen verses themselves are very simple and follow a set form throughout the text:

> In month Arahsamna, 11th day, Venus disappeared in the east. Two months n days it stayed away in the sky. In month Tebeti, nth day, Venus became visible in the west: the harvest of the land will prosper.[3]

Each of the sixty omens recorded upon this tablet applies to the administrative concerns of a turbulent empire: they provide predictions about floods, the availability of food, the activity of kings, and the outcome of wars. Yet, compared to the other, later astrological tablets, the Venus Tablet is simplistic, less sophisticated in its prognostication. However, despite this caveat, it was clearly popular with astrologers for more than one thousand years after its initial formulation, as its presence in Ashurbanipal's library attests.

The historical significance of this tablet resides in its formulation: it represents the earliest known systematic compilation of omens derived from celestial phenomena. Without any apparent mathematical theory or any sense of stellar location other than the planet's relation to the horizon, the ancient Babylonians linked these simple planetary movements to the political and economic affairs of their world.

Here then is demonstrable evidence of the development of a regular astrological study or "discipline." Beginning with these simplistic Venus omens, the study passed through a long development period before finally reaching its zenith with the Enuma Anu Enlil series of complex omen texts.

However, a little caution is required: it cannot be stated definitively that the Venus Tablet represents the beginning of structured astrology. All that we can be sure of is that this tablet contains the earliest list of codified omens so far discovered. Nevertheless, it must be considered probable that had there been any other early codified texts in existence, they should similarly have been incorporated into the later astrological series. Yet, in the series, no evidence of such texts exists.

We are not entirely ignorant, however, of astrological omens that existed prior to the Venus Tablet. Of course it is clear that these omens must have emerged from some preexisting tradition. The astrology of Ammisaduqa's era was almost certainly built upon earlier foundations but, while no great collections of early astrological texts have been found dating from the pre-Babylonian period—the era of the Sumerians—two primitive texts are known to archaeologists. These are perhaps the tantalizing remnants of an ancient tradition about which we know nothing. Someday, perhaps, the exposure of another remote and windswept Mesopotamian tell may reveal a Sumerian library that gives us the answer.

Not all scholars accept these two texts as "astrological," but a reading of them makes it clear that they achieve all the necessary criteria. What is not so clear is whether they represent an isolated astrological omen technique or, on the other hand, represent fragments of some ancestor of the Enuma Anu Enlil series whose other tablets have yet to be discovered.

Of the two texts known, the earliest and, due to its damaged nature, the least satisfactory, dates from the reign of Sargon, king of Akkad from 2334 to 2279 BCE; that is, some seven hundred years prior to the compilation of the Venus Tablet.

> When the planet Venus . . . an omen of Sargon, of the King of the 4 quarters. . . . When the planet Venus . . . so it is an omen of Sargon. . . .[4]

Despite the fragmentary nature of this tablet, it obviously once listed some omens drawn from Venus that were held to affect the king. In addition, its form suggests something of an ordered compilation of omens, thus providing some argument for the existence of a developing tradition of astrological discipline at that early date. Yet, while it is tempting to point to these similarities with the Venus Tablet, the comparison cannot be taken very far. The information is simply not there; all we have is conjecture.

The second tablet that has been discovered dates from the era of King Ibi-Sin of Ur, who reigned, it is thought, for twenty-four years, beginning in 2028 BCE.

> When the planet Jupiter turns his face when rising towards the west and you can see the face of the sky, and no wind blows, there will be a famine and disaster will rule. As Ibi-Sin, the king of Ur, went in chains to Ashan . . .[5]

This omen records an actual historical event: history records that King Ibi-Sin was taken prisoner by the Elamites.

The true implications of these early fragments cannot be ascertained. We do not have, for example, any idea of the particular intellectual milieu within which these omens were produced: we do not know whether these writers were official astrologer-priests attached to the palaces and temples or were lay intellectuals. Furthermore, we do not know the social status enjoyed by these men or women, their importance to the authorities, or the importance of astrology itself. We do not know whether, at that time, astrology had already achieved the intellectual status it was later to enjoy—that of a regular discipline taught by experts in organized schools. And finally, we do not know how these omens were devised, the scientific or philosophical justification through which terrestrial events were directly linked to the planets.

While hundreds of thousands of Sumerian tablets have been discovered, none, apart from the two mentioned, have yet been found that deal with astrology. Significantly, perhaps, all that has survived—or been discovered—of their astronomy is a list of some twenty-five stars. Nevertheless, these fragments argue for the existence of a systematic technical study of the heavens. Indeed, then, an omen technique derived from this, the records of which have not survived, cannot be considered unlikely. We must conclude that further discoveries in the field could completely alter our ideas about Sumerian "protoastrology."

It seems relevant to add another conjecture: these two examples of Sumerian astrological omens emerge from the reign of two Semitic rulers of the Sumerian empire. Perhaps, in some fundamental way, the study of astrology was an expression of the cultural concerns and the psychology of the Semites, later called the Akkadians.

However, there are at least two indications that the non-Semitic Sumerians might have used astrology: a line in the ancient myth describing the birth of Sin, the moon god, reads, "the fate-decreeing gods, the seven of them . . ."[6] While it has been suggested that these seven are the four creator gods of heaven, earth, air, and sea, together with the divine trinity of sun, moon, and Venus,[7] it would seem equally likely that we have here a reference to the seven visible planets. Describing them as harbingers of fate would strongly suggest that an astrological attitude toward them was current. Similarly, in the tale "Gudea's Dream," a strong suggestion of astrological practices emerges. In this dream, a god and goddess appear to Gudea (an ancient ruler of Lagash) and instruct him to build a temple "in accordance with the holy stars."[8]

Despite a certain hesitation with regard to the existence of a formal tradition of astrology in the Sumerian period, the Venus Tablet is proof that, at least by the first dynasty of Babylon, around 1900 to 1600 BCE, astrology had indeed become a systematic discipline. That is, it had become the preserve of a group of highly trained specialists intent upon drawing, from the movements of the planets and stars, omens of significance to the king and the state.

In addition to this, the tablet has importance for the history of scientific astronomy. Written upon it are the first recorded systematic observations of planetary movements. As a result it is a safe assumption that astronomers watched the sky each night for the appearance and disappearance of Venus. And if they watched Venus there is no reason to suppose that they did not watch the other planets as well. Indeed, it speaks well of the accuracy of their observations that some 3,700 years later scholars were able to use them to date the tablet.

It is likely that the information on the Venus Tablet derives from the efforts toward standardization that were characteristic of the reign of King Hammurabi. This king lived about one hundred years before Ammisaduqa and, having inherited the tiny kingdom of Babylonia, proceeded to spend ten years fighting to unify all of Mesopotamia under his rule, thus creating the first empire.

Hammurabi's rule was notable for its persistent attempts to centralize, to standardize, and to unify: he issued his now famous code of laws, all of which were to be held in common by his subjects in the empire. He also began work on standardizing the calendar. His astronomers and astrologers were thus recording all the celestial occurrences in a methodical manner. It seems possible, in the absence of any other information, that here, in the years of Hammurabi's reign, were laid the foundations of the Venus Tablet, its basic form perhaps drawing upon earlier, possibly oral, traditions.

Not content with standardizing the civil and business life of the empire, Hammurabi turned his attention to religious affairs: he began to tamper with the dynasties of heaven. He decided to change the gods around in order that they might better serve the cause of his empire. He elevated the Babylonian city god, a minor deity called Marduk, to be the new head of the Mesopotamian pantheon. Indeed, all the extant religious literature was rewritten under Hammurabi so that it might correctly portray this god's recently demonstrated preeminence.

This elevation of Marduk to the supreme position introduces another mystery concerning ancient astrology. Marduk was identified with Jupiter, which must have been granted the same preeminent status in the sky as Marduk had in the pantheon. Yet, given this exalted position of Jupiter, why then was Venus apparently the first planet to be systematically recorded as a source of omens? Would it not follow that the omens from Jupiter were of greater importance to the state? Or was Venus chosen by astronomical rather than mythological or political criteria? The astrologers could easily observe a cycle in Venus that was not apparent in Jupiter.

With the present state of knowledge we cannot answer this question. Perhaps other tablets that detailed omens drawn from Jupiter did exist in ancient times but have since either been lost or so modified that their residues incorporated within the Enuma Anu Enlil series can no longer be distinguished from later material.

Of course, Venus was a prominent deity in her own right, worshipped in the area for thousands of years before Marduk. Hence, the existence of the Venus Tablet, perhaps more than anything else, provides a demonstration that this prominent position was never seriously placed in jeopardy by the political machinations of Hammurabi.

The conclusion to be drawn from this early evidence of tablets containing astrological omens is that during the beginning of the second millennium BCE there was a considerable industry, not only dedicated to studying and recording the movements of the planets but also to contributing to a gradual development of a series of ordered groupings of related omens. Each star or planet, once identified, had attached to it various ominous phenomena that related its stellar movements to the terrestrial affairs of the king or state.

Following the initial development, evidence exists for the subsequent growth and consolidation of omen texts. One of the experts in this area, Professor Francesca Rochberg-Halton of Notre Dame University, has made a study of the antecedents of the Enuma Anu Enlil series. She has identified sufficient fragments in the various collections held in museums and universities to demonstrate the progressive development of the astrological "discipline" that reached its standard form around the end of the second millennium BCE. Even in the first dynasty period of the Venus Tablet there is evidence of some systematic ordering of other omens on tablets: lunar eclipse omens are organized into logical and consistent groupings. As Professor Rochberg-Halton points out, the "organizing principles" for the omen texts were established, passed down from scholar to scholar through the recopying of text, and eventually "came to represent a scholastic tradition of celestial omens."*

Further proof of this process is to be found not only within the libraries of Babylonia and Assyria but also in the neighboring kingdom of the Hittites to the north in Anatolia. In 1907, near Boghazköy—a town on the trade route linking Mesopotamia with Anatolia—in northern Turkey, the ancient Hittite capital of Hattusas was discovered. Subsequent excavations revealed many written tablets, a number of which concern astrology. Despite their being written in the Hittite script, it became clear that certain of them at least were direct translations from the Babylonian originals.

---

*See Rochberg-Halton, *Aspects of Babylonian Celestial Divination,* page 9. Note too that an early attempt to delineate the antecedents of the Enuma Anu Enlil series was made by Professor Ernst Weidner in "Die astrologische Serie *Enuma Anu Enlil,*" *Archiv für Orientjorschung* 14, pages 175–81.

Shortly before the Second World War one such Hittite tablet was identified and studied by an early pioneer in the history of astrology, the Berlin professor Ernst Weidner. Containing a list of eclipse omens, this tablet was designated "the first tablet of the series." This, as Professor Weidner pointed out, provided proof to scholars that an astrological series of some form existed at that early time.[9] As Hattusas was destroyed in a sudden attack during the twelfth century BCE, it provides a date by which some form of prototype series was in existence.

These Anatolian excavations provided additional evidence for the development of astrology: among a number of other Hittite omen tablets published in 1956 were many that concerned astrology. Of these, one was found that seems to be an introduction to the Enuma Anu Enlil. In addition, some tablets contained solar omens that later appeared in the astrological series, again revealing at least a small part of the development that led up to the final codification of the "discipline's" canonical text series.*

That Babylonian astrological tablets were found not only in the capital of the Hittites but also to the east in Susa, the capital of the Elamites, is evidence of the considerable reputation that Babylonian astrology must have enjoyed even during its formative period in the last half of the second millennium BCE. Among the astrological works dating from this period discovered by archaeologists was a fragment containing both lunar and solar omens of the Enuma Anu Enlil. These omens had been translated from their original Akkadian into the local Elamite language.[10]

In 1927 the French archaeologist Professor Charles Virolleaud, having discovered the site of the ancient Syrian town of Katna, excavated

---

*On page 95 of Laroche's "Catalogue des textes hittites II," entry number 193a refers to a tablet found at Hattusas, KUB IV 63, which holds part of the solar omens of the Enuma Anu Enlil series. It dates from the second millennium BCE. While it does not prove that the series was in existence, it does prove that certain of the omen compilations found in the series predate the fall of Hattusas, thus demonstrating a developmental period. See Laroche, "Catalogue des textes hittites II," *Revue hittite et asianique* 59, pages 94ff.

the temple he found there and discovered a number of baked clay tablets, evidence of the former existence of a library. The next year three additional cuneiform fragments were found at the foot of the mound on which the temple had stood. One of these fragments proved to be an extract from a lunar eclipse tablet of the Enuma Anu Enlil. As it is known that Katna was destroyed by the Hittites around 1360 BCE, it can safely be said that prior to this date not only had part of the Enuma Anu Enlil been compiled but it had enjoyed sufficient popularity for it to have been carried into Syria. Evidence found during the excavations indicated that Katna had been a Babylonian colony, with its temple, like the originals back in Mesopotamia, containing a library with a number of texts on divination, astrology included.[11]

In conclusion, then, it is possible to state that astrology was not formulated in one intensive burst of intellectual activity by the Nineveh priests. Neither was it fully developed in far antiquity to be received complete by the priests of the first dynasty of Babylon. Rather, it developed over an extended period of time during the second millennium BCE. From the series' origins in the first dynasty of Babylon, it has proved possible to uncover traces of a progressive refinement that was to culminate in the standard canon uncovered in the seventh-century-BCE library at Nineveh. Furthermore, it can be shown that the bulk of this development occurred from circa 1700 BCE, the era of the Venus Tablet, until circa 1000 BCE.

Within the tablets of the Enuma Anu Enlil series, we find certain elements of historical information, particularly in the signature lines, that allow for dating and that presumably reflect the historical periods when that particular part of the series was written, codified, or collated. Also, in the same way that the very early tablets contained textual material now known to be historically accurate—the exile of Ibi-Sin, for example—some of the later tablets contain material that relates to political events of the late second millennium BCE. The oldest such fragment mentions the Kassite king Burnaburias II, who lived in the fourteenth century BCE.[12]

A second example refers to King Nebuchadnezzar I, who reigned in approximately 1126–1105 BCE. The fragment briefly mentions his victorious campaign against the Elamites, which, incidentally, had the important result of restoring to Babylonia the statue of Marduk, which the Elamites had captured generations earlier and removed to their capital, Susa.[13] A third example exists in an unpublished text held in the British Museum, which was noted by Professor Weidner; this mentions King Ramman-apal-iddin, who reigned in the eleventh century BCE.[14] Professor Weidner's conclusion was that several astrological traditions developed in parallel and that around the turn of the first millennium BCE these were combined to create the final form of the Enuma Anu Enlil series. This view has received scientific support in recent years through the work of Professors Erica Reiner and David Pingree.

Reiner and Pingree realized that, as with the Venus Tablet, sufficient internal data existed within the astrological series—specifically within tablets fifty and fifty-one—to obtain a probable date for its final compilation into a coherent series. Within these tablets the astrologers made use of certain astronomical discoveries that scholars had already noted existed on tablets recovered from Ashurbanipal's library. In particular these astrologers were familiar with the astronomy from a text recorded upon two tablets called, from its opening line, the mul.Apin ("the star Apin," which together with the star Gamma Andromedae makes up the modern constellation Triangulum).[15] The first tablet of this work lists certain astronomical events that can be verified; these include details of the heliacal rising—the rising at dawn—of certain fixed stars and the culmination and settings of these stars as well as their stellar positions. This has allowed modern scholars to identify virtually all the ancient Babylonian constellations.

This tablet also contained a list of stars that, at a latitude of 36 degrees north (that of Nineveh) and almost directly overhead, cross the meridian—the imaginary circle running from the zenith to the nadir and passing through the north and south points on the earth's equator. As there has been, and continues to be, dispute among scholars over identification of the particular stars mentioned in the texts, Professors Reiner and Pingree decided to employ the Adler Planetarium in Chicago to project the complete constellations across the horizon, thus avoiding the problems associated with the identity of specific stars, in an attempt to discover which date best fit the extant data. They projected more than two hundred stars computed for the dates of 2000 BCE and 1000 BCE, with latitudes of 32 degrees north (Babylon) and 36 degrees north (Nineveh). Their conclusion was that the astronomical data best fit 1000 BCE, at the latitude of Nineveh.[16]

This result suggests that while the astrological omens had long been studied and used by the Babylonians, it fell to the Assyrians in the north to compile the data into the definitive series, the Enuma Anu Enlil.

The historical background to this period suggests a possible reason for this: near the end of the second millennium BCE the Mesopotamian empires began to disintegrate. The Hittite Empire had vanished; the Kassite Dynasty, which ruled over Babylon, had been defeated by the Elamites. Within a few decades Elam too had collapsed into internecine warfare, leaving the area greatly weakened. In the north, however, Assyria was beginning a period of consolidation and prosperity under a succession of strong kings. Yet, despite this initial success, around the turn of the millennium Assyria also fell into disorder and was at its lowest ebb, being reduced to a state a little more than one hundred miles long by fifty miles wide, all of it surrounded by enemies. Yet, although vastly reduced in size, Assyria remained independent and ruled by the same dynasty. Its revival began in 911 BCE, when the newly crowned king began his long fight to recover lost Assyrian territory.

Perhaps, under such circumstances of both fear and hope, the priests and scholars turned with renewed enthusiasm—or energetic desperation—to their greatest predictive science and sought to compile a comprehensive standard work that would aid the astrologers in their advice to the king. And, if this argument is even partly correct, as the fortunes of the state of Assyria improved, so too would the prestige of astrology and its experts.

✳

The series Enuma Anu Enlil varies in length depending upon the astrological school that produced it. While the number of actual omens is presumed to be constant, the number of tablets varies from sixty-eight to seventy, this higher figure being representative of the series issuing from the schools of Babylon and Borsippa.

It was at first thought that the Enuma Anu Enlil was written in faithful replication of ancient originals and passed down through the years in a set form. More recent studies have shown that this was not the case. It is clear that large sections of the series were subjected to reworking and reordering several times. For this reason, examples of the series that derive from different eras cannot be expected to match in all respects. These internal differences are considered to reflect the differing copies produced by the various Mesopotamian astrological schools. On the basis of these differences, Professor Weidner identified five different schools, each of which—in turn—reordered the omen material: those of Babylon and Borsippa, Asshur, Nimrud, Nineveh, and Uruk.[17]

The numbering of the individual tablets is similarly inconsistent, both between the schools and between different examples of the same text within one school. Smaller deviant versions have been found, and these are thought to represent the private work of individual astrologers. It is thought that astrologers would often create their own tablets containing selected extracts from the series, perhaps for personal use or for rapid consultation. Several summaries that have been found quote only a few lines from one or more tablets, while others comprise technical or linguistic commentaries upon the series. It is evident that certain of these extracted summaries became so popular in their own right that they in turn found their way back into the official canon.

Certainly many, if not all, of the Assyrian and Babylonian astrologers had small personal collections of standard Enuma Anu Enlil tablets in addition to other noncanonical texts. It is perhaps to one of these that Ishtar-shumu-eresh referred when, as we have seen, he wrote to the king at Nineveh that his enclosed reading of the omen "is not from the series but is from the oral tradition of the masters. . . . This is not from the series but is non-canonical."[18]

Fundamental to the modern reconstruction of the Enuma Anu Enlil series were the damaged remains of two official catalogs studied and published by Professor Weidner in 1944.[19] The first, from Asshur, is only partially preserved; it lists tablets thirty-nine to sixty and only occasionally gives the opening lines that indicate the contents of each tablet. The second catalog, found in Uruk, is much more important, for it not only provides a list of the opening lines of every tablet but also gives the number of omens to be found on each. The text opens with a short request to the god Anu that he might protect the tablets from damage; Weidner, in a rare moment of humor, takes pleasure in pointing out the demonstrable fact that this god failed in his task.

Due to damage this catalog lists only tablets one to twenty-six before breaking off. However, even this provides useful information about the Enuma Anu Enlil series. In these initial texts two groupings are discernible: tablets one to fourteen are arranged together, as are tablets fifteen to twenty-two. While both these groups deal with lunar omens, the first concerns omens that depend upon the physical appearance of the moon, while the second concerns those drawn from lunar eclipses. The scribe who copied this particular catalog also wrote down the date of writing—which was the evening of February 24–25, 194 BCE, in Uruk.[20] The author adds, by way of an interesting addendum, that he was copying from an ancient and not very well preserved original. We can possibly conclude that if this was all that he had for source material, then, at that late date, the tradition was surely in abeyance.

The entire astrological series—which has not yet been completely reconstructed—is estimated to have contained some seven thousand omens. The existence of the series was first mentioned in print by Professor Archibald Sayce in 1874, but it was not subjected to scholarly reconstruction until the French professor Charles Virolleaud began to publish his work on it from 1903 to 1912.[21] This work was so fundamentally sound that it remains important to this day.

Subsequently, in papers published between 1944 and 1969, Professor Weidner identified tablets one to fifty from the many fragments held in various museum collections. He found, as we already know, that the first twenty-two tablets contained omens derived from the moon, while tablets twenty-three to forty concerned the sun. Tablets forty-one to forty-nine listed meteorological omens, while tablet fifty concerned the planets.

Professor Weidner's work has been continued by the group of experts at the University of Chicago Oriental Institute. Professor Reiner and others have managed to identify the greater part of the remainder of the series. They have found that from tablet fifty until the end of the series concern is placed upon omens drawn from the planets, the constellations, and the fixed stars. The Venus Tablet, which we have already mentioned, is numbered sixty-three on the Babylon list.

Only six tablets now remain to be identified, but from the numerous fragments in existence it is evident that these all deal with the planets and constellations. There was at least one tablet given over to omens drawn from Mars, perhaps tablets number fifty-eight or sixty-six; there was one devoted to Scorpio; and others to Pisces, Cancer, "the Wolf," and Leo.

In the reports from the astrologers to the kings, sections drawn from the series are regularly quoted, which makes it clear that individual tablets existed for the sun, moon, Mars, Jupiter, Venus, Mercury, and Saturn. All but the last two have had one or more tablets identified; hence, at least two tablets, perhaps more, were devoted to them.

Additionally there appear to have been tablets devoted totally, or in part, to shooting stars, the Plough star, Regulus, and the Pleiades. Meteorological omens are also mentioned, and they include omens drawn from instances of fog, thunder, cloud, storm, and perhaps earthquakes—though it is possible that the latter subject had its own separate tablet. Finally, despite the variations in the format and numbering of the tablets consequent upon the many copies made, the basic order of the omens remained constant.

TABLETS OF THE ENUMA ANU ENLIL

Babylonian Version

Tablet 1: Moon's appearance	Tablet 25: Sun's rising?
Tablet 2: Moon's appearance	Tablet 26: Sun's rising
Tablet 3: Moon's appearance	Tablet 27: Sun's rising
Tablet 4: Moon's appearance	Tablet 28: Sun's rising
Tablet 5: Moon's appearance	Tablet 29: Sun?
Tablet 6: Moon's appearance	Tablet 30: Sun?
Tablet 7: Moon's appearance	Tablet 31: Sun eclipses
Tablet 8: Moon's appearance	Tablet 32: Sun eclipses
Tablet 9: Moon's appearance	Tablet 33: Sun eclipses
Tablet 10: Moon's appearance	Tablet 34: Sun eclipses
Tablet 11: Moon's appearance	Tablet 35: Sun eclipses
Tablet 12: Moon's appearance	Tablet 36: Sun eclipses
Tablet 13: Moon's appearance	Tablet 37: Sun eclipses
Tablet 14: Moon's appearance	Tablet 38: Sun eclipses?
Tablet 15: Moon eclipses	Tablet 39: Sun/meteorological
Tablet 16: Moon eclipses	Tablet 40: Sun/meteorological
Tablet 17: Moon eclipses	Tablet 41: Sun/meteorological
Tablet 18: Moon eclipses	Tablet 42: Clouds
Tablet 19: Moon eclipses	Tablet 43: Lightning
Tablet 20: Moon eclipses	Tablet 44: Thunder
Tablet 21: Moon eclipses	Tablet 45: Thunder
Tablet 22: Moon eclipses	Tablet 46: Thunder/Pleiades
Tablet 23: Sun's appearance	Tablet 47: Meteorological?
Tablet 24: Sun's appearance	Tablet 48: Meteorological?

Tablet 49: Winds?	Tablet 60: Venus
Tablet 50: Fixed stars	Tablet 61: Venus
Tablet 51: Fixed stars	Tablet 62: Venus
Tablet 52: Constellation Iku*	Tablet 63: Venus Tablet
Tablet 53: Pleiades	Tablet 64: Jupiter
Tablet 54: Constellations?	Tablet 65: Jupiter
Tablet 55: Constellations	Tablet 66: Mars?
Tablet 56: Mars	Tablet 67: ?
Tablet 57: Mars?	Tablet 68: ?
Tablet 58: Mars?	Tablet 69: ?
Tablet 59: Venus	Tablet 70: ?

*"The Field," consisting of α, β, and γ Pegasi together with α Andromedae. See Reiner, *Enuma Anu Enlil, Tablets 50–51*, page 11.

Implicit within these tablets is a particular and distinctive plan of the heavens that is quite unlike that used today. This ancient prezodiacal concept of celestial geography finds its standard source in the text that we have already mentioned, the mul.Apin.

This astronomical work details a primitive method for locating the moon and planets in the sky. It uses the constellations as a reference point from which the daily movement of the moon and planets can be charted rather than, as today, relating their movement to the ecliptic. Obviously, this resulted in a quite different system from that derived from the use of a fixed zodiac of twelve constellations that straddle the ecliptic. However, as evidence of the influence of this ancient methodology, the twelve constellations used today were among those earlier used as reference points.

In addition to the modern twelve constellations the ancient astronomers used the Pleiades, Orion, Perseus, Auriga, Shinunutu (yet to be identified), "the Swallow" (the western fish of Pisces with part of the western section of Pegasus), and Anunitu (the eastern fish of Pisces).[22]

Additionally these and the fixed stars are further divided into three groups, called "paths": those of Anu, Enlil, and Ea, the gods of heaven, earth, and water.

According to the research of Professor Reiner, these paths were not visualized as three great bands in the sky rather like our present day ecliptic, but they were seen as three divisions of the eastern horizon through which the stars rose.* Thus, these paths could equally be termed *ways* or *gates*.

Facing the eastern horizon, the central path (close in fact to the modern equator) was that of Anu; to the south was the path of Ea; and to the north was the path of Enlil. Each path allowed the entry of "their" stars into the visible hemisphere.

While the omens themselves related the planets, the stars, and the constellations to one another, these relationships remained devoid of any mathematical expression. The terms used to define these stellar associations were all very imprecise. Planets, for example, were seen in conjunction or in opposition, these terms implying simply that they were seen as being close to one another or far apart. Aspects between planets, in the modern sense, were never mentioned.

However, the importance of these connections lay not in the mathematical or observational precision with which such stellar proximity was measured but rather in the relationship itself, for it is the interpretations made from these relationships that form the bases of the Enuma Anu Enlil series.

What is relevant is the meaning that these planetary combinations held for the early astrologers. Why, we may ask, were some combinations seen as beneficial and others as quite the opposite? By what criteria did these early astrologers judge events? And further, what does it mean that a great number of these early statements and techniques

---

*See Reiner, *Enuma Anu Enlil*, pages 17–18. For a complete list of the Babylonian stars together with their modern identifications, when possible, see pages 7–16.

have come down through the centuries and can be found, in one form or another, in any modern text on astrology? Does it indicate validity? Or does it indicate gullibility? And if the latter, why then have not all the teachings survived? By what process of selection have certain of the techniques and interpretations survived while others have been cast aside?

We must begin with the content of the omens, for it seems likely that the basis for prediction may be found in the legends of those gods whose visible presence was the planets and the stars. So it is to those gods, their myths, and their planets that our attention must turn.

7

THE NUMINOUS AND THE MESOPOTAMIAN RELIGION

"Basic to all religion," writes Professor Thorkild Jacobsen, "and so also to ancient Mesopotamian religion—is, we believe, a unique experience of confrontation with power not of this world."[1] Alone among historians of Mesopotamia, he initiates his study of religious development with this highly personal declaration of the fundamental role played by the primal, profound experience, which can be termed *numinous* or *enlightening*—in other words, a direct experience of *divinity*. For Professor Jacobsen, it is with such an experience that religion begins.

The expression of this unique experience must somehow be rendered coherent in order for it to be communicated and interpreted. It must be encapsulated by language into concepts, into symbols, into metaphors. And these concepts, symbols, and metaphors constitute the building blocks of myth.

The mythology of a nation can be viewed as its reflection in the mirror of the heavens, for myth mirrors the hidden side of a nation; the tales of the gods are the tales of a nation's unconscious life expressed in symbolic form.

Through myth a culture seeks to understand and accept the reality within which it lives. These myths arise out of the very deepest layers of the masses and the individual's psychic makeup; they are a symbolic expression of the psyche's innermost processes.

Buried in the unconscious, both individual and collective, are energy patterns that all humankind holds in common; it is these that emerge in myth. The pioneering psychologist Dr. Carl Jung termed these energy patterns *archetypes* and explained that they derived from the *collective unconscious*—that deep psychological level that is shared equally by all.*

Lying within this collective unconscious are *primordial images,* ancient patterns that cause certain resonant motifs to emerge symbolically into the conscious world as myth. The inherent strength of myth lies then in the emotional power that is released within each person through a personal recognition of, and personal resonance with, these emergent archetypal patterns.

Initially unconscious, these patterns flow beneath the surface of consciousness, yet occasionally they can erupt without warning, emerging perhaps in the form of a mass movement or in the person of a demagogue who, crystallizing this unconscious energy, manipulates the public into providing this energy with a focus, with a conduit out into the world.

A common example of this—of a nation's unconscious erupting into the culture—is the process that often leads to war: a leader emerges to focus this national psychosis, and a scapegoat is found that can take the focus of all the ills of the society, which will quickly find itself at war. Then members of society have the chance to act the part of a national mythological war hero—most of whom, it should be recalled, get killed, dying in the arms of their friends.

The tales of heaven are, in reality, tales of earth. Mythology forever

---

*For an introduction to Jung's writings on the unconscious and archetypes, see his *Memories, Dreams, Reflections,* pages 194ff.

connects these two realms, and, of course, astrology's basic premise rests upon this connection. Events in heaven foreshadow events on earth. Indeed, the art of astrology itself can be seen as a means of working with mythology in a practical way.

Without an understanding of myth and its relation to the unconscious, without any insight into the religious aspiration and expression that lies behind the mythmaking process, and without any appreciation of the power of the numinous experience, no scholar working in the field of comparative religion can hope to make any sense out of the endless variations of religious expression. In consequence, many fall into the intellectually secure charade of mere classification: they link common elements as though understanding religion were just another exercise in cross-referencing. They forget the intensely personal, yet universal, experience that is desperately seeking expression through the limitations of language and culture. One of the great historians of Mesopotamia, the University of Chicago Oriental Institute's Professor Leo Oppenheim, scorned the creators of "smoothly written systematizations decked out in a mass of all-too-ingenious comparisons and parallels obtained by zigzagging over the globe and through the known history of man."[2] If, for example, one is looking for the moon, describing and collating the appearance of a million fingers pointing in its direction will not bring one any closer to knowledge of its appearance.

In the progressive relationship of humans with the divine, the experience of the numinous is the ultimate step. Furthermore, despite this primal experience being, by its very nature, beyond description, those who have been through it nonetheless attempt to express or communicate to others their understanding of it, often, of course, in an attempt to guide others toward it. As Apuleius writes, "At midnight I saw the sun shining as if it were noon,"[3] or as the Hermetic text known as the "Poimandres" of Hermes Trismegistus expresses it, "Now fix your thought upon the Light . . . and learn to know it."[4] Even in Old Babylonian times this terminology was current: "Let mine eyes see the sun that I may be sated with light. Banished afar is the darkness, if the light is sufficient. May he who has died the death see the light of the sun."[5] So spoke Gilgamesh to the sun god, Shamash.

Yet despite this, without bringing some knowledge to these passages, we are no clearer. Apuleius recognized this and followed his revelations with the apology "Well, now you have heard what happened, but I fear you are still none the wiser."[6]

The history of religion and literature demonstrates that the only way to overcome the severe limitations of language and communicate an experience so personally profound as that of the numinous is by use of some form of analogy or metaphor. These metaphors then become the primary link connecting this direct experience of the numinous to those secondary religious qualities of faith and a belief in some prophetic scriptural expression. As the human reaction to the numinous experience we have religion—an intellectual tradition that embraces myth, theology, cultic worship, and ritual.

> In the metaphors, therefore, all that is shared by the worshippers of an individual culture or cultural period in their common response to the Numinous is summed and crystallized. . . . In its choice of central metaphor a culture or cultural period necessarily reveals more clearly than anywhere else what it considers essential in the numinous experience and wants to recapture and transmit. . . . [It is this] which underlies and determines . . . the total character of its religion.[7]

A symbol is always more than it appears. Therein lies its power. It can entice our perceptions onward, toward wider horizons. Thus, religious symbols, religious metaphors, seek to draw us further and further beyond the superficial, toward the divine or the numinous.

A study of the religious metaphors and their development during a people's cultural history—the additions and modifications that appear as the culture itself changes—can provide a matrix within which the historical record of political and economic events occurs. The history of the religious metaphors is a history of the evolution of consciousness of the culture. Indeed, to read an ancient myth is a form of archaeology; it provides a direct window into the very basis of that culture.

The divine can be experienced either as *immanent,* that is, as existing in all things equally without distinction, or as *transcendent,* that is, beyond the world, beyond the objects and forms that we see around us. In the ancient Middle East, religion, often using variations on the same mythology, embraced both experiential forms of the numinous. For the Babylonians and the Assyrians, the numinous was experienced as immanent: the power of the gods was considered to reside permanently in an object without denigrating the omnipotence of those gods. Examples of this can be found in numerous Akkadian epics in which the hero, upon confronting a divine figure that spoke through some natural object, saw both the physical object and the divine power as attributes of the one divine being.

This can be seen in the attitude adopted toward the heavenly bodies. The Sumerian word *utu* means both the sun and the power that motivates it—in other words, the power of the sun god is seen as immanent in the sun. Similarly in the case of Venus, the planet is worshipped as being the repository of the goddess Ishtar, who is immanent in that planet and who controls and animates it. They did not, however, believe the planets to *be* the god or goddess.

This belief explains the Mesopotamians' curious attitude toward statues of their gods. The gods were held to be immanent within their images made of stone, wood, or metal. In consequence, daily rituals were performed before these statues by the priests, rituals that entailed cooking and serving elaborate meals for these images twice daily.[8]

During the religious festivals when the statues of the gods were carried out from the city, the population believed that they were carrying the god itself out; for that short period they believed that the god had left the city. Indeed, great calamities were believed to befall any city whose god was lost, broken, or carried off by a foreign invader.

It is perhaps not incidental that the religion of the Old Testament, which opposed astrology, also had a different attitude toward the divine. The chronicle of the Old Testament bristles with fierce denunciations of divination; it is also replete with the angry demands of a god that was experienced, not as immanent, but as transcendent. A god that would communicate through different physical forms—a pillar of fire, for example, or a dark cloud—and yet remain distinct from those forms.

In the story of Moses's confrontation with the divine in the burning bush, it is quite clear that the divine was considered to be distinct from the bush, that the divine was held to be merely using the bush on that particular occasion for its own reasons. As Professor Jacobsen points out, a Babylonian confronted with the same experience would have seen the divine not only as all-powerful but also as being the center of the life of the bush itself.[9] Thus, the Babylonian would have worshipped both the divine and the bush. Conversely, the Hebrews of the Old Testament, insofar as the text can be believed, were never in the habit of worshipping bushes, however often the deity might reside in them.

The religion of Mesopotamia did not maintain the same beliefs, the same cultic practices, or even the same gods over the many thousands of years during which civilization moved from the small Anatolian settlements to the great metropolitan conurbations that grew up on the plains. The religion grew along with the culture. While this growth was obviously slow, it is possible, through a study of the writing that emerged at various periods, to delineate several quite distinct phases in the religious development of the region.

Naturally, the edges of each phase, the transition periods, are indistinct. New literature appears incorporating certain changes without any hint of those processes that might have constituted the formative steps toward the elaboration of this new position.

The earliest type of religion in Mesopotamia, so far as we can tell, involved primarily the worship of fertility gods and goddesses, who ensured that the fields remained productive and the animals healthy. In time, perhaps reflecting the emergence of local warrior kings who ruled over the growing, hierarchically stratified urban communities, the gods also became ordered into a strict social hierarchy, each a specialist in his or her appointed task.

At some point the concept of a ruler god appeared. This god was seen as the king of heaven, who ruled, as did the kings on earth, over a court of many secondary figures.* And, like the kings on earth, this ruler god was appointed by election, by acclamation of all the gods meeting together in a great heavenly hall. Heaven was made, by the storytellers, to reflect the earth. Thus, the social organization and morality in the myths of the gods revealed those social factors that were so vital to the Assyrians and Babylonians.†

Yet, curiously, once the hierarchy of heaven had been established, this then became seen as the foundation for the hierarchies upon earth. The descent of "kingship" from above meant that the "office, not the office-holder, was of superhuman origin."[10] Hence, the source of the Assyrian or Babylonian king's authority was not by virtue of his descent or his dynasty but of his election by the gods. In practice this resulted in a choice of heir on the part of the reigning king: there was no primogeniture in operation, although there was a sense of dynasty. By use of a variety of techniques, including divination, one of the king's sons was chosen as the "crown prince," and until this choice was made and publicly declared, the identity of the heir would be uncertain.

Historians of religion see this development as reflecting, in myth, the social situation of the third millennium BCE. With the gods firmly

---

*Frankfort argues that "kingship originated—not from orderly society but as the product of confusion and anxiety," that the kings brought order out of chaos. See Frankfort, *Kingship and the Gods*, page 236.

†Frankfort maintains that this concept of the "ruler" god, as it was developed by the second millennium BCE, eventually led to monotheism. A monarch should be absolute ruler over heaven in the same way as the monarch was absolute ruler over earth. Thus, a tendency arose to concentrate and consolidate the god's powers, giving rise to the amalgamation of powers in one god. See Frankfort, *Kingship and the Gods*, pages 78–84. See also pages 234ff.

installed as rulers of heaven, the ruler upon the earth—the king—came to be seen as their representative: "After kingship had descended from heaven," begins the Sumerian king list.[11]

The ancient epic of Gilgamesh, king of Uruk, written on twelve tablets, records his being addressed as "offspring [or child] of the gods."[12] The king was the one who carried the responsibility of supervising the various actions desired by the gods; thus, he needed to be aware of exactly what the gods required of him and his city. Here the practice of divination fulfilled a crucial civic purpose: through divination the king was able to know the gods' will. The king had to seek omens, not only to understand portended events but also to discover what the gods required of him.

The turn of the second millennium BCE, argues Professor Jacobsen, coincided with a significant change in the religious perspective of Mesopotamia.[13] During this period, for the first time in recorded history, individuals spoke directly to the gods—they pleaded, requested, begged for success, good fortune, good health—with the expectation that for a moment the gods would drop their cosmic duties and deign to involve themselves in terrestrial affairs for the benefit of the supplicant. For the first time the ancient texts give clear examples of an emerging conception of a personal god, a god directly responsible for individual destiny.

> My god, you who are my father who begot me,
> lift up my face. . . .
> How long will you neglect me,
> leave me unprotected?[14]

So cried a young man in this late Sumerian poem. His prayers were answered, as the poem, with a change of style, continues,

> The man—his bitter weeping was heard by his god,
> When the lamentation and wailing that filled him had
>   soothed the heart of his god for the young man,

The righteous words, the artless words uttered by him,
  his god accepted. . . .
His god withdrew his hand from the evil word. . . .
The demon of fate who had been placed there in
  accordance with his sentence, he turned aside,
He turned the young man's suffering into joy. . . .[15]

Just a handful of texts of this type concerning a "personal" god have been found, dating to 2600 BCE, 2150 BCE, 2000 BCE, and the latest to 1700 BCE. There are no others found until near the end of the millennium. Beyond Mesopotamia this style of text does not occur until relatively later—around 1350 BCE in Hittite material, around 1230 BCE in Egypt, and around the turn of the millennium in Israel.

While the paucity of texts does not allow us to come to any fixed conclusions, the suspicion arises that this was a Mesopotamian religious development that took place during the years straddling the beginning of the second millennium BCE, possibly related to the increasing influence of the Semitic immigrants into the region that culminated in their dominance.

Of this change, Jacobsen says, the concept of the personal religion can be traced "to the beginnings of the second millennium in Mesopotamia" and is embedded in "and limited to the specific relationship of a man to his personal god."[16] This is directly relevant to the formation of a regular divinatory technique because divination provides a channel of communication between the gods and humankind.[17]

In passing it is worth noting that in the case of the culture in Israel, the personal attitude toward religion was extended from the individual to the nation.[18] The nation became a "chosen one," monopolizing the deity and constantly in touch with it through the agency of the Ark of the Covenant. From this attitude a view of history developed that was purposive and meaningful—history was moving toward a future national fulfillment, not simply repeating itself after the passing of a huge cycle of years, as the Mesopotamians believed. To the Israelites, history was linear; to the Mesopotamians, history was repetitive.

Historically there are two interesting points of coincidence between this and the rise of a systematized astrological methodology. The first is that the earliest Sumerian astrological tablets date from about the period of the early texts that describe a personal religion. The second point is that the later religious texts fall within the period of the first dynasty of Babylon, which saw the beginning of the development of astrology. Indeed, the last text discovered was dated to circa 1700 BCE, the beginning of the reign of King Ammisaduqa, whose name is mentioned in the Venus Tablet of the Enuma Anu Enlil.

In the light of this, one should be aware of the possibility of some connection between the two processes—the rise of personal religion and the rise of astrology. Psychologically there are similarities. Professor Jacobsen points out the paradoxical character of the personal approach to deity: while externally the supplicant is giving vent to dramatic expressions of humility and abasement, beneath the surface is a presumption of almost limitless self-importance.[19] The supplicant, for the moment, becomes the center of the universe, demanding the sole attention of the god.

This is not without relevance to astrology, which firmly details the interest of the gods in the earth and, with the much later "natal" birth charts, symbolically details the connection of the gods with the individual. Such birth charts, however, formed no part of Assyrian or Babylonian astrology until some two hundred years after the destruction of the last Babylonian empire. Perhaps, rather, it is from this religious concept that the use of "nativity" omens developed. These had long been used in Mesopotamia.

This type of natal divination procedure inevitably came to include omens that were derived from celestial phenomena.[20] Thus, it is possible that, in some manner that has not yet been discovered by the archaeologists, this led to the recording of the planetary positions at the exact moment of birth in order to determine the fate of the child. At this point was born the natal horoscope, the earliest of which dates to

410 BCE, the period of the Persian domination of Mesopotamia.[21] Of course, this is a very long time after the apparent beginning of a personal religion, and this fact alone demands an explanation.

The Babylonians and Assyrians lived in a world where the past and the future continuously bled into the present. Time itself was seen as cyclical and ever-flowing. This is quite a different perception from that of our Judeo-Christian influenced modern era, where time marches, teeth clenched, onward to a stoically better future. And because of this concept, we remain prey to all manner of millenarian messianic hopes.

In such a fluid universe where past and future, good and evil all ebbed and flowed together, it is only to be expected that all should be regarded as negotiable. If an omen should portend evil, then a ritual would be performed to remove its effects and to appease the god from whom the evil derived. Evil, it was supposed, appeared because an individual or a nation had, however unwittingly, transgressed the will of a particular god or goddess. Consequently, it was necessary to apologize and undergo some form of ritual abasement to prove true contrition before the evil could be averted.

Divination presented astrologers with a conundrum: while evil might be predicted, it was not actually present at the time of the prediction. Thus, the ritual to remove the effect could not yet be applied. It was necessary for the priest and the supplicant to wait until the evil arrived. This was obviously an unsatisfactory course of events—the supplicant awaiting the evil, candles, water, and incense ready, the priest nervously pacing the floor with his magical paraphernalia. Obviously some alternative system needed to be devised.

And, of course, it was: the Namburbi ritual. This was an apotropaic ritual, that is, one designed to avert *threatened* evil. It enabled the supplicant to preempt the evil that was about to descend. Namburbi is a Sumerian word meaning "undoing of it," that is, "ritual for the undoing of portended evil."[22] Its existence and use is a particular adjunct to the Mesopotamian divination technique, for without divination such a ritual would be irrelevant.

That rituals existed to avoid a portended fate requires some investigation into the Mesopotamian's concept of fate, *shimtu*. This is a difficult concept, different from the deterministic view of fate held later by the Greeks and that lies behind the modern Western attitude. Shimtu refers to a disposition that comes from a god, the king, or any individual who has the specific mandate to confer power or privileges.[23] The gods endow mortals with their gifts of power or success; the king can dispose of political offices, land, or privilege; and individuals can assign belongings to their heirs. Shimtu denotes that which is fixed particularly by decree and then is communicated from a higher to a lower social or divine order.[24]

There is though a specifically religious concept of the "establishment of the *shimtu*" for an individual: this is a specific action whereby each person receives from the gods—presumably at birth—their amount of good or ill fortune, thus setting the pattern for the individual's subsequent life.[25] Thus, the later natal horoscope can be seen as a record of one's allotted shimtu.

For most of the last two thousand years, a fundamental premise lying at the heart of astrology has been that of causation: the movements of the planets directly cause specific events upon the earth. Hence, the observation of planetary movement has an immutable determinist quality; from what is observed above will appear, in due course, a series of fated events on earth. While a great many modern astrologers no longer subscribe to this premise, it is still true that it remains the most commonly held assumption.

This belief is an inheritance from the ancient Greeks. They believed in a finite universe, lesser in the hierarchy of creation than the Creator. And, due mainly to Aristotle's influence, they believed that the planets caused direct and physical alteration of events on earth. Precisely how this effect was caused has exercised minds ever after, albeit unsuccessfully.

The Babylonians and Assyrians had no such belief. For them, the existence of celestial (and terrestrial) omens—a celestial event with a correlated terrestrial event—did not, in any way, necessitate any consequent belief either that the celestial events caused the predicted terrestrial events or that the predicted terrestrial events were, in any manner, fated, inevitable consequences of this previous celestial event.*

The anomalous or unusual event that was considered to be significant, or "ominous," and that portended, according to the literature, certain events on earth, was a "sign" or a "warning" of what was possible. It was an indication of what the gods, in their control of fate, had determined should be the outcome. This predicted event, though, could be avoided through magical ritual; it was never considered inevitable.

Professor Rochberg-Halton writes:

> Evidence that notions of causality or fate did not lie in the background of celestial divination comes from the apparent fact that the diviners regarded the omens . . . as neither inevitable nor inexorable. Apotropaic rituals could dispel whatever evil might be predicted. . . . Such "namburbi" rituals were believed efficacious because an event presaged by a given phenomenon was not seen as rigidly bound by necessity or causation. Hence, no fundamental determinism lay at the basis of the Mesopotamian concept (or "theory") of divination. The nature of an omen in a Babylonian text is therefore not that of an absolute cause, but of a warning or sign.[26]

The 140 or more Namburbi texts so far identified all date from the late eighth to the late sixth centuries BCE. Most of them were found at

---

*See Rochberg-Halton, *Aspects of Babylonian Celestial Divination*, page 15. Dr. Rochberg-Halton kindly forwarded me the manuscript of her article "Babylonian Cosmology," to be published in *The Encyclopaedia of Cosmology: Historical, Philosophical, and Scientific Foundations of Modern Cosmology*, edited by N. Hetherington. In it she concludes that "Babylonian astrology . . . never became deterministic and did not require a physical theory of astral influence to explain the significance of celestial omens"; Rochberg-Halton, "Fate and Divination in Mesopotamia," pages 366–68.

the cities of Nineveh and Asshur, although their language suggests an origin in the south, in Babylonia.

Each tablet provides a list of the rituals to be performed for the particular type of evil that threatens, together with the text of the prayer to be spoken in front of the god.*

That these texts have been copied many times is a good indication of the important function that they served in daily life. These rituals also appear in the omen texts, which often have a break in the text where the relevant Namburbi ritual is detailed.

The ritual itself most commonly involved only two people: the supplicant and the priest. It took several hours to perform, although it seems to have been typical practice to perform it in parts over two consecutive days. The site for the ritual needed to be secluded, away from the general hubbub of daily life. Once a suitable site had been chosen, an altar would be prepared.

First, rites were performed to separate the site of the ritual from its surroundings: standards would be raised around the corners of the site, one to each of the four winds. A curtain, for example, or small heaps of flour, might be used to isolate the site. Generally it would seem that some species of magical separation was sought in the same way as a medieval—or modern—magician would inscribe a circle within which to perform his or her rituals.

Following the preparation of the site, the performers would then purify themselves. They washed or bathed, shaved, and then put on clean garments. Then the site itself was purified by sweeping it clean; sprinkling pure water about it; and burning incense of juniper, cedar, or myrrh.

With the site chosen and correctly prepared, the ceremony could begin. Offerings of food or drink would be made to the gods, accompanied by specific prayers to the effect that the portended evil might be

---

*See Caplice, *Akkadian Namburbu Texts,* for translations of the tablets and details of the basic rituals.

destroyed before it could do any harm. These prayers were made mostly to Shamash as god of justice, to Adad as god of wild storms, or to Ea or Asalluhi, the gods of magic.

Finally, at the conclusion of the ritual prayers, the performers would again purify themselves and then perform some small symbolic act to show the "undoing" of the evil, such as the unraveling of a plant or the smashing of a small pot. Then followed a ritualized method by which the supplicant reentered daily life: he was commonly told to leave the ritual enclosure without looking behind him and to take a different road back to his home or to his city, where he should deliberately involve himself in the turmoil of daily life. Entering a tavern was recommended, so that he might drink and talk. And then for some time afterward the supplicant would obey certain dietary rules, avoiding foods such as garlic, fish, or leeks, which were prohibited by the cult, and wearing amulets inscribed with magical formulas.[27]

The Namburbi ritual is, of course, "magical." Magic is a form of intercession with the gods. It relies upon the premise that however omnipotent and remote the gods might be, they too are subject to immutable universal laws. If the magician were to know these laws and be able to operate in accordance with them, then even the gods would be bound to obey.

The task of the magician is to change or redirect nature, and if the future direction of the natural world can be revealed by astrology, then the magician has every opportunity to alter the direction of events, thus creating an alternative future.

With these Namburbi rituals we have left the lofty position of the numinous experience and are within the restrictive and cultic arena of religious dogma. Magical rituals emerge from a particular Weltanschauung, or worldview, one in which universal laws of sympathetic action and reaction exist and can be used by both the gods and humankind. This doctrine of sympathetic action was important to the Babylonians and Assyrians; indeed, it formed the basis of their magical practices.

This idea of sympathetic action is also one of the bases of astrology. As the practice developed, especially under Greek and Roman patronage, each god, each planet, had his or her correct wood, metal, color, number, and image that a devotee would use to seek that god's aid. This procedure is at the heart of the creation of magical amulets and talismanic figures. In time the disciplines of astrology and magic ceased running in parallel and joined together. It can be argued that this process began with the use of the Namburbi rituals to avert negative astrological predictions.

This symbiosis of magic and astrology was to see extensive development over three millennia or more and to end by literally changing the course of Western civilization itself. It was the widespread concept of sympathetic magic, deriving ultimately from the ancient Babylonians, that was expounded in the fifteenth century CE by the Florentine linguist and philosopher Marsilio Ficino, teacher of Botticelli, which, as we shall see, lay at the very heart of the Italian Renaissance.

PART 2

✳

THE MYTHS AND
THE PLANETS

8

SIN

The Moon, Father of Time

The original empire builders of Mesopotamia were the Sumerians. The later Semitic race, the Akkadians, came, it is thought, from Arabia. This influx began very early, for already, at the beginning of the first written records in the fourth millennium BCE, the king list from the first dynasty of Kish reveals Semitic names.

The mythology of the Sumerians was highly sophisticated, with a complex pantheon. In contrast, it appears that the original Semitic religion was based upon just three gods: the moon, the sun, and Venus. Accordingly, when the Semites assumed power over Sumer, at the time of King Sargon in 2334 BCE, while retaining the entire Sumerian pantheon, they substituted at its head their astral trinity of the moon, Sin; the sun, Shamash; and Venus, Ishtar.

There are certain curiosities about this process: originally, it is thought, the Semitic tribes held the sun to be female while considering the moon and Venus to be male. Following upon their adoption of the Sumerian pantheon, they kept the moon as male but the sex of the other two changed: the sun became male and Venus became both male and female simultaneously, later exclusively female.[*]

The moon god—Nanna to the Sumerians, Sin to the Akkadians—remained head of the astral deities. He had been prominent since early Sumerian times, being considered the father of both the sun and Venus—the divine twins. This view of the celestial hierarchy faithfully reflects the ancient concept that day emerged from night, that the sun was born of the moon, that light emerged from the darkness. This Sumerian notion finds expression in the first few lines of the Old Testament, probably one of the most ancient legends still in print and still forming an integral part of a living religion:

> And darkness was upon the face of the deep. And the Spirit of God moved upon the face of the waters. And God said, "Let there be light."

Indeed, the comparison is even closer than the distorted view promulgated by the translations used in the English Bibles. The original word, translated as "God," was in fact the plural term Elohim. Hence, a more accurate translation would give the rendering: "And the spirit of the *gods* moved . . ."

Old Father Time, old "blue beard," whose crescent appearing at sunset heralded the new month, was probably the most important of all

---

*For a discussion on these changes of Venus, see Roberts, *The Earliest Semitic Pantheon,* pages 39–40. Speaking of the male and female aspects of Venus, Roberts concludes that they referred to "the planet Venus under its two aspects as morning star (male = Attar) and the evening star (female = Attart). This distinction was preserved only in the west, however. In the east the masculine form usurped both functions, and the feminine form dropped out of normal use. Nevertheless, the East Semites appear to have retained a memory of the androgynous character of Venus which allowed the Akkadian Attar to develop as a goddess contrary to its grammatical gender." Attar (originally the name of a south Arabian male deity) later transmuted into the name of the Akkadian goddess Ishtar. It is only fair to add, however, that this book comes with a warning: in a review, Aage Westenholz writes of Roberts's work that "it cannot be used without considerable caution." See *Journal of Near Eastern Studies* 34 (1975), page 293.

the astral gods. He ruled over both time and the calendar. His symbol, carved upon most of the statues of the kings, was the lunar crescent— often depicted with a line joining the tips of the crescent, completing a circle. In King Esarhaddon's time, an image of Sin stood at Harran depicting him as seated upon a shepherd's staff and wearing, curiously, two crowns.[1]

Mythology describes his importance in the pantheon, and this importance persisted in the Mesopotamian astrological tradition. Of the sixty-eight or seventy tablets in the Enuma Anu Enlil series, no less than the first twenty-two are devoted to lunar omens. This prominence is also found in the reports from the scholars writing to Kings Esarhaddon and Ashurbanipal, which were found at Nineveh. In Parpola's translations twice as many concerned the moon as any other stellar object. Of those from Babylonia published by Thompson, almost 40 percent address lunar omens.

Sin's actual role in mythology is difficult to define with any precision because his attributes changed over the centuries and many of the texts mentioning him that have survived are copies of older, now lost, originals. It is, strictly speaking, necessary to define the period in which such attributes were apparently current. In Ashurbanipal's time, for example, Sin was regarded as having great wisdom, a depth of knowledge that no other gods could approach.

In fact, later myth records that at the end of each month all other gods would gather to consult with Sin, who would then make all the necessary decisions for the others. Thus, it would seem to reflect a growing tendency to depict Sin as the head of the gods—a role also assumed elsewhere by Enlil (whose meeting hall was the primary divine forum) or later by Marduk (who was also called king of the gods). However, whatever his eventual position in local pantheons, as ruler of time Sin assumed considerable control over life and destiny.

Deriving omens from the moon was a highly complex task. It must have required no little effort on the part of the astrologer and no little knowledge of the great series to select the correct omens. The appearance of the moon alone, while important and often used as an indicator, was only one of the many factors that needed to be taken into account. The day of appearance was significant: did, for example, the moon appear upon the "correct" day—the first, the seventh, the fourteenth, or the twenty-eighth of each month—or did it deviate from this? Was there anything significant about the shape of its crescent—called its "horns"? Were they of equal or unequal length? Were they of equal or unequal brightness? Was the moon surrounded by a halo, and did any other planet, star, or constellation lie within this halo? Were the sun and moon seen together on the correct days or, most ominously, was there an eclipse? Each of these possibilities was systematically written down in the Enuma Anu Enlil tablets, and all the possible predictions from them were listed.

As an analysis of the omens linked to the various phenomena reveals, some appear consistent while others vary widely. As an example of consistency, all the astrologers whose reports have been translated are agreed that if the "horns" are equally sharp and bright, good is portended for Akkad. If, however, one of these horns should be dark, then the prognosis is different: a neighboring country is destined to suffer a revolution. Due to the lack of material, however, a thorough analysis of these attributions is not possible at this stage.

If the sun and moon were seen together on the "correct" day, then the effect was seen as beneficial: "When the Moon and Sun are seen with one another on the fourteenth, there will be silence, the land will be satisfied; the gods intend Akkad for happiness. Joy in the heart of the people. The cattle of Akkad will lie down securely in the pasture-places."[2] Thus the full moon—to which this omen refers—occurring upon its mathematically "correct" day, the fourteenth of the month, indicates a harmony in heaven that, in turn, portends harmony upon the earth.

If, however, there should occur the unfortunate situation in which the sun and the moon appear at other than their "correct" times (the calendar having become out of time with the planetary cycles), then this heavenly disharmony portends a disharmony upon the earth:

"When the Moon appears out of its expected time, the market will be low [it was seen with the Sun on the twelfth]. . . . A strong enemy will overcome the land."[3] Appearances on the fifteenth and sixteenth days, at least, are also seen negatively, invasions of the nation being predicted. While evidence has not yet been discovered, it would seem likely that the other such inharmonious days similarly portended ill for the land.

The fourfold divisions of the lunar month gave rise to a system of sacred days. These, with one exception, lay at the end of each week. Thus, the seventh, fourteenth, the anomalous nineteenth, twenty-first, and twenty-eighth days were considered especially significant and dangerous.[4] On these days it was specified that "the king shall not ride in a wagon, nor speak as a ruler. The Seer shall make no pronouncements in the place of mysteries. A physician shall not lay his hand upon a sick person."[5]

That these commands are reminiscent of the Jewish Sabbath is not gratuitous, for it seems likely that the Old Testament concept of the Sabbath was derived from this Mesopotamian idea of sacred days. Of these four sacred days each month, one was particularly significant and accorded a greater importance than the others. This was the fourteenth day, the day of the full moon, which was given over to rejoicing and prayer. The name given to this day was Shabattu, and it is from this that the Hebrew word Shabbat and the English term Sabbath derive.

The ancient Hebrews were no strangers to the cult of the moon god, Sin. Evidence suggests that this ancient cult was the original inspiration for the Hebrew religion and thus for significant parts of Old Testament theology. The book of Genesis records that Terah, father of the patriarch Abraham, left his home city of Ur planning to settle in Canaan, but reaching the trading city of Harran, he settled there. These two cities, Ur and Harran, were the supreme centers of the cult of Sin. Furthermore, as we have seen, it seems that there was a later tendency in the cult of Sin to make him the head of all the gods, perhaps even subsuming the pantheon, hinting at the development of a primitive monotheism—the propagation of which was Abraham's forte. Such an incipient monotheism can be seen in the actions of Nabonidus, the last king of Babylon, who tried unsuccessfully to convert Harran's moon worship into the national cult of Babylonia. In the summer of 1956, excavations uncovered three laudatory stelae he had erected at Harran that glorified Sin as "king of the Gods."[6]

Certain other appellations given to Sin support such a pivotal role: he has received praise as "father, who holds all the life of the land in your hand"; "Father, the source of all things"; and "Lord who determines the destiny of Heaven and Earth."[7]

It is possible, though, to carry this argument a little further. Some scholars have suggested that the worship of Sin remained deeply entrenched in the ancient Israelites, that they brought this worship with them when they departed Harran for the land of Canaan. The infamous cult of the golden calf, for example, was probably dedicated to Sin. It is argued, too, that the name of Mount Sinai itself—below which the golden calf was worshipped and upon which Moses received the stone tablets of the law from a jealous male deity—derived its name from Sin, thereby suggesting that it was an already established cult site.*

A major source of moon omens, recorded in the astrological reports to the kings Esarhaddon and Ashurbanipal, was the observation of planets or stars falling within the halo of the moon. This, in modern terms, signifies a conjunction. The halo is caused by a cloud of minute ice crystals in the upper atmosphere, which, because of their crystalline shape, refract the light of the moon to form a circular band around it.

Saturn falling within the halo of the moon was invariably recorded as indicating peace for the kingdom, truth spoken by all, and security

---

*The name Sinai means "the mountain belonging to Sin." See Bailey, "The Golden Calf," pages 114–15.

for the king. Curiously, so far as a modern astrologer would be concerned, the benefic Jupiter falling in this position portends quite the reverse—hostility ruling throughout the land and the king besieged in his palace. Further, at least one tablet mentions that the moon and Jupiter together portended an "unpropitious" event.[8] Mars being close to the moon was similarly given a negative interpretation. Several of the letters make it clear that destruction of cattle was foreshadowed, that the king would die, and that his lands would be reduced. By what terrestrial mechanism was not spelled out, but it was presumably the result of an invasion.

Only rarely do the reports mention constellations falling within the moon's halo, but those that do also provide clear predictions. Cancer, for example, was considered beneficial, while Taurus and Scorpio were seen as very negative. Taurus especially was singled out as a harbinger of evil.[9] And Scorpio, as today, received a negative report. This is an extraordinary prejudice that, to date, has been maintained for almost three thousand years, perhaps more: "When at the appearance of the Moon, the constellation Scorpio stands within its right horn, in this year locusts will swarm, they will eat up the harvest."[10]

The fixed stars too find occasional mention in the reports as having fallen within the moon's halo. Aldebaran in this position, it was reported, brought truth and justice to the land, a quality also attributed to Saturn. Regulus falling in a similar position was said to make pregnant women bear sons rather than daughters.

The next source of moon omens derived from the observation of the brightness of the moon. If the moon was bright, then benefits were portended for the kingdom: the crops would prosper, the people would have enough food and drink, and, as the report states, they would express their happiness through dancing. Unfortunately, virtually the same predictions were produced for the occasion that the moon is dark: "Moon at appearance is bright, crops of the land will prosper"[11] and also "Moon at appearance is dark, land will eat plenty."[12] It appears that some information was lost or garbled early on in the formation of the astrological series, and this error was transmitted uncorrected by later scribes overawed by the antiquity of their tradition and thus unwilling to introduce any changes or even corrections. Professor Rochberg-Halton comments that "the authority of the [Enuma Anu Enlil] text rested primarily on its antiquity"[13] and that the astrological series "could not be radically changed."[14]

Assyrian scholars saw their world as essentially divided into four: first there was Assyria itself (the kingdom of Akkad) and, to the north, the kingdom of Subartu. Both of these lay within the modern state of Iraq. To the east, in what is today Iran, was the perennial enemy, Elam. To the west, in Syria, was the land of Amurru—the Amorites. This fourfold division on earth was reflected, so they believed, in a similar division on the face of the moon. In consequence, lunar omens were connected to one or more of these kingdoms, depending on which part of the moon was involved in the ominous event.

One tablet, probably quoting from the astrological series, records in detail the lunar geography as defined in the texts: "The omen of all lands: the right of the Moon is Akkad, the left Elam, the upper part of the Moon is Amurru, the lower part is Subartu."[15] These directions cannot be related to the geographical reality, and so it is difficult to see by what species of logic these characteristics were derived.

One of the most menacing occurrences in Mesopotamian astrology was that of an eclipse, either lunar or solar. While eclipses of the sun were the supremely malevolent event, those of the moon, while more common and less dramatic, were nonetheless regarded with considerable foreboding. Indeed, of the lunar tablets in the Enuma Anu Enlil, almost 40 percent were dedicated to eclipse omens.

The scholar who has the greatest expertise on the eclipse omens of the Enuma Anu Enlil is Professor Francesca Rochberg-Halton, who received her doctorate at the University of Chicago Oriental Institute. She studied under Professor Erica Reiner, who along with Professor Leo Oppenheim had for many years been intrigued by the tablets of celestial divination. Professor Rochberg-Halton's chosen dissertation topic was the lunar omens found on tablets fifteen to twenty-two in the series. Her dissertation was later augmented and published in 1988 as *Aspects of Babylonian Celestial Divination,* a work from which we have had several occasions to quote already.

Professor Rochberg-Halton's detailed study of this material led her to conclude that these omens were very probably the first to be systematically collated into a text collection, thus, incidentally, suggesting that the earliest codification was perhaps not the Venus Tablet after all. She found, in the British Museum's holdings, four Old Babylonian eclipse omen texts, all of which seemed to draw upon a "single corpus of eclipse omens."[16] These, she suggests, are forerunners of the Enuma Anu Enlil. That at least some of the compilations were already old and respected by the end of the second millennium BCE is demonstrated by the final text of tablet twenty in the astrological series. It was copied, so the text reads, "according to a writing board of the 11th year of Adad-apla-iddina, king of Babylon."[17] This date translates, depending upon which system is used, to about the year 1058 BCE.

Certainly the examples held in the Nineveh libraries, some of them written around the end of the second millennium BCE, derived from earlier originals. We have already had occasion to mention tablet twenty of the series, which was copied in 1058 BCE.[18] Tablets twenty and twenty-one also reveal their antiquity by mentioning in their texts certain geographical references to states that ceased to exist after the end of the second millennium BCE.[19]

The eclipse tablets are highly systematized and seem to cover every possible combination of an eclipsed moon with celestial, meteorological, or terrestrial phenomena. While it is possible that many of the eclipses themselves were derived from actual events observed, some at least—for example, in tablet twenty—could not have occurred as they appear in the tablet.[20]

Omens were drawn from an assorted combination of factors: from the direction of the eclipse; from the dominant color; from the part of the moon that was covered by the eclipse; from the duration of the eclipse; from the coincidence or not of the eclipse with its predicted date; from the appearance of the moon's "horns" at the time; and from its occurrence upon a given set of special dates.

Apart from these physical variations there was another large group of omens that were derived from the combination of the eclipse with other events that happened simultaneously. Such events include a meteor falling at the same time, a planet near the moon at the time, a wind blowing from one of the four directions, thunder, lightning, and an earthquake.

Overall, the prognosis for eclipses was negative; an eclipse presaged only ill for the world. Tablet sixteen of the Enuma Anu Enlil gives a representative sample of the menacing effects predicted:

> *"The land of the prince will be destroyed."*
> *"The land will suffer calamity."*
> *"The king will die."*
> *"The land will go to ruin."*
> *"The gods will become angry."*[21]
> *"Pregnant women will miscarry their unborn."*
> *"There will be a devastating flood."*
> *"The people will sell their children for money."*[22]

Astonishingly, a great number of these attributes have survived the three thousand years or more since they were recorded and are today, in astrological books, commonly available and still associated with lunar eclipses. Tradition still holds eclipses to be malefic and retain the following attributes, all of which are identical with those in the Assyrian astrological series:

> *"causes the death of some king"*
> *"causes pestilence and many evils among mankind"*
> *"causes abortive births"*

"damages the seeds of the earth"
*"thunders and lightnings [sic]"**

All these statements are found in a popular early twentieth-century book by the astrologer Raphael. His book, while slightly archaic in its language, is still in print and readily available. That the specific statement of the Assyrians, declaring that an eclipse threatens to cause pregnant women to miscarry, has survived intact for so long, is a cause for some amazement.

Not all eclipses were held by the Babylonians to be negative. Certain ones that occurred during the evening watch—the first watch of the night, from sunset to midnight[†]—in Nisannu, the first month, seem to have been regarded as favorable. That which occurred upon the fourteenth day (its "correct" day) indicated that "the harvest of the land will thrive."[23] The fifteenth day was regarded as similarly fortunate. Why this should be so cannot be gleaned from the surviving texts. There may conceivably be some significance in the fact that the important Babylonian spring festival ended on the thirteenth day of Nisannu. Other eclipses that were believed to bring benefits were those that occurred on the fourteenth, fifteenth, sixteenth, and twentieth days of Abu, the fifth month.[24]

Among the plethora of dire predictions there is one other category that is explicitly auspicious. This is a curious group that is based on the eclipse appearing to be red. This color seen during a lunar eclipse is caused by sunlight refracted by the earth's atmosphere reaching the surface of the moon and causing it to have a yellow or reddish appear-

_____

*See Raphael, *Mundane Astrology,* pages 63–66. The basic source for Raphael would seem to be William Ramesey's *Astrology Restored,* pages 308–9. This was published in 1653 and was the first mundane astrology book published in English. While Ramesey often mentions his source as being Ptolemy, this material is not mentioned by the latter. No study has yet been done on the other sources that Ramesey might have had available.
†The Babylonians divided each night into three equal "watches": the evening watch, the middle watch, and the morning watch. Each watch consisted of four hours. See Rochberg-Halton, *Aspects of Babylonian Celestial Divination,* page 44.

ance.* Invariably, these proved advantageous: "prosperity for the people"[25] or "the harvest of the land will thrive."[26] This procedure of imbuing the color associated with an eclipse with astrological significance had a later currency far beyond Mesopotamia. A millennium later the Greek astrologer Ptolemy mentions it in his *Tetrabiblos,*[27] and, farther afield, this methodology is found in Indian astrology.[28] Other colors associated with eclipses are mentioned only in later copies of tablets sixteen and seventeen: white, black, red, yellow, and variegated or, alternatively, dark. These too are found in Ptolemy.

Very few eclipses were recorded as having planets or stars associated with them. Within the Enuma Anu Enlil series, only tablet twenty has a consistent inclusion of the two. In this tablet there are four references to eclipses in association with Venus, one with Mars, one with the constellation "the Eagle," which is Aquila, and fragments of text mentioning an eclipse apparently including Orion. Only Mars is additionally mentioned: once in tablet nineteen and once again in tablet twenty-one. Of hundreds of eclipse omens only seven include planets and one, possibly two, include constellations. This is a curiosity for which, at present, we have no explanation.

The effect of these planets was considered to be beneficial. A combination with Venus, called in the texts Dilbat, drew the prediction that "the son of the king will enter the house (or the throne) of his father."[29] This statement is explained in the text as meaning that a king would die, but his people would be well and the future of the state would be good following a period of anarchy. It seems, therefore, to refer to a beneficial change of monarch. Another expresses the benefits as "the king, the city, and its people will be well. The foot of the enemy will be kept away from the land."[30] Of the three eclipses involving Mars, only one omen has survived, that this contact would cause the cattle to die.[31]

The constellation Aquila is mentioned as being involved with an eclipse on two occasions, but no prediction is given. The particular lines

---

*For an explanation of this and a discussion of the relevant omens, see Rochberg-Halton, *Aspects of Babylonian Celestial Divination,* pages 55–57.

read more as a plain report of an observed event.[32] A single fragmented text remains that mentions Orion but without reporting whether the constellation was included in an eclipse. The suggestion is, though, that it was.[33]

A search of the astrological reports to the Assyrian kings elicits a little more information. Two texts mention an eclipse in conjunction with Jupiter, Venus, and Saturn. Both relate to the eclipse of April 21, 667 BCE. What is unique in this case is that the existence of the three planets was seen as beneficial, was seen as counter-acting the normal evil of the eclipse. The writer, Balasi, states that "the king should not be afraid of this eclipse!"[34]

In time, of course, and by virtue of some as yet undiscovered process of cultural and mythological evolution, the moon became feminine, the symbol of the mother goddess Selene to the Greeks, Isis to the Egyptians, and Mary to the later Christians. Where and when this sexual transformation occurred has never been established, but these are essentially lesser queries. The important question is why?

9

SHAMASH

The Sun, Judge of Heaven and Earth

Assyrian mythology, as it had evolved by the reign of King Ashurbanipal, expounded an elaborate pantheon of gods and goddesses, whose interrelationships formed complicated celestial dynasties, identical to those complicated family entanglements that existed among the rulers of Nineveh or Babylon. Sin, the moon god, was considered to have fathered many children, among which were the twin brother and sister—Shamash and Ishtar—respectively, the sun and Venus.

Shamash, the sun, was the great lord who watched over both heaven and earth and who ruled over the living and the dead. His role is expressed by the many titles applied to him, among which were Determiner of Fates and Architect of the Cosmic Designs. In magical or cultic rituals such as the Namburbi he was revered as the Supreme Judge, the head of the Divine Court of Justice, to whom an application might be made in order that a release from misery or injustice might be granted. In this capacity Shamash condemned the wicked and released the innocent from their unjust bondage. Sacred to him was the pure tamarisk wood that was used to craft his statues that stood in the temples. His symbol was the equal-armed cross, often held within a circle.

The extant myths depict the sun as playing only a minor role in celestial events. This is surprising, given that the sun plays such an obvious role in human life; however, because the Mesopotamian calendar was based not upon the sun but upon the moon, it could be that his portrayal never became crafted beyond that of a supporting role.

Despite this, Shamash always at least held a significant position in the Assyrian iconography. On many statues of the kings, the divine symbols are prominently displayed: above the king's head are carved the crescent for the moon, the eight-pointed star for Venus, the bent tongs for Adad, and the crown for Enlil, along with the symbol for Shamash, the equal-armed cross. Indeed, this solar symbol is unique in commonly being repeated on the body of the king himself. Around his neck the king wears, like a modern military decoration, the cross pattée of Shamash. The impression given is that this constitutes the visible sign that the king was Shamash's earthly proxy—and the mention in a text of the king being called the Sun of the People lends some credence to this.[1] It is in fact likely that this is a true to life representation, that the king wore such a symbol around his neck as part of his normal royal regalia. Again, this evident prominence given to Shamash makes his minor status in the mythology all the more difficult to comprehend.

This minor role of the sun in mythology appears to be reflected in the reports from the astrologers found in the Nineveh libraries. Again, though, we must be cautious, for we have no idea how much information has been lost both in the original destruction of Nineveh by the Medes in 612 BCE and in the primitive excavations of the nineteenth century.

---

[1] According to one report, the "cross is the emblem of the god Nabu" and "the dignity of the crown prince lies upon the cross." See Parpola, *Letters from Assyrian Scholars,* 318, volume 1, page 275. Nabu is the "crown prince" of the gods; hence, it can be seen as a possibility that this emblem of the cross pertains in some way to the recognition of the heir to the throne. Parpola corrects a translation in his volume of notes to read: "The king my lord knows that on the ground of this association the cross serves as the badge of the crown prince" (ibid., volume 2, page 330).

In the published reports we find only a small number of references to Shamash, but in support of the argument that there may have been a loss of data, no less than twelve tablets in the Enuma Anu Enlil are devoted to the sun. This is a strong indication that the astrological tradition accorded Shamash considerable importance, almost equal to the moon.

The task of compiling a correct list of omens drawn from the sun is made uncertain by a terminological peculiarity of the ancient scribes: they often used the same name for both the sun and Saturn; both are regularly called Shamash. This identification was clearly expressed much later by the Greek historian Diodorus Siculus, who explained that, to the Babylonians, Saturn was considered to be "the star of the Sun."[2]

This identification has led to a number of confusing statements: one report states the apparent absurdity that should the sun be seen during the midnight watch, then one should expect a great destruction of the population. At first this appears to be arrant nonsense. How could it be possible for the sun to appear at midnight? The answer is that this tablet, garbled as it may have been by scribes, actually refers to Saturn, as "Sun of the night."

The possibility of misinterpretation endured as this ambiguous terminology was maintained by the astrologers throughout the centuries. Plainly there was never any suggestion that this imprecise term should be clarified, although, according to the reports, it is clear that even the astrologers themselves sometimes recognized the potential for confusion. One correspondent, recording a conjunction of Saturn with the moon, added an interpretation drawn from omens of the sun with the moon. Evidently recognizing that the king would query this, the astrologer prefaced his interpretation with an explanation: "Saturn is the Star of the Sun" and added "Saturn is the star of the king too."[3]

This ambiguity then makes the following intriguing prediction impossible to assign definitively, either to the sun or to Saturn: "When *Shamash* reaches its zenith and goes forward, the reign of the

All-powerful king will be long."[4] It is tempting to see this as referring to the sun, thus giving an early example of the astrological tradition well established in later times: the coronation of a king should take place at noon when the sun is at the midheaven because, by astrological principles, this portends a prominent and successful leadership. Unfortunately, this particular Assyrian tablet could just as well be referring to Saturn. Even then, Saturn at the midheaven for a coronation could, by modern astrologers, be read as "a long reign for a powerful and just king who rules firmly"—depending on the aspects.

The occurrence that truly unnerved the ancient rulers and their advisers was an eclipse of the sun. For this reason the ancient kings were determined that their astrologers should be able to predict such events well in advance. This was a vital task in order that time might be available for the correct preparatory rites, which, they hoped, would minimize the effects. That these eclipses were expected to augur a sinister and malevolent period throughout the empire is disclosed in the omen literature: they almost always denoted invasions of the enemy with the consequent destruction of the population and crops.

The reports from the astrologers contain a number of warnings of imminent eclipses. From the thirty-four years from 681 to 647 BCE, there were ten solar eclipses and thirty-eight lunar eclipses potentially visible from Nineveh.[5] Naturally, the king took the advent of these personally. He was, after all, the Sun of the People, so an eclipse was perceived as a direct attack by the gods upon the king.

As we have seen, the ancients, ever pragmatic, believed these astrological portents to be warnings of impending evil, warnings that the particular god had been angered and was demanding satisfaction. Unfortunately, the usual method of averting these negative influences by recourse to the Namburbi ritual was not considered suitable in the case of eclipses. These particular rituals were not sufficiently powerful to ward off the increased evil promised by a solar eclipse.

While ordinary fate could be cheated or redirected, eclipses were such momentous events that the fate portended simply could not be avoided. Their effects would be felt upon the earth whatever ritualistic pleas and entreaties might be raised by the priests. The inexorable quality of such an omen is indicated in a report to Esarhaddon regarding a solar eclipse witnessed by the astrologers at sunrise on May 27, 669 BCE: the correspondent stated that, unlike a lunar eclipse, there was no apotropaic ritual to be used against it.[6]

Masters of negotiation—as though dealing with the gods was no different to dealing in the marketplace—the Mesopotamians, almost impudently, devised a way out of this impasse: if such irrevocable evil was directed against the king, then they would change the king. They would arrange to choose a "substitute" king to sit upon the throne during the period of the negative influences and absorb into himself all the expected evil, thus, incidentally, making clear the superiority of the office of kingship over the man who occupied it.

The creation and coronation of a substitute king were described in various reports that were available to archaeologists from the very early days of Mesopotamian excavation. The reports also mentioned that at the end of the ritual period the substitute would "go to his fate." What this fate was has been a matter of dispute among archaeologists and historians. Some, like René Labat, have argued that "going to his fate" refers to the substitute being ready for any "fated" death that might await the king. Sacrifice was not intended. Others see no particular difficulty in accepting the possibility of human sacrifice on the part of the Assyrians.

The early lack of explicit details as to this fate allowed for some doubt on the part of scholars. For many years the position adopted was that the eventual fate of this substitute was unknown. Even though the reports gave dark hints of ritual human sacrifice, there was a marked reluctance on the part of certain historians to accept that such sacrifice played an important role in the culture, which, as research had progressed, was increasingly viewed as too sophisticated and scientifically competent for such barbarism. This attitude persisted even though human sacrifice was well attested both in Europe and the Middle East at the time.

However, all doubt would seem to have been definitively removed by a recent translation of a text that was unavailable to Labat and others:

Damqi . . . who had ruled Assyria, Babylonia and all the countries died with his queen . . . as a substitute for the king. . . . He went to his destiny for their rescue. We prepared the burial chamber. He and his queen have been decorated, treated, displayed, buried and wailed over. The burnt offering has been burnt, all omens have been cancelled and numerous *namburbi* rituals . . . ceremonies, exorcistic rites . . . chants [and] scribal recitations have been performed in perfect manner.[8]

Clearly, this substitute and his queen, and perhaps even his "court," were all killed at the end of the ritual period—normally one hundred days. Indeed, it has been suggested that some of the elaborate "royal" burials discovered with much attendant publicity were in fact those of the substitutes rather than the actual kings.

An examination of the various tablets that mention the enthronement and fate of the substitute kings indicates the basic outline of the procedure involved. In Assyria, at least, it was evidently a common practice to provide a citizen with a prominent temple office, one that involved him regularly in temple rituals that brought him into close proximity with the cult and the gods. This man was the candidate for king substitute when an eclipse of the sun threatened.

A common man should, as before, be appointed to the office of the bishop, to present the regular offerings in front of the dais. . . . When an eclipse afflicting the land of Akkad takes place, he may serve as a substitute for the king.[9]

It seems that the need for such a substitute was not infrequent. As we have seen, ten solar eclipses over thirty-four years would suggest a requirement for one substitute every three or four years.

Once the astrologers had predicted a solar eclipse, then an inevitable series of events ensued: first a Namburbi ritual was performed—despite its powerlessness in this situation—following which the substitute king was enthroned by means of a ritualized coronation ceremony. The substitute then sat upon the king's throne and slept in the king's palace. At least one substitute, and perhaps all of them, was required to travel after his coronation at Nineveh to the old capital of Akkad, where he was enthroned again. Where the real king went during this time is not recorded.

Immediately following his coronation the substitute king went and stood before a statue of Shamash, where he recited a number of ritual statements in order to take upon himself every omen that was considered to apply.† This task completed, the substitute then proceeded to rule over all the lands and cities of the kingdom—though, it appears, in silence. The substitute kings were not expected to utter a single word of command or even to speak at all when questioned[10]: "a man clad in the king's robes with a diadem upon his head, sitting silently upon his throne. They asked who he was, to which he gave no answer."[11] To support him during his brief reign, he was even supplied with a queen—also, it appears, a substitute.‡

The number of days during which the substitute should remain king seems to have varied. The full term was agreed at one hundred days. Why this particular period, we are not told—but a lesser term might be served if, for example, the predicted eclipse did not occur. Normally, however, the full term would be served, after which the substitute would, ominously, "go to his fate."

---

*See Parpola, *Letters from Assyrian Scholars,* 279, volume 1, page 227. The most comprehensive investigation of Assyrian and later sources for information regarding the substitute king is found in ibid., volume 2, pages xxii–xxxii.

†Mar-Ishtar wrote to Esarhaddon: "The substitute king . . . sat upon the throne. I made him recite the scribal recitations before the Sun-god, he took all the celestial and terrestrial omens on himself, and ruled all the countries." See Parpola, *Letters from Assyrian Scholars,* 279, volume 1, page 227.

‡The text, column A, line 20, reads "the young woman shall become the woman." See Lambert, "A Part of the Ritual for the Substitute King," page 110.

After the substitute king had been killed—perhaps by poisoning[12]—his throne, table, weapon, and scepter were burned and the ashes buried "at their head," an enigmatic statement that might refer to the dead king and queen. Following this it was considered that the purification of both the land and the true king was accomplished. However, to complete the task, a series of six paired wooden statues was constructed. On the left hip of each was written a variety of formulas, each text following the basic form of: "Depart, evil. Enter, good." Each of the six pairs was then buried: one pair each at the gates of the palace, at the gate of the shrine of Shamash, in the palace bedchamber, and at the palace court.[13] With this, life could return to normal—until the next eclipse.

Clearly considerable disruption was caused to the kingdom during the period of the substitute. However, it is certainly possible that during the period that the king had given up the office of power his advisers maintained the right to issue the requisite commands to allow the country to operate on a daily basis. The refusal to allow the substitute to speak would seem to be a measure aimed at avoiding any disruption to the daily life by ill-considered or ignorant actions on the part of this temporary king. We can, perhaps, have some sympathy for the citizens of Akkad in the year 671 BCE, when the enthronement of substitutes was twice believed to be necessary—on July 2 and December 27. Both the substitutes were killed.[14]

In addition to the eclipses, the Enuma Anu Enlil tablets detail a number of other methods for deriving omens from the sun. There are those omens drawn from the physical appearance of the sun, from the rising of the sun, and from the association of the sun with meteorological events. However, very few of these find any mention in the astrologers' reports, and so, lacking a full translation of all the relevant tablets, it is not possible to draw any firm conclusions as to the interpretation of these solar combinations. However, it does appear that in practice little significance was attached to these additional omens.

One event that does find mention in several reports is that of a halo surrounding the sun. Not surprisingly, the usual prediction is for rain. A modern meteorologist would see the rationale behind this because such a halo is formed by ice crystals in the atmosphere.

In conclusion, apart from one report referring to astrologers keeping "the watch of the sun," the only other omens from the sun result from what modern scholars would term *parhelia*. A parhelion is a spot of intense light seen in the sun's halo, a "false sun." The ancient astrologers believed that if, for example, a parhelion should stand in the path of the sun, then this augured well for the kingdom, and in consequence benefits could be expected. If, however, multiple parhelia should be seen, then the reverse was the case, and cattle and game would be destroyed. And if the sun should be at its zenith and coincide with a parhelion, then the king, it was written, would in anger go to war.[15]

10

ISHTAR

Venus, Queen of Heaven

Of all the ancient Mesopotamian deities, probably the most widely known is the goddess Ishtar. She is frequently invoked in the same breath as Isis, Demeter, Persephone, and other mother goddesses. Yet, unlike the later Greek and Roman goddesses, her ancestry is complex and her cult even more so. In fact, when dealing with the ancient texts themselves, rather than commentaries upon them, quite a different view of Ishtar emerges, a perception at some variance to that normally presented by those who obviously prefer their gods and goddesses to inhabit a well-ordered pantheon and to exhibit well-defined and consistent characters. Unfortunately, with the Mesopotamian deities, such is not the case.

Ishtar manifested both male and female attributes. A tablet dating from the time of Ashurbanipal states that Ishtar of the evening star was female, while Ishtar of the morning star was male.[1] Considerable variation existed on a local level as well. While Ishtar's official cult center was Uruk, an ancient city dating from Sumerian times, her following was very widespread, with a statue to her standing in almost every city.

There were, however, certain differences between them: each statue of Ishtar—that in Nineveh, for example, or perhaps that in Uruk—was held to be different, distinct, and endowed with certain unique qualities.

All through the Middle East there have been many exemplars of female goddesses, and Ishtar seems to have gradually subsumed them all, absorbing their features into herself. For this reason her position in the pantheon and her importance varies greatly from era to era. As a result it is impossible to create a portrait of Ishtar in the same way as one might a Greek goddess.

Part of Ishtar's complexity is derived from her origins: she was a mixture of both Sumerian and Semitic deities. The original Sumerian astral deity linked to the planet Venus was known as Inanna—from whom, parenthetically, we derive our modern name Jenny, possibly one of the oldest surviving personal names. When the Semitic tribes gradually moved into Mesopotamia, they brought with them a deity associated with Venus, but in their case it was a male deity called Attar. After the Semitic immigrants had become dominant in the region, their Venus god became replaced by the native Sumerian goddess.

The complexity and importance assumed by Ishtar is exemplified by the wide variety of derivative forms of her name that can be found throughout the Middle East. The Semitic god from southern Arabia, Attar, gave rise to the masculine Ashtar, then, under the influence of the Sumerian culture, the feminine Ishtar emerged. The southern Arabian god Attar also had a feminine aspect, called Attart, later becoming Astart or Asteret. The Canaanite goddess Ashtoreth is a corruption of the latter form, the Greek rendering being Astarte. From Astarte came the Greek Aphrodite. By Assyrian times, insofar as we can tell from the records, the change of sex from Attar to Ishtar was final, although certain vestigial male forms lingered on.

See Roberts, *The Earliest Semitic Pantheon,* page 39, and Heimpel, *Catalogue of Near Eastern Venus Deities,* page 21. However, Heimpel notes (page 22) that Astarte was never identified with either Venus or the evening star, at least until relatively recent Byzantine times.

Ishtar was the third deity in the astral triad. She was considered, by Ashurbanipal's reign, to be the daughter (and firstborn) of Sin, the moon; twin sister to Shamash, the sun; and sister too of both Erishkigal, the much feared queen of the underworld, and Tammuz, the dying and resurrecting god who was later to assume such prominence. Ishtar was the queen of heaven, the beautiful goddess of love, sexuality, and childbirth. Conversely, she was also the terrible goddess of war; it was to her that Solomon sang,

> Who is this arising like the dawn
> fair as the Moon,
> resplendent as the Sun,
> terrible as an army with banners?[2]

It was for worshipping the goddess that Solomon was condemned in the Old Testament.

There were many ways of symbolizing Ishtar, but the most common symbol in Assyria was the eight-pointed star and thus, perhaps, for her the number eight was sacred. There is a curiosity, however: her name, in cuneiform, is also the symbol for the number thirty. In some esoteric manner, known only to the ancient priests, this number and Ishtar were connected. Unfortunately, no vestige of any ancient gematria has been found that could illuminate this point or indicate the numbers associated with other deities.

It is certainly possible that the later medieval eight-sided churches, such as the Knights Templar built, dedicated to the European mother goddess, Mary, are a continuation, through Middle Eastern contacts, of this Ishtar symbolism. Certainly the Knights Templar were famous for their prowess as warriors, and it would not be out of character for their cult to have viewed Mary as a species of war goddess.

The Templars' patroness was Mary in the form of the Black Virgin. It was under her auspices that their spiritual mentor, Saint Bernard, had received his primary spiritual vision. It is most likely that the medieval Black Virgin was an ancient Middle Eastern goddess who had been given a Christian overlay. Many of the early Christian sites of the Virgin cult had grown up about an ancient black statue of a goddess with whom legend often associated a tale of a miraculous discovery.*

The Mesopotamian Ishtar temple complex had both living accommodation and its own farmland in order to support a feminine hierarchy that was distinguished by both office and social class. At the top was the high priestess, who was often a daughter of the king. It was she who took the role of wife to the god in the annual sacred marriage, which was consummated in order that the lands might remain fertile. Serving below her were at least two grades of priestesses.

A further group of women attached to the temple were the so-called temple prostitutes, of which there were two types, reflected in Ishtar's titles of *qadishtu* or *harimtu*—both meaning "whore." The former were the temple "sacred prostitutes," while the latter were "business girls" operating from commercial brothels.[3] It was by the former title that Ishtar was worshipped as patroness of the many temple prostitutes. As their goddess she also held the names Queen of the Windows and She Who Loiters About, which gives some indication that the lifestyle of prostitutes has not changed over the succeeding millennia.

Sacred prostitution formed an important part of the cult of Ishtar. It is of interest that the qadishtu also played a part as wet nurses, perhaps because they were often exposed to pregnancy. In addition, prostitution of the commercial rather than the sacred variety was also linked to the temple; it formed part of the organization's business activities. The temple administration would commonly grant the franchise of some prime site over which the temple had rights—a stretch of busy canal, for example—and in return would gain a proportion of the girl's earnings.*

*See the work on this subject by Ean Begg, *The Cult of the Black Virgin*.

"The Babylonians have one custom in the highest degree abominable," wrote the Greek historian Herodotus in the fifth century BCE.

Every woman who is a native of the country is obliged once in her life to attend at the temple of Venus, and prostitute herself to a stranger. Such women as are of superior rank . . . go to the temple in splendid chariots, accompanied by a numerous train of domestics, and place themselves near the entrance. This is the practice with many; whilst the greater part, crowned with garlands, seat themselves in the vestibule; and there are always numbers coming and going. The seats have all of them a rope or string annexed to them, by which the stranger may determine his choice. A woman having once taken this situation, is not allowed to return home, till some stranger throws her a piece of money; and leading her to a distance from the temple, enjoys her person. It is usual for the man, when he gives the money, to say, "May the goddess Mylitta be auspicious to thee!" Mylitta being the Assyrian name for Venus. The money given is applied to sacred uses, and must not be refused, however small it may be. The woman, not suffered to make any distinction, is obliged to accompany whoever offers her money. She afterwards makes some conciliatory oblation to the goddess, and returns to her house, never afterwards to be obtained on similar, or any such terms. Such as are eminent for their elegance and beauty do not continue long, but those who are of less engaging appearance have sometimes been known to remain from three to four years, unable to accomplish the terms of the law.[4]

Herodotus had visited Babylon and was certainly an eyewitness to the events he described, albeit a questionable reporter. Archaeologists have not found sufficient evidence to support all his assertions, particularly his statement that it was a general rule whereby all women were required to have a sexual experience in the temple at the hands of a stranger. It is now generally considered that he had misunderstood the

situation and was describing rather the lifestyle of the qadishtu women.
However, the truth may, as often, lie somewhere in between. From a
small archive discovered at Sippar, a tablet was noted in 1973 that for
the first time presented some unambiguous evidence for the granting of
sexual favors by Babylonian women as part of the service that they owed
Ishtar.[5] These particular married women, attached to the army, were
"attending to the needs of military personnel."[6]

That no stigma was attached to any man who visited the temple
women is evidenced by a marriage contract that has survived. It specifies first that the man being wed should remain faithful to his wife by
not taking another woman. However, it then allows that he might go
to the city for the purpose of having sex with a qadishtu.[7] Given the
rudimentary medical knowledge of the times and the indisputable evidence for the existence of venereal disease, it might be supposed that
this latter would be exacerbated by the sexual aspects of the temple cult.
No specific details are forthcoming about this potential problem except
that an Assyrian medical text, when speaking of the symptoms of venereal disease, insists that its occurrence showed "the hand of Ishtar,"[8]
which, if we can read this in a narrow sense, might indicate that the
disease resulted from a visit to a temple woman.

It was written that Ishtar was responsible for the woe that love
and passion brought to men, distracting their minds from such socially
encouraged tasks as serving in armies and acquiring money. A man
finding himself caught in the passion of love, and seeing his wealth
disappearing through pleasure seeking, could approach the priests or
priestesses of Ishtar and request that they perform a magical ritual
designed to free him from Ishtar's pernicious embrace and thus allow
his inflamed desires to subside. Whether the same opportunity was
open for women is something about which the texts remain silent.

Among the surviving reports from the astrologers to the Assyrian kings
only some twenty are found that mention Venus and, of these, many
exist only in fragments. In consequence, we lack all but the barest

details regarding the character of omens drawn from Venus, apart, that is, from the simplistic material within the Venus Tablet. Fortunately, one tablet is sufficiently well preserved to provide a number of detailed omens:

> If the goat-star [Venus] approaches Cancer, there will be peace and reconciliation in the country, and the gods will have mercy on the country. Empty storage bins will become full, the crops of the country will recover, the pregnant women will perfect their embryos, and the great gods will keep the sanctuaries of the country in order.[9]

These attributes are repeated in the other remaining fragments, and assuming them to be at least partially representative, we can conclude that a major omen drawn from Venus contacts pertained to fecundity: the successful pregnancies of women and the growth and harvesting of crops. Such an explanation is in character; Ishtar's domain included procreation as well as agricultural fertility.

Apart from this one text, the information provided by the remainder is minimal and hardly allows any conclusions to be drawn about the ancient view of Venus's role in astrological *omina*. All we have are statements that Venus becoming visible in the fifth month or in the eleventh month—probably the modern Leo or Aquarius—foreshadows prosperity of the crops, as does Venus moving within the constellation Virgo. The reverse, a disastrous harvest, is the prediction drawn from Venus failing to become visible in the eighth month, perhaps to be identified with the modern Scorpio. Even worse is predicted on the occasion that Scorpio receives an explicit mention: it is specified that should Venus enter this constellation, then all the crops will be destroyed by winds and floods. Thus, we can loosely summarize the position: if Venus is not in Scorpio when it is supposed to be, then the harvest is disastrous; if Venus is in Scorpio, then the harvest is destroyed. The position is nothing if not comprehensive.

Ishtar's military aspect also finds expression in the astrological tablets, though, to be fair, warfare is the subject of a large number of omens drawn from a variety of planetary sources. Should Venus enter the constellation Libra, for example, then a war is predicted—one that will go badly for the empire. It is not insignificant that modern astrologers seem to have inherited at least one element of the theory that lay behind the formulation of this omen: warfare traditionally is still placed under the rulership of Libra. There are other indications of impending war: if Venus should disappear in the first or fifth months or, conversely, appear in the fifth month, then conflagration was considered imminent. The war that was expected to follow upon the disappearance of Venus in the first month would, the texts state drily, prove disastrous for the king, whereas in the wars that were associated with the latter two events, he was expected to win.

Of course, as we have seen above, if Venus appeared in the fifth month, not only was a successful war imminent but simultaneously, in a species of astrological non sequitur, the crops would be successful. By which criteria the astrologers decided upon one of these disparate predictions for their reports to the king remains a mystery. We have no record of them admitting defeat and sending both.

The harmonizing effect of Venus, an important part of the attributes allocated to the planet by modern astrologers, is clearly expressed when, for example, the planet is seen in conjunction with an eclipse. One text, reporting an impending lunar eclipse, adds that Venus, Jupiter, and Saturn would all be present within it. Rather than being recommended to perform a Namburbi ritual, the king is informed that he need not fear this eclipse.[10] A second text describing another lunar eclipse in conjunction with both Venus and Jupiter expresses omens that are favorable to the king.[11] It would thus seem likely that Venus and Jupiter, with or without Saturn, are here seen as very powerful protectors of the king and kingdom, able to remove or render inoperative the evil normally associated with an eclipse.

It would be interesting if we should find textual support for the presence of one or both these planets in a solar eclipse, thus obviating the need to install a substitute king on the throne. A statement one way or the other on this point would allow a direct judgment to be drawn about the relative strength of planetary omens with respect to terrestrial ritual.

At the moment, the existence of Namburbi and substitute king rites indicates the primacy of terrestrial influence: the will of the operator can alter or avoid the fate portended by omens from above. But how certain of success were the ancient priests? Exactly how malleable did they think the universe was? A statement about the relative merits of either ritual or the presence of Venus or Jupiter to remove the danger of an eclipse would begin to resolve this question. It is certainly possible that in the future a text might be found or identified that deals with this point, and we shall learn a little more about the ancient concept of fate as a result.

The remaining omens from Venus are inconclusive: one tablet only mentions omens derived simply from a station of Venus—an event that precedes both a period of retrograde motion and the return to direct progress about forty days later. No further distinction is mentioned, yet as this event is rather common—occurring every eighteen months— one would expect somewhere to find some further differentiation of Venus stations perhaps drawn from the different months in which they took place or the different planets or constellations in whose proximity they were observed. Certainly the general framework of the omens in the Enuma Anu Enlil series is of such a structure that would suggest a methodical organization of omens in this manner. However, nothing of this sort has been found.

All that survives on this single Babylonian tablet that we have is the bare comment that a station of Venus indicated that the prince— presumably the crown prince—would live a long time and there would be justice in the land.[12]

The royal dynasty gets a further undifferentiated mention in tablet fifty-one of the Enuma Anu Enlil: if Venus should rise early in "its month," then the king would have a long life, whereas if Venus should rise late in "its month," the king would soon die. This suggests the dangers attending upon any errors made in establishing the working parameters of the national calendar, for if the astrologers had, for some reason, chosen the months wrongly—perhaps having failed to intercalate a month—then this event, of dire consequence to the king and by extension to his astrologers, would take place. How the king would view a prediction of his death derived from an astrologer's error in calculating the calendar can only be guessed at, but it is fair to imagine that if the astrologer merely lost his position and had to make bricks for a living like the unfortunate Tabia, he could be considered fortunate.

The last omens to be mentioned are those derived from the conjunction of Venus with Mars: "if, when Venus rises, Mars is seen near it, then the king's son will enter the palace and take the throne." Thus, according to this statement, the event was seen as a direct threat against the king by one or other of his sons. This prediction can also be understood as the king dying and being succeeded by his son. It would therefore seem, as we shall see, that this omen probably derives more from the presence of Mars than of Venus. This conjunction, though, is certainly seen as negative in another text: it predicts that the crops would be ruined either by a flood or by an enemy trampling through them.[13]

It is clear that a number of the ancient omens associated with Venus have survived to appear again in the astrological tradition inherited by modern astrologers. Of course, the prime role of Venus—the rule over women and all things feminine—still remains closely identified with the planet. This we should not be surprised about, as the Greek and Roman writers, who are our sources, stressed this aspect. However, it is the survival of the less obvious aspects that is interesting.

The ancient concern of Venus with the success of the harvest finds an echo in the modern attribution of commodities and the commercial resources of the nation under the rule of Venus. The martial quality of Venus in the past, the rulership of armies and invasions, has also survived: war, treaties, and allies are today still part of the role of Venus.

Finally, the concern of Venus with justice throughout the land finds its corollary in the modern acceptance of Venus's rule over the law courts.*

These correspondences are very close, proving that with Venus, the astrological values have successfully passed across several thousand years from ancient Babylon to the present—albeit in a slightly modified form.

---

*For the modern attributions, see Watters, *Horary Astrology,* pages 44–45.

11

NINURTA

Saturn, Brother to Mars

Saturn is "the author of melancholy," writes astrologer William Ramesey in his work, *Astrology Restored,* which in 1653 was one of the earliest astrology texts printed in English.* If Saturn is seen to be "well fortified" and "Lord of the year," then, he explains, this signifies "that the people will build houses, that the earth shall be fruitful and that people shall be honoured, wealth will be increased and effort shall be rewarded." If Saturn is weak in this position then "there shall be much cold . . . and men shall sustain much sorrow, losses . . . and great damage by storms, wind and rain. . . . He is cold, dry, melancholic, author of solitariness."[1] All in all, Ramesey gives us the distinct impression of some determinedly dour deity who lies heavily upon humankind, too fat to move, too ill to laugh, and too angry for compassion.

This dour view of Saturn has reached into the twentieth century. The English astrologer Margaret Hone, in 1951, produced a work that for many years remained the standard text for trainee astrologers. In it

---

*The first published text was six years earlier: William Lilly's *Christian Astrology.*

she contends that Saturn holds "the power to limit or control life" and stresses that it is the source of "the sternness of fate."[2]

Astrologers have long feared Saturn. Tradition has maintained its identity as a symbol of limitation, of restrictive structure, of repressive fate. As a result it was seen as a negative influence because, the unspoken assumption goes, people do not enjoy limits being imposed upon them. However, modern astrologers' embrace of depth psychology has changed the approach to this symbol: limitation and structure are now understood as essential for growth. Saturn, the stern judge, has become instead the firm and steadfast teacher.

The ancient astrologers saw Saturn quite differently. To the Assyrians and Babylonians he was not a stern and cold patriarch but a conquering hero. Saturn, in the earliest legends, battled with the ancient powers of chaos that had erupted from the primeval womb to recover the stolen tablets of law. And possession of these gave control over destiny.

Saturn and Mars, the divine brothers, were both warrior gods. While the planet Saturn, called Sagush in the astrological letters, was never formally identified in the texts with a deity, it is generally understood as the planet of Ninurta, also known as Ningirsu, Ninib, or Ninurash.* In fact, Saturn and Mars were in such close alliance that the Babylonians and Assyrians sometimes declined to identify them separately. An example of this celestial congruence appears on a relief that archaeologists excavated at the city of Kish, the cult center of the war god. It shows the head of the war god flanked by the symbols of both Ninurta and Nergal (Mars), each of them depicted with a sun disk—for both also shared certain qualities of the solar deity.[3]

Ninurta's primary mythological role was that of the conquering hero who waged war on behalf of the gods. His story is told in

*Saturn is recorded as d (meaning dingir, or "god"), Ningirsu, or—as the planet is normally written in the astrological reports—Sagush (meaning "constant"). See Reiner, *Enuma Anu Enlil*, page 14.

myth so ancient that it certainly predates the appearance of writing. While many details of the story have not yet been reconstructed, the basic plot as we understand it is as follows. In ancient times the eternal laws had been written by the gods upon the "tablets of fate." Possession of these tablets conferred the power over fate upon the owner. Originally they were held by Enlil, who wore them upon his breast. One day at dawn, after Enlil had removed the tablets in order to wash, they were stolen. The thief was the winged dragon of storms called Zu, who was in league with the great sea-dwelling dragon of chaos. Such was the fear instilled in the gods by these creatures that none was prepared to pursue them and fight for the recovery of these vital tablets.

Only Ninurta finally had the courage to step forward and volunteer for this formidable task. After a search he located the nest of Zu in the mountains and saw the tablets hidden within it. He managed to rescue the tablets and brought them back to the great meeting hall of the gods, where, in gratitude, he was awarded custody of the tablets. Thus Ninurta became overseer of fate and destiny—known, as we have seen, as shimtu to the ancient Assyrians.

The images of Ninurta, carved upon boundary stones and stelae, molded in clay or inscribed upon cylindrical seals, were combinations of the eagle with certain weapons. The ancient solar symbol of the eagle, often standing upon a pillar, was the primary representation of Ninurta. Variations often occur: the symbol might be a weapon with an eagle's head or an eagle with a lion's head and, occasionally, we find an eagle with two heads facing in opposite directions. This odd symbol still survives in European heraldry today. Whether there is any chthonic symbolic resonance is impossible to tell.

Ninurta was not always portrayed in animal form; he was, at certain times, portrayed as a man holding in his hand a seven-headed weapon. It has been suggested that this could be a symbol of the seven celestial gods, but for what reason they would be depicted in this form is unclear. Perhaps the portrayal is illustrating how Ninurta held the gods' fates in his hands?

There are two apparent associations of Ninurta with the Old Testament. Both involve an opposition to the spread of this Mesopotamian cult. One of Ninurta's titles was Lord of Swine; to him the pig was sacred. It is arguable that here we might see the origins of the biblical proscription of the consumption of pork, for by forbidding the consumption of this meat, Ninurta is effectively insulted and rejected. Indeed, to abstain from pork could be the mark of a person who also abstains from the worship of this god.

The second association appears in the book of Amos. This prophet is fulminating against his people for their widespread worship of the god Sakkut (translated as "Moloch" in the King James version of the Bible), a practice that he promised would bring invasion and exile.[4] Now the cult of Ninurta, both as a war god and as a sun god, spread westward from Mesopotamia, and as sun god he was considered specifically to embody the god of the rising sun, "he who opens the gate of sunrise." As god of sunrise, one of Ninurta's titles was Sakkut—the very same opposed by Amos. We can be confident then that Ninurta's cult was well entrenched among the Israelites during the time of the prophets—the eighth century BCE, about a century before the reign of Ashurbanipal in Nineveh.

Although quotations found within the astrologers' reports clearly point to there having been at least one tablet of the astrological series wholly or partially devoted to omens from Saturn, this tablet has not yet been discovered. In consequence, the only sources available for information at the present time are the reports themselves. As with so many of the planets, only a small number referring to Saturn exist: of the 358 astrological reports published by Parpola and Thompson, only twenty-six mention Saturn. How representative of Saturn are those attributes quoted is a question that cannot at the moment be answered. We can only hope that many more tablets escaped destruction and now await identification among the huge holdings in the world's museums.

While utilizing these astrological reports should at least allow the clarification of certain basic astrological attributes, unfortunately they do not, for there is yet another source of uncertainty. Around 56 BCE, the historian Diodorus Siculus wrote down all he understood of Babylonian astrology. During the course of his explanation he mentioned that the planet Saturn was "the most conspicuous and presages more events and such as are of greater importance than the others."[5] He then adds that Saturn "they call the star of Helius [the sun]."[6] As we have seen, this is recognition of the archaic and potentially confusing Mesopotamian practice that the sun and Saturn were often both referred to as Shamash in the texts.

The earliest known description of the characteristics ascribed to Saturn is found in the Babylonian creation epic, the *Enuma Elish,* which was collated into its definitive form during the first dynasty of Babylon. Some have suggested a date of around 1800 BCE.

. . . the star [Saturn], star of law and order . . .[7]

To modern astrologers this is a very familiar attribution, for the characteristics allocated to Saturn today include precisely the same traits: Saturn is "discipline and whoever enforces it."[8] This is further proof that early Babylonian mythology can be found forming an integral part of the astrology of an age existing almost four thousand years later.

By far the most numerous category of astrological reports from Nineveh that mention Saturn are those that also include the moon. They deal specifically with conjunctions between the two:

When a halo surrounds the Moon and Saturn stands within it, they will speak truth in the land: the son will speak the truth with his father. Welfare of multitudes.[9]

That such a conjunction is consistently seen as predicting truthful speaking is demonstrated by three other reports that state the same conclusion.[10] Additional information is provided by a note to one of these reports, which vouchsafes the information that this particular conjunction promises a "secure foundation for the king's throne and justice throughout the land."[11] This last assertion is the same as the "law and order" attribute found in the creation epic. A second text makes the connection explicit: Saturn is identified as "the star of Truth and Justice."[12]

A second type of omen is derived from conjunctions of Saturn with the moon. These concern the king and the state over which he rules, in the case of the Nineveh reports, Akkad.

> Last night Saturn drew near to the Moon. Saturn is the star of the Sun. This is its interpretation; it is lucky for the king. The Sun [Saturn] is the king's star. . . . When the Sun [Saturn] stands above or below the Moon, the foundation of the throne will be secure; the king will stand in his justice.[13]

A further report specifies that Saturn is the "Star of Akkad" and lucky for the king.[14]

There are a number of ways in which this state of national security and justice is expressed in the astrologers' reports: "The land will be satisfied. . . . The cattle lie down securely. . . . The gods intend happiness for Akkad." All of these comments confirm the impression that Saturn was a benevolent planet, important to the well-being of the kingdom.

Certain texts concerned with Saturn provide omens that, in the present state of our knowledge, are at variance with those in other reports. Without further material or the translations of the Saturn tablet in the Enuma Anu Enlil, we have no way of knowing whether the omens they express were from this series and were thus canonical or were from a noncanonical, perhaps oral, tradition.

One text, for example, gives for a conjunction of Saturn and the moon the reading that "robbers will rage."[15] This is seemingly anomalous—if justice is ruling the land, the usual interpretation of moon and Saturn, how can robbers rage? Further examples, if we could find them, may make the sense clearer and resolve the evident contradiction, but for the moment this text stands alone as an apparent anomaly in the body of reports.

One curious attribute of Ninurta has survived the millennia to reappear, associated with Saturn, within modern astrology books. This is his relationship with the rocks of the earth. Typically, in a modern astrological text that deals with "mundane" attributions, Saturn's rule will include "coal, its mines and miners. Lead, foundations of buildings . . ."* The clear implication is that Saturn rules over certain heavy or dense minerals. This seems to have a connection with Ninurta: certain fragments of Sumerian myth survive that speak of the stones of the earth being hostile to Ninurta, who was eventually forced to battle with them. Once he had defeated and subdued them, he dealt out their fates, good or bad. Chalcedony, for example, was given a bad fate in that it was destined forever to be carved and split by chisels. Marble, on the other hand, was awarded the privilege of being used for the building of temples. Some twenty minerals, not all of which have been identified, were listed as being under the control of Ninurta.[16] Could it be from this legend that the later astrological attribution found its source?

There are two further attributions to mention: a general famine is predicted from a conjunction of Mars and Saturn,† and Saturn in Leo is mentioned as portending a three-year period in which lions and jackals will roam, attacking and killing with such license that the traffic of people and goods becomes seriously disrupted.[17]

---

*See Watters, *Horary Astrology,* pages 48–49. Her source for this would appear to be William Ramesey, who gives a very similar listing.

†See Thompson, *Reports of the Magicians and Astrologers,* 103, page liv. Note that the text reads "Mars reaches the path of the Sun" and later explains (rev. 4) that this "path of the Sun" refers to Saturn (as the star of the sun).

In conclusion, it is clear that for the Assyrians and Babylonians, Saturn ruled truth and justice along with law and order, which factors were seen as important in maintaining stability throughout the land of Akkad. The prime mover of the law was the king, and Saturn also provided omens concerning his well-being and the basic foundations of his rulership. These benefits, though, augured by Saturn's conjunctions with others, could be negated should the planet ever be in conjunction with Mars. This latter combination at least was seen negatively and was considered to foretell famine and hardship.

It is fair to say that there is little in these ancient descriptions of Saturn's influence that cannot be found in a modern astrology book. Saturn today is said to rule over the "foundations of the state" and "the limits of socially or legally permissible conduct."[18]

On Saturn and Mars together the English astrologer the late H. S. Green writes: "Unfortunate for the Monarch and the Government; serious difficulties in national life; discontent on the part of the people."[19]

It does seem evident that much from ancient Babylonia has survived the last three thousand years to find a place in the astrology books used today, which encapsulate a continuation of the ancient intellectual tradition.

12

NERGAL

Mars, Lord of the Dead

Mars was always identified by the ancient astrologers with the god Nergal, brother to Ninurta.⊙ Like Ninurta, it seems that Nergal was originally a solar deity, though, in contrast to his brother, Nergal was considered evil, lord of both the fires of hell and the heat of the fierce summers that destroyed both humans and crops.

Nergal's earliest known name was the Sumerian Lugalmeslam, which translates as "King [Lugal] of the lower world where the Sun lay at night." Mythology explains why this was so. In a very early tale referring to a time of great antiquity, even by Sumerian standards—we find the story of Nergal and the underworld. The plot opens with all the gods gathered together in heaven for a great feast.

The gods wished to invite Ereshkigal, goddess of the underworld, to their gathering. As they knew that she would refuse to leave her domain, they instead suggested that she send an emissary to accept her share of the food. Ereshkigal duly sent an envoy, who presented himself

---

*To the scholars who wrote the tablets in the Assyrian library, Mars was known as Nibeanu or d.Ugur.

at the door of the feasting hall of the gods. Upon seeing the envoy, all the assembled deities rose from their seats to greet him. All of them, that is, except for Nergal, who remained firmly seated. This was understood as a direct insult to the goddess.

When Ereshkigal heard of this she was filled with anger and demanded Nergal's life. She insisted that the gods deliver him down to the underworld so that she might have the pleasure of personally executing him. Nergal appealed against this demand but found that he could not escape his fate. However, after his entreaties, by way of compromise, he was permitted to make the journey accompanied by fourteen companions—one for each of the doors in Ereshkigal's palace.

Nergal traveled down into the depths of the earth, and when he reached the palace he placed one of his companions on guard at each door. He then rushed the building and, finding the envoy whom he had ignored, quickly killed him. He continued into the throne room, where he found Ereshkigal. Seizing her by the hair, Nergal dragged her to the floor and was about to slice off her head when, with tears, she begged to be spared. She would become his wife, she cried, if only he would let her live. Nergal was moved by her pleas and had a change of heart. With a gesture of tenderness he dried her tears and agreed to her offer. And so, from that time onward, Nergal and his wife, Ereshkigal, shared rule over Arallu, the underworld. From that time onward, Nergal was also a god of the underworld, god of the grave, and judge of the dead.

Nergal's mythological connection with death appears in the astrological reports, where there are numerous references to Mars precipitating widespread disease or carnage. In addition, like his brother Ninurta, Nergal appears in mythology as a war god, lord of battle. There is, too, no doubt that this attribute was also attached to his planet, for in the reports there are many references to Mars causing an invasion of enemy troops, for example, "When a planet and Mars stand facing one another, there will be an invasion of the enemy."[1]

Other more specific combinations also find occasional mention.

If Mars was conjunct with Jupiter, for instance, then it was predicted that there would be widespread devastation of the kingdom. This perhaps suggests that the modern "expansive" role of Jupiter in astrological interpretations was also valid in ancient times.

Nergal was also considered to be the god of plague, fevers, and pestilence, and these attributes find frequent mention. To the Assyrians at least, general tragedy such as a plague striking the nation was, it would appear, tantamount to Mars declaring war upon them. Many of the texts mention the result of Mars's unfavorable actions being "a bed of warriors," this description being a highly poetic image of the plague dead, especially so as it was common for a whole army to be struck down by such a disease. And as we shall see, this association of Mars with plague is still held today.

Mythology records that the god Enlil entrusted to Nergal the cattle of the field. This attribute is manifested in the reports, where many omens link the movement of Mars to the fate of cattle: "When a halo surrounds the Moon and Mars stands within it, there will be destruction of cattle."[2] However, it seems that not only cattle were considered to be affected by movements of Mars. Another text states that Nergal rules over commercial prosperity, in fact the price of basic commodities in the market.[3] This leads to the possibility that we should see Nergal not as ruler simply over cattle but over all animals that were husbanded for commercial slaughter.

Although, as we shall see, the astrological symbol for the crown prince is Mercury, he too is said to be affected by Mars, and the most evil position for the planet to assume is if Mars should enter the greatly feared constellation of Scorpio. During this time the danger to the crown prince is manifest: "Mars has stood within Scorpio: this is its interpretation. When Mars approaches Scorpio, the prince will die by a scorpion's sting or will be captured in his palace."[4]

Many of the characteristics given to Mars by the Babylonians and Assyrians have remained attached to that planet despite the passing of thousands of years. Any readily available modern astrological text will list war and battle among the planet's concerns, but perhaps this is not so surprising given the strong residue of Greek mythology in modern life. Less obvious are the more arcane rulerships.

Among the traditional associations with Mars listed by astrological writers in the early part of the twentieth century are not only war and violence in general but also plague, epidemics, and fevers. And, as ruler of the sign Scorpio, Mars reaches back to its very earliest mythology and is still considered to preside over death and the underworld. However, as we shall see, since the 1930s this latter attribution has been progressively subsumed by Pluto.

Even more arcane is the strange Mesopotamian link between cattle and Mars. Extraordinarily, this has survived the millennia as well. While the majority of Western astrologers today would place cattle and cattle markets under the rulership of Venus,[5] Mars, as ruler over abattoirs and butchers, in this way controls the fate of commercial beasts that are slaughtered for the market.*

There is something remarkable about this minor and generally unknown attribution surviving for such a long period of time. It is yet another indication of how valuable astrological texts were to those scribes and scholars who so carefully copied, recopied, and translated the material from the Mesopotamia of three thousand and four thousand years ago. And there is something remarkable about the fact that this information is still in print. Whether one grants the assertion any validity or not, from a purely aesthetic point of view, in the history of ideas, it is a satisfying situation.

Since the 1970s astrology has progressively focused less upon an individual's future than upon an individual's perception of reality. The birth chart is seen as not only revealing an individual's personal reality but

---

*See Mayo, *The Planets and Human Behaviour,* page 162. The original source for this would seem to be Ramesey, *Astrology Restored,* page 54. See also Lilly, *Christian Astrology,* page 67, repeated in 1911 by Pearce in *The Text-Book of Astrology,* page 89. Curiously, this attribution is not mentioned by Barbara Watters, H. S. Green, or Raphael in their books on the mundane aspects of the planets. It would seem that for many modern astrologers Scorpio/Pluto has taken over this attribution. For example, Barbara Watters places butchers under Scorpio (*Horary Astrology,* page 29).

also pointing out those areas in his or her life where modification, compromise, and nurture could usefully play a part in the realization of individual potential. In other words, it is used to aid an individual to make the utmost of all potential talents. Thus, the birth chart is seen as a map of individual potential rather than some occult diagram of fated destiny.

This modern attitude obviously owes much to the psychological thought of the last half century, as well as to a modern interpretation of very ancient alchemical, magical, and Hermetic philosophies.

The transmutation of the individual, the magus using the stars to change his life, is the point of the discipline. And it is perhaps fitting that a planet that modern astrologers regard as a powerful symbol of this urge to transmute one's life is Pluto, unknown to the Babylonians and discovered only recently, on January 21, 1930.

Of relevance is that Pluto, in his modern incarnation, contains a synthesis of the attributes of the brothers Nergal and Ninurta, Mars and Saturn. Pluto is the arbiter of fate, like Ninurta, and ruler of the underworld, like Nergal. Pluto is also held to rule over Scorpio, that constellation or sign that was so feared by the Mesopotamians, perhaps because for them it symbolized all that they were pushing away from themselves with their civilization—the chaos, the darkness, the unknown. But now, with the appearance of Pluto, astrology is confronting the depths, its own womb. Perhaps this is its true challenge.

Finally, it should be recalled that both Ninurta and Nergal battled with goddesses: the goddess of chaos on the one hand and the goddess of the underworld on the other. The two goddesses are aspects of the one entity, as, of course, are Nergal and Ninurta. The feminine, having been conquered, was thrust far beneath the surface yet, as was apparent to all, still retained its strength. Today, with Pluto receiving more attention as a symbol worthy to represent the transformation of personality, the deeply hidden feminine aspect of this destructive energy is beginning to appear once more in the light of consciousness. As one modern astrological writer puts it, "in the astrological Pluto we are confronting something feminine, primordial and matriarchal."[6]

13

MARDUK

Jupiter, Savior of Babylon

The god Marduk was gone. He was locked up, imprisoned within the sacred mountain. And his loss caused chaos to erupt throughout the dusty city: the marketplaces were thrown into turmoil, angry fights and loud disputes broke out among the restless population, slaves rather than their masters assumed control in every household. Quickly the streets became filled with rushing people frantically seeking their god. They raised their faces to heaven and cried aloud, "Where is he? Where is he held captive?"

Then, suddenly, in the midst of this turmoil, galloping horses smashed a pathway through the streets, pulling an empty chariot, which careened and bounced around the corners. Gilded and ornate, this chariot was the god's own. Driverless, bouncing out of control, it was dragged at high speed along the sacred road crossing the city until it exited at a furious pace from the gate of Ishtar to race toward the Akitu temple beyond the city walls. Behind the chariot a single priestess followed. She bewailed the disappearance of the city's god. The whole city was afraid, for with no god to protect it, it could fall into chaos. "Find Marduk" was the urgent cry heard in the streets.

If their god were not found, evil would quickly take over. And so in desperation and in fury passed the fifth day of the great spring festival at Babylon.

In ancient Babylonia and Assyria the arrival of spring heralded the beginning of the year. The first month, Nisannu, began with the evening nearest to the spring equinox upon which the crescent moon was first visible.

The priests of Babylon would wait, studying the sky each evening, until the crescent moon was seen. Then they would officially declare the beginning of the month. In modern times this date can vary between March 13 and April 11.

Nisannu was a special month for the Babylonians, and its first eleven days were occupied by a great religious festival that touched the very ancient and yet still insecure roots of Mesopotamian society. It touched, perhaps, those fears of chaos and savagery that have lingered on since humankind first began living in settled communities, long before written records existed.

During those eleven days of rituals, both public and private, the rights of the king along with the stability and strength of the civilization itself were first called into question and then symbolically reasserted—as though disintegration were so close to the surface that only a deliberate and conscious regular revocation could hold chaos at bay. And so, symbolically, within prescribed limits, this festival allowed the primordial chaos a chance to emerge once again, briefly, to tear aside the fabric of civilization built by order and hierarchy. It emerged to be again defeated, for another year.

In Babylon the central personalities of the festival were Marduk (Jupiter), the chief god of the city, along with his son, Nabu (Mercury). Similar spring festivals are known to have been regularly held in the cities of Asshur, Nineveh, Ur, Uruk, Dilbat, Arbela, and Harran, far away on the route to the Mediterranean.

Excavations at Babylon have revealed a text of the festival that gives details of the ceremonies performed on each day. Regrettably, like so many of the tablets found, it was badly damaged, with the consequence that only the details for days two to five are complete. As a further caution we must remember that this gives only the ceremonies performed in Marduk's temple in Babylon, the Esagila. Whether there were any associated public rites is unknown, but there must surely have been. Perhaps someday they will be discovered.

Additional information can be gleaned from a variety of other texts that allude to, or give details of, various rites occurring on other days. A collation of these sources has enabled a general but limited reconstruction of events to be made. It became clear that, in essence, the festival comprised two important rites that, it seems, were anciently seen as separate festivals—the sacred marriage and the events at the Akitu temple. However, by the turn of the first millennium BCE, at least, these were combined into one long and complex spring observance.[1]

A small number of intriguing texts that have been found reveal that behind the public events of this and other state rituals lay an esoteric explanation understood only by initiates. Their form is often simple: each succeeding event in the public ritual is followed by an explanation of its inner meaning:

> The King, who wears jewels on his head and roasts goats.
> :He is Marduk, who carried firewood on his head and burnt the sons of Enlil and Anu in a fire.[2]
> The ox and the sheep which they throw alive to the ground . . .
> :That is Kingu and his seven sons when they were smitten.[3]

Other such texts detail the mystical numbers associated with each god, the plants, the metals, the precious and the semiprecious stones. These works give a brief glimpse into what must have been a rich and complicated secret tradition, accessible only to the privileged few. To ensure this, each text ends with a warning. "A secret of the great gods. May the initiate instruct the initiate. Let the uninitiated not see."[4]

The first four days of the spring festival were filled by various preparatory rites that methodically set the stage for an increasingly intense religious celebration. The rituals for the first day are no longer extant, but they were perhaps not dissimilar to those of days two and three, details of which have survived.

Both these days began with the high priest, who, after a ritual cleansing, entered the temple of Marduk to stand alone before the god's statue and recite a long prayer. This prayer began by praising Marduk's triumphs in defeating all his enemies and concluded with a plea for a blessing upon the temple, the city, and the people.[5] Once this was completed, the rest of the day passed with the normal observances in the temple, the daily meals being served to the statues of the god along with the associated rituals.

On the third day, however, events took a slightly different course. Following the morning prayer to Marduk, skilled craftsmen were called and ordered to construct two small wooden figures. One figure was depicted holding a snake, the other a scorpion. Once completed, these figures were then covered with gold and jewels. The remainder of the day passed in the same way as the two before.

It was not until the fourth day was reached that a change began, a shift of emphasis to move the festival into deeper waters until it would reach the point where it would involve more than those concerned with the inner workings of the temple and would progressively erupt beyond those confines until it dominated the entire city.

Day four began early: three hours and twenty minutes before sunrise, the high priest rose, ritually washed, recited special prayers, and then walked to the temple forecourt, where, in the company of others, he awaited the rising of the constellation known to the Babylonians as "the Acre." This constellation's rising was celebrated by the chanting of a special litany. Following this, nothing is recorded until the evening, when for the first time in the festival the creation myth, the *Enuma Elish,* was recited in its entirety by the high priest to the statue of Marduk.

This epic poem, written significantly upon seven tablets, was as close to a sacred book as the Babylonians possessed. It is thought that this work was a compilation of earlier texts and traditions that were then woven together around the turn of the second millennium BCE, specifically for use in the Babylonian cult of Marduk. Perhaps we can see here the work of Hammurabi and his great desire for unification and centralization. The epic is interesting not only for its mythological content but also for its literary quality, which gives considerable information about the development of the Mesopotamian intellectual tradition.

A literary and religious text such as the *Enuma Elish* has important implications. First, it establishes as canonical its synthesis of traditions, which, once in such a fixed form, is saved from reinterpretation and change. It can also be distributed to all parts of the kingdom to convert local cults—once of equal importance to that of Babylon's Marduk—into provincial cults of less significance than the new official observance. In this way, the cult can serve the purpose of political unity. Standard texts and myths can bring a very powerful psychological pressure to bear upon the population, such that any divergent or contrary thought becomes tantamount to heresy and is punished.

On this fourth day of the festival the creation epic was read only in the privacy of the inner sanctum of the temple of Marduk. It was not, so far as the evidence we have reveals, read at this stage to the general public. A problem of understanding this festival arises out of the very nature of the surviving texts. None of them specifically mentions any involvement of the public in any part of the festivities. This must be considered unlikely, and undoubtedly a consequence of the specific motivation behind the writing of the texts we have. They were a guide for the priests of the temple. It is unlikely that the rituals described are the only ones observed; rather, it would appear more likely that the instructions for the public observances have not survived. It is inconceivable that four days of such an important festival could go by without public awareness and participation. We are in the position of attempting to understand all the rituals of Christmas, for example, using only the text of a nativity play. Would we be correct to use this as proof that the public had no involvement other than observing a small group of actors on a single day?

The fifth day was marked by a curious ritual humiliation for the king. It marks this day as one of atonement. It began with the high priest chanting prayers to Marduk as the god who is immanent in all the planets, albeit under different names.[6] This is seen by some scholars as early evidence for a monotheistic tendency in Babylonian religion. A line in the *Enuma Elish* echoes this: "Marduk . . . to thee we have given kingship over the totality of the whole universe."[7]

After a purification of the temple, the king entered the inner sanctum and stood before the statue of Marduk. The escorting priests then left, allowing the king to be alone with the god. Then the high priest appeared and, approaching the king, removed his royal insignia—the scepter, the ring, the sword, and the crown—and placed them on a seat at the base of the god's statue. Then the high priest slapped the king firmly in the face and pulled sharply on his ears. It was considered a very good omen if this should cause tears to come to the king's eyes. The king was then required to kneel before the god and declare that he had not neglected the temple or the city, that he had not sinned during the past year, and that he had not offended any people who were native-born citizens of the "free" cities Nippur, Sippar, Asshur, and later Harran. Following this confession and prayer, all the royal insignia were handed back to the king, and his face was struck a second time.

It would appear that the point of this ritual was to affirm that royalty was the preserve of Marduk, that it was a gift to the king that could be revoked at any time should the king transgress the sacred laws.

Later this same day, workmen began to prepare an offering table with a canopy of gold, which was placed in the section of the temple dedicated to Marduk's son, the god Nabu (Mercury), who was due to arrive the next day. At this point in the festival Marduk, his part perhaps played by the king, was considered to be a captive "in the mountain," that is, in the temple tower. Thus began the descending chaos for the city with the population desperately seeking their lord, but he was nowhere to be found. And so the fifth day of the festival drew to a close with the citizens unsettled and fearful. The final moments were filled with sacrificial blood: in an early evening ritual, in the temple court, the king and the high priest sacrificed a white bull while chanting a prayer that began "Divine Bull, splendid light that illuminates the darkness . . ."[8]

On the next day, the sixth of the festival, Nabu—who was to rescue the captured god—arrived in Babylon. His statue was placed in his chapel, which lay within Marduk's temple. The two gilded wooden figures that had been constructed on the third day were placed in his chapel also, facing Nabu's statue as it was borne toward the site. As this statue came closer, a swordsman beheaded the two figures, which were then thrown into a fire. The meaning of this latter rite is unclear, but it appears to be some ritual method of preventing evil befalling Nabu.

With this establishment of Nabu in his father's temple, the existing tablet breaks off, and the remainder of the festival must be pieced together from various alternative sources. One thing, though, is certain: for the remainder of the festival, the presence of the king was vital. The records indicate that on the occasions when the king was absent, the festival had to be canceled. This is one argument in favor of those scholars who maintain that the king not only attended the rituals but took an active and important part in them, perhaps as counterpoint to the high priest, as in the "humiliation" ceremony, or perhaps through acting the part of Marduk in some ritual dramas.

The seventh day remains almost a complete mystery. While other sources indicate that it witnessed the rescue of Marduk from his "mountain" captivity by Nabu, no details of the procedures involved have survived. The eighth day, however, is slightly better served by the sources. On this day the statues of the gods that had been carried to Babylon were assembled in the Hall of Destiny. For the first of two occasions, future destiny was determined. It is in this hall, upon this occasion, that Marduk was ritually elected king of the gods and thus given unlimited powers.

The details of the procedure at Uruk are known. In the morning of the eighth day, the statue of a servant of the gods was carried down into the temple court, where the gathering was to take place. This statue was placed in front of the statue of Anu, the sky god. Then the statues of the rest of the gods, in strict order of rank, were carried to the court and placed in their correct positions. A bowl of water was offered to Anu and his wife for their morning wash, and then a gold plate filled with meat was served, first to Anu and then to the others.

The arrangement of the statues of the gods was conducted by the king, who, holding a shining staff, successively called for each deity to come from his or her chapel in the temple and then, taking each god by the hand, led them to the correct position in the court. While this assembly was being held we are told that a "hush of reverence" passed over the city. The people were required to show no anger or thought-lessness in order that any negative influences might, in this way, be averted. What occurred, if anything, once all the statues were assembled is unknown, but it must surely have symbolically represented the recapture of the tablets of fate, although, in this case, Marduk would have been the heroic deity credited with the victory, thus taking over the role formerly ascribed to Ninurta.

By contrast the ninth day was one of celebration with the triumphant procession to the Bit Akitu, the special temple beyond the city walls. The procession began in the morning, led by the king with his court and accompanied by music and burning incense. Once it reached the Bit Akitu, a great banquet was held to celebrate Marduk's victory over the goddess of chaos, Tiamat.

Why this special temple for the New Year ceremonies lay beyond the city walls has not been explained in any extant tablet, and it remains a mystery. Excavations at the Assyrian capital of Asshur revealed that the shrine lay some two hundred meters beyond the ramparts. It was a significant establishment, surrounded by its own gardens and containing a large courtyard planted with trees and shrubs. The largest room the archaeologists found was a hall some one hundred feet long, which may have been the site of the celebration banquet. Archaeologists have surmised that the answer to the mystery about this temple being beyond the city walls may perhaps lie in its independence, for if it lay beyond the walls, then it could be considered beyond the jurisdiction of the city god—a good place, then, for often competing gods to gather and feast without fear.

At the conclusion of this banquet the procession returned to Babylon, and, while scholars cannot be definitive about this, it seems most likely that this, the evening of the ninth day, was when the sacred marriage was celebrated. This union of the god and goddess took place in the "room of the bed," a special shrine on top of the vast seven-staged ziggurat, Esagila. A priestess, perhaps the high priestess, took the place of the goddess, and scholars are divided over whether the king took the place of the god. Some, including the historian Herodotus, suggest that this was a symbolic event, with the single priestess spending the night alone. Others consider it more likely that the king and the priestess physically consummated the marriage, acting the part of the gods.

Marduk occupied a prime position in Babylonian and Assyrian mythology as effective savior of the world. Accordingly his planet, Jupiter, written either as "Sagmegar" or "mul dingir Marduk" (the star of the god Marduk) in the texts, occupied, with certain exceptions, a similarly beneficial position in their astrology. In modern astrological practice Jupiter is seen as benefic, that is, its considered effect in general is to encourage an advantageous possibility to emerge. It is said to be the planet of good luck and material advantages. The seventeenth-century astrologer William Ramesey—source for much modern astrology—concurs: "Jupiter when he is Lord of the year . . . the king shall do justice. . . . The people also shall be in a good and prosperous condition, and shall receive good from their King and Superiors, and they from the people, and the year shall be healthy, plentiful and good."[9]

This attitude toward Jupiter would appear to have its source in the ancient astrological texts. For the Babylonians and Assyrians Jupiter was certainly a benefic planet, the most dramatic example of its beneficial powers being revealed in a statement concerning its involvement in an eclipse: "Jupiter stood in the eclipse; it portends peace for the king, his name will be honourable"[10] and "The Series has said as follows in connection with this Nisannu eclipse: If the planet Jupiter is present in the eclipse all is well with the king, a noble dignitary will die, in his stead."[11] Jupiter's influence removed the evil, removed the need for any Namburbi ritual or substitute king. Jupiter, Marduk, calmed the disharmony in heaven and restored order, just as he did at the beginning of time and each year in the spring festival. However, the quote from the Enuma Anu Enlil suggests that the evil was not destroyed but was merely averted, even though the king and kingdom remained untouched without further magical aid.

The land of the kingdom too could benefit from Jupiter's involvement in events. Depending upon the particular occurrence, Jupiter could portend a good harvest, peace and security, sufficient rain for the farmers, and success in military campaigns: "When Jupiter stands fast in the morning . . . angry gods will be favourable with Akkad, there will be copious rains, plentiful floods . . . corn and sesame will be plentiful."[12]

A quality also associated with Jupiter was that of acting as a "conduit" to the gods, one that was uncluttered and could reach directly to the relevant deity. This perhaps was picking up on some of the qualities of Marduk as champion and chief of the gods: "When Jupiter goes with Venus, the prayer of the land will reach the heart of the gods."[13] This is speaking of a conjunction between Jupiter and Venus. However, the same quality appears in an omen derived from the observation of Jupiter: "The gods will give peace, troubles will be cleared up, and complications will be unraveled. . . . The gods will receive prayers and hear supplications; the omens of the magician shall be made apparent."[14]

The final benefit to be noted is conferred by Jupiter appearing brighter than usual—as a result of atmospheric conditions unknown to the Babylonians and Assyrians. On this occasion "the king of Akkad will go to pre-eminence"[15] and "the weapons of the king of Akkad will prevail over those of his foe."[16]

This would seem to be a clear equation of Jupiter (Marduk) in heaven with the king on earth. As Jupiter apparently grew brighter, that is, more prominent in heaven, so too would the king grow more prominent and successful on earth. That his success was coupled with the nation's success is evinced by another text, which vouchsafes, "When Jupiter grows very bright, that land will eat abundance."[17]

Jupiter's role was not always seen as beneficial: it had a dark, destructive side that could be revealed under certain conditions—by a conjunction with the moon, for example: "When a halo surrounds the Moon and Jupiter stands within it, the king of Akkad will be besieged."[18]

Further examples make it clear that the combination of the moon with Jupiter was seen negatively: invasions, the death of a king, commercial restriction, and widespread social hostility.[19] It is clear that this aspect was considered as most "unpropitious." We can understand, then, the reasoning behind the report that simply states bluntly: "Jupiter stood within the halo of the moon. Let them make a nambulbi [sic] ceremony."[20]

A number of other unpropitious omens from Jupiter are mentioned in the reports from the astrologers. Jupiter entering the constellation of Taurus, for example, indicated that the "good fortune of the land passes away" or that the farm animals do not have many young.[21] If Jupiter should enter Orion, then pests would devastate the harvests;[22] if it should pass by Regulus, then war would arrive and the throne would be seized by an enemy;* and if Jupiter should

---

*See Thompson, *Reports of the Magicians and Astrologers,* 272, pages lxxxvii–lxxxviii. See also Parpola, *Letters from Assyrian Scholars,* 13, volume 1, page 9, for a variant on this: "If Jupiter passes Regulus and gets ahead of it, and afterwards Regulus, which it passed and got ahead of, stays with it in its setting, somebody will rise, kill the king, and seize the throne."

enter Sagittarius, there would be great destruction throughout the kingdom.*

Finally, the conjunction of Jupiter with Mars was considered unfortunate: "When Jupiter stands in front of Mars, there will be corn and men will be slain, or a great army will be slain. . . . There will be devastation in the land. . . . The king of Akkad will die. . . . This omen is evil for the lands; let the king, my lord, make a nambulbi [*sic*] ceremony."[23] It seems as if any conjunction to Jupiter was regarded by the ancient astrologers as a direct challenge to their king and, by extension, to their land. This same text adds firmly that "evil" would come to the nation if Jupiter and any planet were together.

Whether such celestial movements can be read literally is still a matter for argument, but certainly some reports seem to indicate that, at least on some occasions, a literal reading is correct. One text states unequivocally the connection between a celestial challenge and one upon the earth: "When Jupiter advances on Regulus . . . so another will rise up and kill the king, and seize the throne."[24] Regulus has long been named the Royal Star, called by the Assyrians Sharru, which means "the king." Jupiter then, in this text, is assuming the role of a strong challenger to the reigning monarch, symbolized by Regulus.

This negative side of Jupiter has, to a certain extent, survived to be passed through medieval and Enlightenment Europe to appear in modern texts. William Ramesey writes that all the beneficial qualities of Jupiter could be reversed if the planet "be weak," that is, badly aspected.[25] For the modern astrologer an afflicted Jupiter suggests immoderation, hasty action, disharmony, and injustice throughout the land.[26]

One mystery does remain with Jupiter: it is not a dominant, presiding force in astrology, either ancient or modern. It is a source of astrological data in the same way as the other planets. The astrological texts

*See Thompson, *Reports of the Magicians and Astrologers,* 190, page lxvii. The text speaks of Jupiter entering Pabilsag, which is Sagittarius, perhaps with one star from Ophiuchus. See also Reiner, *Enuma Anu Enlil,* page 14.

do not reflect the mythological, which, on the contrary, show the pre-eminent position of Marduk. Of course, Marduk was deliberately, and for political reasons, raised to his ruling position in the pantheon of gods. He was raised there during the first dynasty of the Babylonian kings to underline and consolidate their power. Yet, even one thousand years later, Jupiter does not have this position in astrology. Are we seeing here a much older, pre-Babylonian tradition of Jupiter revealed in the omen texts? A tradition whose god has been changed but whose relative importance has not? Until more discoveries are made, we cannot know for certain.

14

NABU

Mercury, Scribe to the Gods

Curiously little is known of the cult of Nabu. This is especially surprising because it is clear that during the first millennium BCE Nabu's cult became so widespread and so popular that it began to rival that of Marduk. Indeed, the cult is believed to have survived into the Christian period—to the fourth century CE. Yet so few documents have been found that describe any rituals or texts integral to his cult that this major god essentially remains a mystery to us.

The center of Nabu's cult was the Babylonian city of Borsippa, situated by a lake near the Euphrates River about ten miles south of Babylon, which generally dominated it politically. Borsippa's existence is recorded from the beginning of the second millennium BCE. Nabu's temple, the Ezida, held a notable library to which Ashurbanipal sent his men in their search for unusual tablets. Unfortunately, Borsippa has not been extensively or scientifically excavated by archaeologists.

Nabu's cult, however, seems to have arisen rather late. While he is first mentioned during the reign of Hammurabi, it was only around the turn of the first millennium BCE that Nabu became god of Borsippa and at the same time replaced the earlier Sumerian goddess, Nisaba or Nidaba, as the deity presiding over wisdom, writing, and accounts, and as the patron of scribes and writing. He became sufficiently popular for the later kings to have a formula mentioning their support of the temples of Marduk and Nabu stamped upon each of their building bricks. And he became sufficiently widespread for the prophet Isaiah to complain about him.*

Nabu was the messenger of the gods "without whom no plan is initiated in heaven."† His name means literally "herald," which was later repeated by the Roman Mercury, herald of the gods. The similarities do not end there; Nabu was considered to reflect the rapid motion of the planet Mercury and thus had the attribute of swiftness.[1] His symbol, carved upon stelae, was most commonly the writing desk, but he was also represented, on occasion, by a mason's chisel or a measuring rod.[2]

Nabu's divine role is not described in the creation myth, the *Enuma Elish,* which was formulated early in the second millennium BCE, yet he appears in the texts associated with the great spring festival as son of Marduk and divine scribe. He was also the one who, on the seventh day of the festival (the seventh of Nisannu), rescued Marduk from his imprisonment. Then, on the eleventh day, when the gods assembled to decide the destiny, the fate, of the world for the next year, it was Nabu who recorded them.

Although simple, this story gives an unexpected insight into the origins of a popular modern (and medieval) astrological technique: that of casting an astrological chart for the moment of the spring ingress—the moment that the sun enters Aries—in order to predict the events of the coming year.

Why should such a chart for the sun's entrance into the first sign of the zodiac determine the character of the subsequent year? The answer would seem to lie in the ancient Babylonian festival and its associated mythology. For if, as they believed, the fate of the coming year was

---

*Isaiah 46:1–2: "Bel is crouching. Nebo cringing. Their idols are being loaded on animals, on beasts of burden, carried off like bundles on weary beasts. They are cringing and crouching together, powerless to save the ones who carry them, as they themselves go off into captivity." Bel is Marduk and Nebo is Nabu.
†See Langdon, *Semitic Mythology,* page 158. For the most comprehensive survey of Nabu, his titles, and the extent of his cult, see Pomponio, *Nabu.*

determined by the gods, then, through their interpreters—the planets—this fate would be declared to all who had the ability to read it.

The sky was considered to be the Book of Heaven, Shitir Shame, and hence in the sky this fate is to be read. Thus, at the beginning of the year, the fate for the coming year could be read in the movements of the planets. And this is precisely what a modern astrologer is doing when an ingress chart is cast. Modern astrologers still retain vestiges of the Babylonian spring festival. And that the Assyrians also had some prototype of this ingress chart is revealed by one statement in the reports translated by Professor Thompson: "When Jupiter appears at the beginning of the year, in that year its corn will be prosperous."[3]

From 1846 to 1855 the explorer Henry Rawlinson—who had earlier climbed the rock of Behistun to copy the cuneiform inscriptions—conducted a number of excavations in Iraq. One of them, in the summer and autumn of 1854, was the first to be conducted at Borsippa, where he uncovered the remains of the temple of Nabu. As his workers dug their trenches farther down into the mound, uncovering layer upon layer of the outer wall of the terraced temple, Rawlinson noticed something odd: several of the stages seemed either to be made of different colored bricks or to have been covered by a substance imparting different colors to them. It appeared evident to Rawlinson that this was the result of a deliberate attempt, on the part of the Babylonian constructors, to impart a different color to each successive stage of the temple.

This temple was a ziggurat tower made up of seven stages, the first being 272 feet square and 26 feet high. This stage had a coating of black pitch about half an inch thick. Above this the next stage, of the same height, was made of red bricks. Above there were stages of a light yellow brick, a gray brick, and one, the second highest, was covered with a vitrified layer of "blue slag." As Rawlinson writes:

I was soon struck with the coincidence, that the colour black for the first stage, red for the third, and blue for what seemed to be the sixth, were precisely the colours which had belonged to the first, third, and sixth spheres of the Sabaean planetary system . . . were the colours which appertained to the planets Saturn, Mars and Mercury, by whom those spheres were respectively ruled![4]

The Sabaeans were a religious group during the sixth to tenth centuries CE who were based in Harran, a major city on the route from Assyria and Babylonia to the Mediterranean. They had retained much ancient star lore from the past, and it pervaded their writings, which were available in the Arab world.

Struck by these parallels, Rawlinson then looked again at some artifacts he had discovered. The ancient Babylonians were in the habit of burying, at each corner of the foundations of a new building, an inscribed cylinder recording details of the king or other prominent person under whose auspices this construction was carried out. Rawlinson had found two of these: the cylinders, which were identical, recorded not only "that the Temple was dedicated to 'the planets of the seven spheres'" but that it was called "the stages of the seven spheres."[5]

Rawlinson then felt justified in proposing the following reconstruction: that each stage of the temple was dedicated to a different planet and that each was given this planet's color. Noting that the order of the planets for the Sabaeans was Saturn, Jupiter, Mars, sun, Venus, Mercury, and the moon, he suggested that the first stage, that upon the ground and coated with jet-black pitch, was dedicated to Saturn; the second, of red-brown bricks, was dedicated to Jupiter; the third, of brighter red bricks, to Mars; the fourth, to the sun, though he could not distinguish any color difference in the bricks; the fifth, of yellow bricks, to Venus; the sixth, covered by a vitrified blue layer, to Mercury; and the seventh stage, to the moon, although, as with the fourth stage, he could not detect any color difference here. He suggested that the fourth stage had originally been covered with a gold veneer and the seventh with a silver.

While subsequent excavations over the succeeding century or more have revealed certain other temples with remains that suggest that some or all of their stages were colored, no further evidence has ever been discovered in the tablets that could prove that Rawlinson's interesting speculations had a basis in fact. His thoughts cannot, even today, be dismissed, and time may yet prove him correct. Indeed, as we shall see, his looking to the Sabaeans for clues was not without justification.

In the reports found in the Nineveh repositories, Mercury was written in the Sumerian figures GU.UD, often translated as *Gud*. It was pronounced in Akkadian as *Shihtu,* which means "jumping," and is perhaps a reflection of its speed in relation to the other planets. Its most well-known effect was to cause rain; one of the prayers given on day five of the spring festival mentions "the star Gud which causes rain."[6]

This depiction of Mercury as a "rainmaker" receives confirmation in the reports: "When Mercury is seen in Iyyar, a flood will come and benefit the fields and meadow lands."[7] It is useful to remember that for the Mesopotamians a flood was, in general, of benefit to the country so long as the water control systems were not overwhelmed. The corollary to this is revealed in another report: "When Mercury appears in Elul, there will be a heightening of the market, an increase of cereals."[8] For if the land received a plentiful rainfall, then the farmers would have a good harvest, meaning that the markets would be filled with high-quality produce. This same omen also reports that aspects of Mercury suggest that "cattle will be numerous in the fields" and that "sesame and dates will prosper," the clear inference being that Mercury affected the production and sale of basic agricultural commodities.

Apart from these commercial aspects of Mercury, omens drawn from this planet played a particularly important role in the organization of the palace for, as the reports state unequivocally, "The planet Mercury is the crown prince."[9] This clearly derives from the mythological role of Nabu being the son of Marduk.

Any variation in Mercury's appearance or movement affected the crown prince and his duties. A number of reports are concerned with the correct time for the prince to enter the palace and meet the king, the implication being that there was a strong stricture against the king's heir and the king being in the same place at the same time. However, if the planet was particularly bright, then this was one of the most advantageous times: "The planet Mercury is very bright; as it is the star of the crown prince, it means fortune . . . for the king and the crown prince. The crown prince is to enter into the presence of the king."[10]

The connections between these ancient attributes of Mercury and those used by modern astrologers are not immediately apparent. Yet beneath the ancient symbolism are the seeds of the modern. While it is true that Mercury today no longer has any connection with rainmaking, it would seem that the effect of this rainmaking, the bountiful harvest and active markets, is the beginning of one of the modern attributes of Mercury—that of ruling commerce and markets. While large companies and multinational commerce are represented by other factors for modern astrologers, Mercury is still seen as ruling the marketplace itself, where buying and selling is done directly.[11] This includes stock and commodity markets and even the "horse-trading" done on a daily basis by bankers and politicians. One can see how this derives from the ancient Babylonian and Assyrian city marketplaces.

Of course, while the astrological reports do not mention anything to do with predictions for the part of society that fell under the patronage of Nabu, the scribes, this mythological attribute of Mercury finds its way into modern astrology. Today Mercury also rules over writing and communication.[12]

During this survey of the Babylonian and Assyrian gods and their links with the planets we have had occasion to note certain minor attributes that, rather than having fallen by the wayside, have remained associated with the planets until the modern day. Often these attributes seem curious, even weird. Mercury is no exception. In modern astrology Mercury rules thieves. Can we see a beginning of this idea in the following report from the eighth century BCE? "When Mercury is visible in Kislew, there will be robbers in the land."[13]

15

ASTRONOMY

The mul.Apin

In the popular imagination, the Middle Eastern sky stretches upward, forever deep and forever clear. The blood-red evenings gradually fade into a night where each star glistens with its crisp light. Beyond, the desert silence is broken only by the crackle of wood fires and voices murmuring over coffee and roasted lamb. It is true, and romantics will pray that it remains ever so, that the Middle East can be exactly as this dream would have it. Quite often it can—if one can ignore the intrusion of rusty water trailers, battery-powered televisions, portable gas cookers, and roving military helicopters lopping past like predatory pterodactyls—quite often, but not always.

It is easy to forget that a very simple practical problem confronted the ancient astrologers at the very outset. How were they to view the first rising of the moon when the horizon was totally obscured by clouds, dust, or sandstorms? As one Assyrian astrologer laments, "They watched the Moon; the clouds were dense, and the Moon was not seen."[1]

This was a crucial and critical difficulty, for in order to maintain control over the calendar—one of the major tasks accorded the astrologers—they needed to know, with some precision, the day and the time upon which the new moon would appear and initiate a new month.

There is a tone of defensiveness in various letters from the astrologers to the king, written to explain why they had not been able to ascertain the exact beginning of the month or the rising of a planet. One senses their relief when the astrologers were able to report that "when the Moon appears on the first day . . . the land will be satisfied."[2] In other words, the lunar month was in harmony with the calendar month. Their reactions are testimony to the political pressure they were under. The king required an accurate calendar; if the astrologers could not maintain this, then their status, their position at court, was under serious threat.

This constant pressure upon the astrologers was undoubtedly the major factor that stimulated the development of Babylonian astronomical techniques, for the only means by which the astrologers could overcome the incertitude presented by the practical difficulties of observation was by devising an effective means of calculating, in advance, the first appearance of the new moon. In this way they could, also in advance, decide whether it was necessary to intercalate an extra month and so bring the civil calendar back into harmony with the lunar. Naturally, in order to do this they needed to gain an understanding of the cyclical movements, at least, of the sun and moon.

The technical advance necessary for this could not occur in a single stage. First, the celestial movements needed to be plotted accurately in order to build up sufficient data to make the existence of stellar cycles apparent. For this task the question of stellar location becomes crucial. Movement can be plotted only in relation to something fixed. Thus, the moon and planets needed to be located in space relative either to some geometrical constant—such as the ecliptic—or to the fixed stars. Some form of celestial cartography was needed.

Initially, in the early second millennium BCE, stellar geography was a very primitive affair. In the Venus Tablet of Ammisaduqa, this planet was located no more accurately than by its proximity to the horizon. But with time the means of location became more sophisticated.

The astrologers writing to the royal court in the first millennium BCE would often relate planets to each other, to the moon, or to the fixed stars or constellations. In addition to this a certain amount of rudimentary relative measurement was demonstrated, using as measures of stellar distance "fingers" or "cubits": "Mars . . . has approached one hundred and fifty cubits nearer to the constellation Libra," for example.[3]

By means of their primitive timekeeping and constant observation, the astrologers eventually discovered the long-term movements of the sun, moon, planets, and stars, thus allowing them to begin to predict their future positions. No specific date can be placed upon this important discovery, but evidence within the tablets themselves would place it near the end of the second millennium BCE.

Nevertheless, many difficulties remained, not the least being the difference in viewpoint between Babylonia and Assyria. Because of the 4 degrees difference in latitude between the two cities, a planetary rising could be seen in Babylon before it was visible in Nineveh. This was no doubt the cause of the rather defensive letter from an astrologer in Nineveh to King Esarhaddon:

> As regards the planet Mercury . . . "I have heard it can be seen in Babylon," he who wrote this to the king, our lord, may really have observed it. His eye, however, must have fallen on it. We ourselves have kept watch but we have not observed it. One day it might be too early, the other day it might lie flat in the horizon. Our eyes should indeed have fallen on it.[4]

Gradually Mesopotamian science progressed until the astrologers were able to predict these events in advance. But even then perfection eluded them: "When the Moon out of its calculation delays and does not appear . . ." begins one rather sad explanation.[5]

Apart from the aesthetic or scientific considerations, an accurate calendar was important for agriculture in order that farmers might know precisely when the seasons began. When at an early stage the

calendar remained erratic, with no noticeable regularity about the inter-
polation of intercalary months, the calendar could not be relied upon to
indicate the beginning of the various seasons correctly. In other words,
when the calendar said it was spring, it might, in fact, still have been
winter—or just as easily summer. In consequence, farmers, in order to
be certain about the seasons, did not rely upon the civil calendar but
instead depended upon changes in the weather and watched for the rising of certain stars and constellations. The usefulness of these as markers for the seasons must have been realized very early. The fifth tablet
of the creation myth, the *Enuma Elish,* begins with the determination
of the astronomical boundaries for the year: "Marduk," it states, "determined the year, defined the divisions; for each of the twelve months
he set up three constellations."[6] A similar procedure was recognized by
the ancient Greeks: the poem attributed to Hesiod, "Works and Days,"
contains a number of these stellar markers for agricultural use.*

These sets of constellations were standardized into four groups and
recorded on tablets now known as the *astrolabes.* A number have survived, the earliest dating from around 1100 BCE.[7] On these the stars
are listed in three columns, each column holding twelve stars. For each
month three stars are listed—one star each for the paths of Ea, Anu,
and Enlil.[8] Originally, it is thought, these were recorded upon a circular table divided into twelve segments and three concentric circles, thus
giving thirty-six sections, each containing one star.

Each of the thirty-six sections not only listed the star but also held
a number. Archaeologists pondering upon their significance soon realized that these numbers were related in some manner to the length of
the day. It was finally discovered that they gave the weight of water that
should run out of a water clock during the period of day or night. The
highest number recorded was four, and this was associated with the ris-

---

*For example, lines 383–84: "When the Pleiades . . . are rising, begin your harvest, and
your ploughing when they are going to set." And lines 597–98: "Set your slaves to win-
now Demeter's holy grain, when strong Orion first appears." See Hesiod, "Works and
Days," in *Homeric Hymns and Homerica.*

ing of Orion in month three, which was summer. Thus, in summer four *mana* of water—around four pounds—would run out of the water dock during the day, whereas in month nine, which would be winter, only two mana were recorded as necessary.[9]

By later standards these astrolabes were not very accurate, but they clearly fulfilled a need and were produced over a long period; examples have survived from both Assyria and Babylonia ranging over a span of one thousand years. Yet, despite their evident success, the desire for more accuracy remained.

Greater accuracy was difficult in the period before mathematical techniques were introduced into astronomy. The practical instruments that the astrologers employed to supplement their observation of the heavens remained very rudimentary: a water dock to calculate the passing of time and a gnomon or sundial that marked the change in the year by means of the changing length of its shadow.

The water dock was very simple and measured time relative to a given weight of water. The Babylonian and Assyrian astrologers must have used a system similar to the later Greek and Roman timepiece called a *clepsydra*. Designs differed, but essentially it comprised a vertical container holding water that slowly ran out of a small hole at the bottom into a larger bowl equipped with a wooden float. As the water passed into the bowl, the wooden float rose up its side, which was marked with the hours.*

The accuracy of the astrolabes was improved during the years preceding the turn of the first millennium BCE. The sum total of astronomical knowledge at this time was contained in a two-tablet compilation called, from its opening line, the mul.Apin.† The astronomy

---

*Two mana sufficed to last the night at the summer solstice, three mana at the equinox, four mana at the winter solstice. See Neugebauer, "Water Clock in Babylonian Astronomy," page 40.

†While some of the standard literature states that this series appeared on three tablets, the latest work on mul.Apin demonstrates that only two tablets were used. See Hunger and Pingree, *MUL.APIN,* page 8.

contained in the tablets has been shown to date from 1000 BCE or earlier by Professors Reiner and Pingree at Chicago's Adler Planetarium.[10] However, of the forty different examples of the text known—none complete in itself—only two contain a date, the earliest being from 687 BCE. This, then, in the absence of any further information, must mark the earliest point at which we can be certain that the information had been arranged into this compilation.

The mul.Apin consists of astronomical information placed under a number of groupings. Curiously, though, while this information obviously comes from elsewhere and has been brought together in the mul.Apin probably for the first time, there is little indication about these sources. It is difficult to believe that all previous texts were destroyed once the mul.Apin was compiled, but it is just as difficult to believe that none of these sources has been found in the various specialist libraries that have so far provided today's scholars with raw material. Once again, we are confronted with an area needing further research and discovery.

The mul.Apin is grouped into eighteen sections. These include a list of fixed stars divided into those of the paths of Ea, Anu, and Enlil; the dates when the thirty-six fixed stars and constellations rise in the morning; the planetary periods; the seasons, equinoxes, and solstices; tables of the period of the moon's visibility; rules for intercalation; gnomon tables detailing shadow lengths; and weights of water for their clocks. The tablets also contain omens drawn from comets and fixed stars.[11]

There is one further section contained in the tablets that is perhaps the prototype of an important later astronomical concept. The mul.Apin gives a list of all the stars in the "path of the moon," that is, stars that lie in the apparent path along which the moon moves through the sky. As Professor Bartel Leendert van der Waerden notes, "the text states explicitly that not only the Moon, but also the Sun and other planets move in the 'Moon's path' defined by these constellations." The list of eighteen constellations is given in the text.[12] It seems that this number of constellations used to mark the "moon's path" gradually fell to twelve—the same twelve that later became the signs of the zodiac.

The "moon's path" was a zodiacal belt 12 degrees wide within which the sun, moon, and planets all moved. While the zodiac as a regular mathematical division of the sky was not yet established, this concept of a celestial "path" probably represents the final stage before its invention. Perhaps all that remained was to formulate the ecliptic—the center of this belt—a line marking the apparent path of the sun.

The second-century CE astronomer and astrologer Claudius Ptolemy writes that he had access to eclipse records dating from the era of Nabonassar, king of Babylon from 747 to 734 BCE.[13] However, he complains about the lack of reliable planetary data. He remarks that the ancient observations were made with little competence because they were concerned solely with the appearances and disappearances of planets and stars, all of which, he laments, were difficult to observe.[14]

Despite the apparent confidence in astrology, astronomical observation, and prediction as exemplified by the Enuma Anu Enlil and the mul.Apin, doubt obviously still remained. Astrologers were, it seems, seeking greater accuracy in their predictions from the omens and in their maintenance of the calendar. Perhaps they were driven by fear of the king, or maybe they were compelled by that obsessive curiosity that companions the intellectual process itself. Whatever the cause, the astrologers effected a remarkable and astounding change of perspective. They began, as it were, at the beginning. They began as if nothing could be taken for granted any longer. They began to compile the "diaries," the *nasaru sha gine,* or the "regular watching."

These texts record, in a systematic manner, both celestial and terrestrial events, and list, for periods ranging from several days to several months, all the major events observed in the heavens, the sky, society, commerce, and politics. There are two basic types of diary. Some were the "short diaries," so called because they were used by the professional observers to record their regular daily observations. These cover short periods of under a month. By physical variations in their inscriptions they reveal that the same tablet was used night after night. In order to inscribe the small day tablets they needed to be kept soft and malleable. The usual process adopted by the scribes was to wrap the tablets in wet cloth, which delayed the process of drying. Some obviously began to harden prematurely because on these the final lines of cuneiform text are scratched onto the surface rather than being inscribed with the wedge-shaped impressions of the stylus.[15] Once written, these short texts then served as raw data for the compilation of the larger and more elegant summaries that covered longer periods of up to a year.

Each diary records the length of the month and the details of the evening upon which the crescent moon is first visible. They contain other details about lunar events, the first and last appearance of the planets, their stations, and, in the later diaries, the relevant zodiacal signs. Dates of equinoxes and solstices were also listed, together with records of the appearances of Sirius. Then all other astronomical phenomena that struck the scholars as significant were added: the conjunctions of the moon and planets with fixed stars or less regular events, such as the appearance of comets or meteors.

Less exalted information was also recorded: the weather, for instance, together with wind direction and strength and the level of the river. The world of ancient commerce also found a place: written at the end was the market price—the amount that could be purchased for a shekel of silver—of such basic commodities as barley, dates, sesame, and wool, together with any price changes that occurred during the months in question.

The same tablets also listed the zodiacal placement of the important planets for those months and the political events—battles, deaths, treaties—that had taken place, albeit with an emphasis upon events in Babylon, the city in which all the diaries we have were written. In addition to all this information, they also recorded any unusual natural occurrences, an earthquake, for example, or something as mundane yet as ominous as a fox having run through the gate into the city.[16] These diaries represent an important window upon ancient life.

The earliest known diary is represented by a fragment dating from

652 BCE, during the reign of Ashurbanipal.[17] The next, a later copy of the presumed original text, bears the date "Year 37 of Nebuchadnezzar," which is 568 BCE, almost a hundred years later.* A hundred and fourteen years more pass before the next appears, in 464 BCE. Only three more are represented that century. But, starting with a diary of 392 BCE, their numbers increase significantly, and many more are found, until the last, which is dated at around 60 BCE.[18] In all, about 1,200 of these texts and fragments of texts exist, the preponderance being in the British Museum, which purchased the majority in the nineteenth century from antiquities dealers in Baghdad.

It is unlikely that the diary of 652 BCE represents the first and only time that century that such information was recorded. It must surely be viewed rather as an example of an established genre rendered unique solely by the caprice of history. While it is true that there is a gap of almost a century before the second example appears, this in no manner precludes the possibility that diaries once existed for all or many of the intervening years. In fact, it is more likely that the form was well established in Ashurbanipal's time and continued, so far as was possible, in a systematic manner until the ultimate demise of the temple organization responsible for both the daily observations and their recording.

The overwhelming impression given by these diaries is that they represent an attempt to create a database. Indeed, what other rationale could there be for the methodical and detailed recording of all this information? It seems reasonable to suggest that these diaries indicate how, over the course of time, the astrologers had reoriented astrology and added new and more specific techniques to it, finally arriving at the point where they found the loose and nonmathematical Enuma Anu Enlil obsolete and primitive. To put it plainly, I suggest that the

---

*See Sachs and Hunger, *Astronomical Diaries,* volume 1, pages 47ff, and Van der Waerden, "History of the Zodiac," pages 96–97. The actual tablet preserved is a later copy of information dating to 568 BCE. While Professor Van der Waerden states that it "appears to be a faithful transcript of an original," it is necessary to be aware that material could have been added at the time of copying.

astrologers were aware that they had inherited a predictive tradition that was faulty. While the tradition itself had sufficient intellectual momentum, credibility accorded by its antiquity, and apparent practical value to justify their maintenance of it, they were aware of the need to revitalize it. Perhaps they were, in a way, embarking upon a search for connections that might exist between planetary and terrestrial events. Were they, I wonder, beginning to reject the cosmological ideas of their own tradition in favor of a more deterministic approach?

Whatever the causes, do not think it too fanciful to suggest that the implication of these diaries is that they represent evidence of a methodical attempt to collect data in order to seek some empirical link between celestial and terrestrial events, with the probable aim of eventually codifying these links and creating a new, "modern," scientifically and mathematically rational astrological corpus—a new Enuma Anu Enlil perhaps?

It is evident that the seventh century BCE was a time of intense activity and discovery by the Assyrian and Babylonian astrologers, and further, that all the elements were in place both for the entry of mathematics into astrology and astronomy and for the discovery of the regular zodiac and the natal birth chart. All that was needed was some catalyst, some new perspective that could initiate these potential changes lying dormant beneath the surface. That catalyst was to appear in the sixth century BCE in the form of an invading army. Babylon was to be conquered by the Persians.

PART 3

✳

The Aftermath

16

THE INVASIONS

Late in September 539 BCE, beside the river Tigris in the area of modern-day Baghdad, two armies faced each other.

Nabonidus, king of Babylon, had recently returned from ten years' campaigning in Arabia, but his experienced army, commanded in the field by his son, Belshazzar, was seriously outnumbered.[1] Opposing Nabonidus and his army were the massive forces of Cyrus II, king of Persia, who had invaded Babylonian territory some weeks earlier. There was but one possible outcome: Nabonidus was to be the last king of Babylon.

The seeds of this impending defeat, which had its roots in religion, had been sown many years before. Nabonidus, whose mother was the high priestess of Sin at Harran, had early in his reign developed a devotion to this god and cult to the point where he was evincing a tendency toward monotheism. As we have already noted, archaeologists have revealed evidence that he worshipped Sin as the supreme god: inscriptions carved at his command at Harran show that he regarded Sin as "King of the Gods" and "Greatest of the Gods."*

---

*See Gadd, "Harran Inscriptions of Nabonidus," pages 47, 49, 51, 57, and 59. "Sin, king of the gods, lord of lords of the gods and goddesses" appears on page 65.

Whether Nabonidus was actually thinking of monotheism or rather of simple political unity, it appears that he was intending to unify his kingdom under the worship of one supreme deity. Certainly the later anonymous author of the hostile "Verse Account of Nabonidus" thought so.[2] He complains bitterly that Nabonidus had built a temple to Sin in Babylon and had canceled the annual New Year festival, thus rejecting the worship of Marduk. One fragment in this account states bluntly, "the King is mad."

This account further reveals that Marduk delivered Nabonidus up to Cyrus because of this rejection. It states explicitly that Marduk chose Cyrus to become the "ruler of all the world."[3] In return for this approbation, Cyrus restored the statues of the gods and goddesses back to their proper temples and "brought them back to life because their food is served to them regularly!"[4]

This work is evidently a production of the Persian propaganda department, seeking to prove that Cyrus thus had divine sanction for his conquest. It would seem, though, that most of the native inhabitants of Babylon tended to agree. The "Nabonidus Chronicle," a less obviously partisan production, records that in the seventh year of his reign Nabonidus canceled the New Year festival, and it was not reinstated until ten years later, the year in which his kingdom was invaded by the Persians. The clear implication is that this festival was reinstated under pressure in an attempt to regain the support of the Babylonians, but they had already turned their sights toward Cyrus.

The Babylonian and Persian armies were facing one another and battle was about to erupt when the military governor of Assyria and his entire contingent abruptly changed sides. This was the end for Nabonidus. The Assyrian governor, Gobryas, had evidently been in secret negotiations with Cyrus, who then attacked, defeating the Babylonian army and killing Belshazzar. The combined forces then attacked Sippar, which fell without a struggle. Nabonidus, in residence there, fled. Gobryas and the combined army then attacked Babylon, which, after a short resistance, also surrendered. Nabonidus was soon captured and from that point fades from the historical record. Seventeen days later, in October 539 BCE, Cyrus entered the city as conqueror. Eight days later the Assyrian governor, Gobryas, conveniently died—of what, is not recorded.

Babylon was neither looted nor destroyed by Cyrus's invasion: he maintained control over his troops and thus gained even more goodwill from the conquered population. Neither did he change any of the religious or administrative institutions, except that at the subsequent New Year festival, his son, Cambyses, ritually received the divine approval of Marduk prior to taking over as governor of Babylonia. Thus was the Persian dynasty's hold over the Babylonian Empire consolidated.

The ensuing period of Persian domination, which lasted more than two hundred years, maintained and encouraged the existing intellectual and civic activity so that it further flourished under this apparently benign rule. Even the writers of the Old Testament, not normally noted for their tolerance of foreign pagan rulers, allowed Cyrus a favorable press—for setting free the Jewish exiles who had been brought to Babylon as captives by Nebuchadnezzar forty-seven years earlier.[5]

Stability and economic prosperity were maintained throughout the reign of Cyrus's son, Cambyses, but upon the latter's death rebellions broke out across the empire. After two years of internecine fighting, the rebels were finally defeated by a relative, Darius, who then became king and instigated another long period of stability. To commemorate this victory over his enemies Darius ordered a great monument to be carved in cuneiform upon the rock at Behistun, the same rock upon which Henry Rawlinson risked his life to make copies of the ancient inscriptions.

The period of Persian rule brought about an important advance in the practice of astrology—the adoption of mathematical discipline. While the Babylonian year normally, as ours, contained twelve months, it was necessary occasionally to add a thirteenth intercalary month to bring the calendar back into harmony with the seasons. These interca-

lary months were added whenever the astrologers considered it necessary, without any apparent systematic order—that is, until 529 BCE.
From this date regularity was observed in the intercalation of months
that, with three exceptions, was maintained until 73 CE, the latest date
for which we have records.[6] This is evidence that the astrologers had
gained a much greater understanding of the celestial cycles upon which
calendrical regularity depended.

The search for regularity in stellar movement continued with the
discovery of the *synodic periods* of the planets. The synodic period is the
period between consecutive conjunctions of a planet with the sun, as
seen from the earth. Additional to this was the concept of the *sidereal*
period, which is the length of time taken by a planet to pass through the
entire twelve signs of the zodiac and return to its starting point. These
in turn led to the formulation of larger planetary periods that were used
for predicting future movements. The period used for Saturn, for example, was fifty-nine years, being made up of two sidereal periods, each of
twenty-nine and a half years—or fifty-seven synodic periods. Similar
accurate periods for all the planets were fixed early in the Persian era,
and together with the mathematical techniques, this knowledge was
used to calculate future planetary movements.[7]

Around this time, too, the planets became established in zodiacal
signs rather than in zodiacal constellations. Mathematical concerns had
led to the sky being uniformly divided up into twelve signs of equal
length. It is thought that one of the major factors contributing to this
development was the need to calculate the future movements of the sun.
Unlike the moon and planets it could not possibly be related to the
fixed stars—there being none visible during the day. Once established,
the names of the zodiacal signs were derived from, and identical with,
the names of the zodiacal constellations, which leads in some cases to
uncertainty over which is being referred to. For this reason it is difficult
to be sure when the first use of the zodiac occurred.

Nevertheless, a tablet recording Venus setting in the sign Pisces
dates from 446 BCE,[8] and the Babylonian diary for 464 BCE used

both zodiacal signs and fixed stars to coordinate stellar geography.* In addition to these and in order that no doubt should remain regarding the possible confusion of constellations with zodiacal signs, a tablet dated 454 BCE mentions "Mercury's last appearance in the east in the end of Aquarius."[9] This terminology makes it quite clear that here the zodiacal sign is being specified.

While these tablets indicate the use of the zodiac, none offers any indication regarding its form. However, an even earlier text provides both the first mention of the zodiac and the first indication that it was divided mathematically into twelve regular signs. This is a Babylonian moon text that dates from 475 BCE, sixty-four years after the capture of the city by Cyrus.[10] According to Professor Van der Waerden, the data contained in this text cannot be understood without the existence of a regular zodiac.[11] It is, though, fair to conclude that the zodiac had already been devised prior to the writing of this tablet, suggesting a date for the discovery at around the beginning of the fifth century BCE.

Astrology, during this era, not only modified its structure as a result of adding mathematical techniques but also altered its orientation. We find a remarkable and radical shift in the concerns of astrology. It changed from the political, mass-oriented "mundane" astrology to that in which the individual was important. This change reflected one that had occurred in society as a result of the Persian invasion. Professor Van der Waerden, an expert on the early history of astrology, argues that just as there is a close connection between the classical Babylonian astrology of the Enuma Anu Enlil and the Babylonian polytheistic religion, there is also a corresponding relationship between the astrology based upon a natal horoscope and the monotheistic Persian religion—Zoroastrianism.[12]

Natal astrology would not have arisen, argues Professor Van der Waerden, without a change in cosmological perspective. An important

---

*See Sachs and Hunger, *Astronomical Diaries,* volume 1, page 55. Van der Waerden, in *Science Awakening II,* page 125, mentions that of 419 BCE, but his comment, published 1974, has been superseded by that of Sachs and Hunger.

part of this new perspective, he believes, was supplied by Zoroastrianism. The basis of this religion is found in the writings of Zoroaster, which reveal a supreme god, Ahura Mazda, together with a concept of an individual immortal soul that has a free choice between good and evil. Professor Van der Waerden sees this doctrine as influencing the Greeks through Pythagoras and Plato. He writes, "I believe that . . . Persian myth had a decisive influence on the rise of birth horoscopy."[13]

The first known natal chart, from Babylon, dates from 410 BCE, probably April 29.[14] While it uses the zodiacal signs, it does not reveal any use of degrees. It states merely that the particular individual was born at that date and then simply states the signs within which the moon and planets were to be found. It ends, apparently, with a prediction, although the damaged state of the tablet does not make this reading certain.

This is one of six charts published in 1952 by the late Professor Abraham Sachs, and it is still the earliest known. The subsequent five natal charts all date from the Greek period of domination, the earliest being from Uruk, circa April 4, 263 BCE. This differs from the first in now mentioning the specific degrees of the sign within which the planets were placed:

Year 48 of the Seleucid Era, month Adar, the child was born. That day the sun was in 13.30° Aries, the moon in 10° Aquarius, Jupiter at the beginning of Leo, Venus with the sun, Mercury with the sun, Saturn in Cancer, Mars at the end of Cancer.[15]

After a break of several lines caused by damage, a number of specific predictions are given:

He will be lacking in wealth. . . . His food will not suffice for his hunger. The wealth which he had in his youth will not remain. The 36th year he will have wealth. His days will be long in number.*

---

*Note that because of damage to this tablet, Sachs indicates that a number of the words are not certain. See Sachs, "Babylonian Horoscopes," page 57.

The next three tablets range from 258 BCE—which produces both a conception and a birth date—to 235 BCE, which gives zodiacal degrees for the sun and all the planets, the moon alone being without a mathematical placement. This latest tablet, also from Uruk, records a number of predictions:

> Jupiter . . . in 18° Sagittarius. The place of Jupiter means: His life will be regular, well; he will become rich, he will grow old, his days will be numerous. Venus in 4° Taurus. The place of Venus means: Wherever he may go, it will be favourable for him; he will have sons and daughters. Mercury in Gemini, with the Sun. The place of Mercury means: The brave one will be first in rank, he will be more important than his brothers.[16]

During the course of the fifth century BCE, the Greeks first appeared to become seriously interested in the systematized Babylonian astrology. It is true that there was an earlier awareness of *omina* derived from celestial occurrences; Homer gives many examples, but they were very simple and had no apparent relation to contemporary Babylonian practice. However, in time Greek intellectuals realized the necessity of studying within the ancient intellectual traditions of other places. To what extent the Greek scholars were already studying and working in Assyria and Babylonia during the latter years of the native dynasties, and to what extent they continued to do so during the period of Persian domination, is not known. But some scholars were certainly there.

A famous example—though he is unlikely to have been the first—was Pythagoras, who was born around 558 BCE* and was thus nineteen years old when Cyrus took Babylon. If we can believe his later biographers, Pythagoras at age twenty went to study in Egypt. He remained

---

*Gorman argues this date against the more common 569 BCE. See Gorman, *Pythagoras*, page 49.

there for about twenty-five years, until he was captured by the Persians, who invaded under Cambyses in 525 BCE. Pythagoras was then taken in captivity to Babylon. While there he was taught for some years by a leading Zoroastrian priest, Zaratas, and was received into the highest esoteric mysteries of Zoroastrianism, which included, so the chronicles state, the doctrine for which Pythagoras is famous—that of the musical harmony of the universe.

Yet the truth about the origins of this doctrine might owe more to the Babylonians themselves than the Persian Magi. Professor Van der Waerden notes the parallels between the measurements of distances between stars and the doctrine of the Pythagoreans. He comments that "the Pythagorean 'harmony of the spheres' presupposes that the distances between the planetary spheres have the ratios of simple whole numbers. These speculations might well be related to Babylonian cosmology and number speculation."[17] Indeed, it is legitimate to suggest that this doctrine might have formed part of some esoteric teaching of the Babylonian priests. And what else might they have taught? Some form of proto-Kabbalah associated with their curious Tree of Life? Some version of the reincarnation teaching that was later promulgated by Plato?[18]

It is recorded that, prior to his death in 399 BCE, Socrates encountered a "magus" who had come to Athens. This astrologer made a number of predictions to Socrates, including that of his violent death.[19] This information comes from the Greek philosopher Diogenes Laertius, who was about age thirteen at the time. If his comments are accurate, natal horoscopes were being used in Greece at the beginning of the fourth century BCE.

Plato, a probable student of Socrates and spiritual heir to Pythagoras, evidently had good contacts with Babylonian thought, although there is no record of his ever having studied in Mesopotamia. According to a manuscript discovered in the ruins of Herculaneum—which was destroyed along with Pompeii in the eruption of Mount Vesuvius—shortly before his death in 347 BCE, Plato met with an astrologer, a

"Chaldean."[20] Plato's dialogue the *Timaeus* was a gospel for the Greeks of the eastern cosmological speculation and knowledge. In this dialogue Plato deals with the immortal soul, astrology, reincarnation, the mathematical harmony of the universe—all creations of the Divine Architect. His dialogue the *Epinomis* is in the same tradition and has been described as "the first gospel preached to Hellenes of the stellar religion of Asia."[21]

Cicero provides some literary evidence of early knowledge of horoscopy in Greek intellectual circles. He writes that a pupil of Plato, Eudoxus, who was later to earn himself a reputation in astronomy, was very critical of astrology, proclaiming that "no reliance whatever is to be placed in Chaldean astrologers when they profess to forecast a man's future from the position of the stars on the day of his birth."[22]

Assuming that this writing to which Cicero refers was correctly attributed, it would indicate that Babylonian natal astrology—the drawing up of horoscopes of individuals—had, upon its arrival in the Greek world, met with some opposition from the astronomers. This hostility is interesting, for it testifies to a division between astrologers and astronomers, whereas in classical Babylonian days the two professions were identical.❾ It also supports an early fourth-century BCE date for the introduction of Babylonian horoscopic techniques into Greece.

The Greeks truly arrived in Mesopotamia with the invading army of Alexander the Great, who, on October 1, 331 BCE, defeated the Persian army and shortly thereafter rode triumphantly into Babylon. Subsequently, thousands of Greeks arrived to visit, study, or live in the new cities that were being founded in the wake of the conquest. Many studied astrology at the astrological schools that flourished. Archaeology has proved the existence of two Babylonian teachers who

---

❾It also testifies to a change in attitude to the divine—the astronomers no longer saw the heavens as indicating the will of the gods.

were mentioned later by the Greeks: Kidinnu, called by the Greeks Cidenas, and Nabu-rimannu, known as Naburianos.[23] According to the classical writer Strabo, other schools were in operation in Uruk and Borsippa.[24]

After Alexander's death in 323 BCE, his empire was divided up by his generals. The eventual winner of Babylonia was the general Seleucus, who dated his "Seleucid" era from April 3, 311 BCE.

The Greeks were concerned with the individual and individual freedom. Their ideological traditions were founded upon the independent city-states, which, until the mid-fourth century BCE, had never been subject to any central authority. They were used to freedom and the questioning of all authority. By contrast, the Mesopotamian tradition was conservative, having arisen in a society that was strongly centralized. The consequence was that the Greeks introduced theory. They were not content simply to predict celestial movement; they wanted to know *why* these movements occurred in this way. They wanted a rational, intellectual explanation for events in the natural world. These differences can be seen in their opposing attitudes toward astronomy. The Babylonians showed little enthusiasm for theory. While the Greek astronomers sought the expertise to predict the planetary positions at any point in time, the Babylonians were content with being able to calculate certain events in the planetary cycles: risings and settings, retrograde motion, stations, and oppositions.[25]

We should not then be surprised to find the "scientific" side of astrology and astronomy receiving so much attention during this Hellenistic period. The great number of diaries that have survived from this era testify to this, as do the text ephemerides, the oldest of which—inevitably incomplete—dates from year 4 of the Seleucid era: 307 BCE.[26] If the missing piece were to be found, it would probably prove to date from year one. These texts continued for hundreds of years, the latest dating from Seleucid era 353, or 42 CE—about the time Saint Paul began preaching his Christianity at Antioch.[27] In fact, by this time Babylonia had long been under Parthian rule, and so the scribes who continued dating their tablets to the Seleucid era were perhaps making some variety of political point.

From this time, too, comes a text bearing the only known illustrations of the constellations and the zodiacal figures. One depicts the seven stars of the Pleiades, together with the moon god Sin standing between the "horns" of a crescent moon and the bull of Taurus.[28] A second bears, on the front, Jupiter depicted as an eight-pointed star and a drawing of Hydra with the lion of Leo standing upon it. On the reverse there is a depiction of Mercury, the star Spica, and Virgo as a woman holding an ear of corn.[29] Beneath these illustrations are twelve divisions, one for each sign of the zodiac. Each of these signs is, in turn, subdivided into a microzodiac, thus producing a division of 2.5 degrees, or two-and-a-half days. Finally, each zodiacal sign carries a comment regarding its astrological significance.[30]

Berosus was a priest of Bel in Babylon who, sometime after 281 BCE, left for the West. He settled on the island of Kos, which was already renowned as an intellectual center. Well-established tradition has it that Berosus brought to Kos all the knowledge of the Babylonian astrological tradition, which thus enabled it to be studied by the Greeks. He achieved such fame with his divination and predictions that, according to Pliny, the Athenians raised a statue in his honor.[31] Subsequently, the Stoic philosophers—beginning with Zeno, who died in 264 BCE—approved of astrology, and thus thereafter it gained rapid entry into the Greek intellectual world.

The astrologers knew that, with the change in perspective wrought by the advent of the individual natal horoscope, new analytical techniques needed to be discovered. That this was the case is demonstrated by a tablet found at Uruk and undated except that it can be attributed to the Seleucid period. It is very similar to modern astrological "cookbooks"; that is, it lists predictions for a systematic combination of planets. This could be evidence for the development of a new type of codified standard text but, unlike the Enuma Anu Enlil, based upon natal astrology:

If a child is born when Jupiter comes forth and Venus had set, it will go excellently with that man; his wife will leave.

If a child is born when Jupiter comes forth and Mercury had set, it will go excellently with that man; his oldest son will die.

If a child is born when Jupiter comes forth and Saturn had set, it will go excellently with that man; his personal enemy will die.

If a child is born when Jupiter comes forth and Mars had set, it will go excellently with that man; he will see his personal enemy in defeat.

If a child is born when Venus comes forth and Jupiter had set, his wife will be stronger than he.

If a child is born when Venus comes forth and Saturn had set, his oldest son will die.

If a child is born when Venus comes forth and Mars had set, he will capture his personal enemy.[32]

This procedure (if not the predictions) is familiar to modern astrologers. It is a list of the effects expected from opposition aspects. Those for Jupiter and Venus noted here are augmented elsewhere in the text by those for Mercury, Saturn, and Mars. Also discussed is the effect of certain fixed stars appearing at birth.

Two questions arise from this tablet. The first is that, given such a list of oppositions, are there elsewhere, as yet unrecognized, lists of conjunctions and perhaps other aspects—trines (120 degrees), squares (90 degrees), or sextiles (60 degrees)?

The second question is suggested by the list of fixed stars rising at birth that the text also contains. We must ask how much more of a step is the concept of the zodiacal sign rising at birth. In other words, the ascendant. Not much more, I would argue.

Unfortunately, as is so often the case, evidence is lacking. No example of an original astrological chart showing the use of an ascendant is known prior to 4 BCE.* However, literary evidence can perhaps push the date for

*See Neugebauer and Van Hoesen, *Greek Horoscopes,* page 17. This is one of the Oxyrhynchus papyrii and gives a birth of approximately 9 a.m., Scorpio rising.

the first use of the ascendant back a little further: Balbillus, the astrologer to Roman Emperors Nero and Vespasian, writes of two early charts: December 27, 72 BCE, and January 16, 43 BCE. For both of them he provided an ascendant. The source of the data could have been his father, Thrasyllus, who was also an astrologer, serving the Emperors Tiberius and Claudius. The actual computations used, according to Professor Neugebauer, would not have preceded 22 BCE and were perhaps later, but they indicate that the ascendant had entered astrological practice a decade or so into the Roman imperial era.[33]

By this time Alexandria and Athens had long replaced Babylon as the great centers of learning and religious syncretism. Those philosophers working in the tradition of Pythagoras and Plato, later becoming known variously—according to their allegiances—as Neoplatonic or Hermetic philosophers, held that works such as the *Timaeus* and, for the latter, the writings attributed to Hermes Trismegistus, were gospels of the highest truth. These mystical philosophers were a major force in the classical intellectual world until the Christians finally made their lives untenable. Yet they still retained their respect for Babylonian astrology. One of the greatest of their number, and head of the Academy at Athens in the fifth century CE, Proclus, referred in his commentary on Plato's *Timaeus* to the Babylonian astrologers "whose observations cover whole cosmic periods and whose predictions are irrefutable both for the individual and public events."[34]

The Academy at Athens, also known as the Platonic Academy, was closed in 529 CE by the order of the Emperor Justinian. The last philosophers, hounded by the Christians, moved east, accepting what proved to be a temporary abode at the court of the Persian king. Finding their situation uncongenial, they departed from Persia to an unknown destination. It has been argued that they found their final refuge within the walls of that city dedicated to the moon god, Harran.[35]

17

HARRAN

City of Temples

Harran stands guard upon the ancient road that links the Persian Gulf to the Mediterranean. For thousands of years, as the Babylonians and Assyrians extended their empires, the city grew in wealth and power, benefiting from its commanding position upon this important commercial and military route.

The city survived the millennia, remaining both important to trade and true to its traditions even during the political and economic vicissitudes that witnessed the destructions of Babylon, Nineveh, and many other ancient imperial cities. Its end was long delayed: it did not finally arrive until almost 1,900 years after that of Nineveh. In 1259 CE, during the Crusades, Harran was taken by the remnants of a Mongol army that two years earlier had fallen violently upon the Muslim states. Finally, in 1271, the Mongol forces were defeated and Harran was abandoned "but for the birds in their nests."[1]

All that remains of Harran today is a forlorn collection of crumbling ruins standing in the southern Turkish desert about twenty-five miles southeast of Urfa, the ancient Edessa. A nearby village holds the last descendants of the ancient citizens. Yet, despite its present-day economic insignificance, it remains revered in Islamic, Jewish, and Christian traditions as the staging post for the patriarch Abraham on his journey from Ur to Canaan.

In ancient times, however, despite its commercial and strategic importance, Harran's true fame reposed in its cultic significance: it was the center for the worship of the moon god, Sin, whose temple was one of the most famous in antiquity.

During the later Christian and Islamic eras, Harran remained a pagan light shining out in a region fully converted by the increasingly intolerant monotheistic faiths. It remained a city dedicated to the planets: within the four kilometers of defensive wall lay seven temples, for the sun, the moon, and each of the known planets.

Harran preserved at least part of the learning of ancient Mesopotamia into medieval times, preserved and augmented it. Influences came to Harran from Iranian, Egyptian, Greek, and Roman sources; all added their knowledge to the Babylonian substrata. Yet all these newer influences were pressed into the service of a very ancient cosmological conception: that the planets were conduits for divine energy and that this divine energy could be used by anyone trained in the requisite knowledge.

Each of the star temples in Harran was a type of "talisman" designed to draw down the influences of the god into itself. The ancient Babylonians and Assyrians believed that the god was immanent in his or her statue, and the builders of Harran took that idea a stage further. Their temples themselves, not just the divine images, were built in such a way that the entire structures would be infused with the presence of the god, that god to whose planet the temple was dedicated.

In talismanic magic, a deity's power is attracted into or coerced into a physical object, where that power resides in concentrated form. The aim, in the case of the architects of Harran, was to create the conditions for this divine power to affect, directly and profoundly, any person who might worship within the temple. It is, perhaps, analogous to a huge spiritual lens that might magnify and concentrate the powers from above.

The temples of Harran were renowned throughout the classical world, a pagan world increasingly under threat from Christianity. Harran's temples continued to function even after such paganism was proscribed by the Christian emperors of Rome and Constantinople. Following the closure of the Platonic Academy at Athens, as we have noted, the teachers Damascius and Simplicius, together with their companions, went into exile and sought a place of refuge. Until recently their fate remained a mystery. In 1986 the French professor Michel Tardieu produced good reasons for accepting that they finally settled in Harran and there founded a Platonic academy that survived at least into the tenth century CE, when it was visited by the Arab writer al-Masudi.[2]

In time, Christianity was displaced by evangelical Islam; the pressure continued. A number of Arab writers commented upon Harran's temples, but unfortunately their accounts do not always coincide. Neither do their brief asides on human sacrifice in these temples; these must be taken with complete skepticism.*

Central to Harran was the temple to Sin, the moon god. This was variously described as round, pentagonal, or octagonal, with its cult image made of silver upon a pedestal with three steps. Its associated color was white. This temple was destroyed and rebuilt on three occasions during the first millennium BCE, the last standing until its destruction, according to one Arab writer, in 1032 by the Muslims, who then built upon the site. It is curious that this cult to a moon *god*

---

*The basic European source for the accounts of the Harran temples is Chwolsohn, *Die Ssabier und der Ssabismus*. This has never been translated into English. One brief account exists in translation: Stapleton, Azo, and Husain, "Chemistry in Iraq and Persia in the Tenth Century AD," pages 398–403. For a more recent summary see Kollerstrom, "Star Temples of Harran," pages 47ff. The work by Professor Tamara Green, *City of the Moon God*, covers many of the uncertainties demonstrated by previous scholarship and explores the intellectual context within which Harran was embedded.

should have continued so long after the classical world had worshipped a female moon deity: Selene.

In addition to the temple of Sin, there was at least one and probably two other temples to the moon beyond the walls of Harran, one of them to the moon goddess, initially perhaps to the consort of Sin (Ningal) but later attributed to Selene. It was following a visit to this that the Roman emperor Caracalla was assassinated in 217 CE.

The temple to the sun was described as square and golden. The image of the god was of gold, hung with pearls and wearing a crown. It stood upon a pedestal six steps in height. Its associated color was yellow.

Mercury's temple was hexagonal without and square within. The cult image was cast in an alloy made from a mixture of all the other metals, its hollow interior filled with mercury. It stood upon a pedestal of four steps. The color associated with Mercury was brown.

The temple to Venus was triangular but with one of the sides longer than the other two. The image of Venus stood upon a pedestal of five steps and was made of copper. The associated color—in which the temple was possibly painted outside and inside—was blue. Within the temple were many different kinds of musical instrument. These were played continually by women attendants or priestesses, who dressed in white.

Mars had an oblong temple that was colored red. Weapons were hung upon its walls, whether internally or externally is not clear. Mars's image was constructed of iron and raised upon a pedestal of seven steps.

The temple to Jupiter was built upon a triangular base with a pointed roof. The stone used in its construction was green, and the walls were painted this same color. The image of Jupiter was made of tin and sat upon a throne raised upon a dais of eight steps.

Finally, the temple to Saturn was hexagonal and built of a black stone. It had black curtains hung about it, whether outside—rather like the Ka'aba at Mecca—or inside, again the context does not make it clear. The cult image was of lead and stood upon a throne raised upon a dais nine steps high.[3]

While these temples to celestial bodies made up the heart of Harran, there were various others: one temple stood to the "First Cause"; another was built to the "First Reason"; one was to "World Order"; another to "Necessity"; and there was a "Temple of the Soul."[4] It seems, too, that in addition to the temple to Mercury, there was another dedicated to Hermes Trismegistus.[5]

The last star temple that survived within the city walls of Harran was destroyed in medieval times; some commentators put this during the period of 1063 to 1086;[6] others report that one moon temple survived until the Mongol invasion.[7] Whatever the truth about this, however, beyond the walls of Harran there was still at least one pagan temple reported operating as late as 1200 CE.[8]

Of interest is that from the beginning of the twelfth century until 1146 the nearby county of Edessa was held by the Crusaders. They never managed to take Harran itself, although they ranged freely about the countryside. These European knights must have been exposed to the pagan beliefs, literature, and ritual endemic to the area. Archaeology has revealed an ornamental archway carved in the Crusader style, indicating that Western artisans may have found their way into Harran.* The extent to which these ancient beliefs could then have found their way to the West is an intriguing historical mystery. What is certain, as we shall see, is that these ideas had already traveled to Constantinople.

---

*Apart from the existence of this arch there is no documentary evidence to suggest, as do Lloyd and Brice, that the Crusaders ever held Harran; in fact, all the evidence suggests the reverse. Nevertheless, the existence of this carved arch demands explanation. It is found in a room within the castle abutting the southwest tower. This room was rebuilt at a "late date in the history of the building." It may be that this archway came originally from the cathedral of Hagia Sophia in Edessa, destroyed in 1149 CE by Nur ed-Din, who transported much of its stone to Harran for building work on the mosque, which he was enlarging. It would not be unreasonable to suppose that some of this stone was also used in the castle. See Lloyd and Brice, "Harran," pages 79 and 102, and illustration on page 103.

✳

Harran has never been comprehensively excavated. It was first visited by European archaeologists in the mid-nineteenth century and was subsequently visited by a number of scholars and enthusiasts, including T. E. Lawrence. No excavations were conducted, but certain of the remains were surveyed.

It was not until 1950 that the first scientific investigation was mounted. On July 9 of that year the British archaeologists Seton Lloyd and William Brice arrived to spend three weeks making a comprehensive survey of the site and copying inscriptions. They did not, at that stage, intend to conduct any excavations.[9]

Lloyd and Brice surveyed and mapped the city wall and gates, the remains of the castle, and the great mosque, where they found an inscription to Saladin. Nowhere on the site, though, did they find any remnants of Harran's many temples. They reported that "the prevailing character of the visible ruins is Islamic."[10] The sole exception to this was the ruin of a large basilica church, partly built over by later Islamic structures. They did find traces of earlier occupation, either carved stone reused by Islamic masons or a small number of potsherds that could be dated to Greek or Assyrian times. However, they concluded that only systematic excavation could find anything more of the pre-Islamic periods.

In May of the following year, another trip was taken to the site by the British archaeologist D. S. Rice.[11] He partially excavated the southeast gate of the castle, primarily to recover the remaining parts of an inscription that a local inhabitant had discovered. It eventually proved to record the ruler of Harran in 1059. This was the sole extent of fieldwork undertaken at this time.

Rice did not return until July 1959, when he was accompanied by four colleagues from England and two Turkish museum officials. They excavated into the great mosque, cutting some thirteen trenches. In the ruins they discovered a small fragment of a cuneiform tablet that translated to "As to E.Hul.Hul, the temple of Sin, king of light of heaven and earth, my lord, I verily made it great."[12] Rice and his colleagues concluded that they were close to the site of the temple of Sin.

They discovered a further curiosity that might be connected: after digging beneath remains of residential buildings dating to the medieval Islamic period, they moved immediately into a level containing Iron Age remains but no buildings at all. The only construction noted was a brick platform. They did not arrive at residential remains until they dug down to a level that contained Middle Bronze Age remains. Perhaps this platform formed part of the court of an ancient temple—perhaps the temple of Sin?

While it would seem that the archaeologists were coming close to finding one of the temples, and one would assume that sufficient enthusiasm existed to support another series of excavations, nothing more happened for twenty-seven years. Meanwhile, Rice died in 1962. Then, in 1986, an American expedition from the University of Chicago Oriental Institute, under Professor Lawrence Stager, arrived at Harran to excavate on and near the mosque. Unexpectedly, even before all the members had arrived at the site, the Turkish authorities stepped in and insisted on such restrictive practices that the American professor abruptly abandoned the entire excavation. The ruined mosque and the nearby Islamic graveyard were now regarded as sites to be protected from the shovels of Western unbelievers. Since that time, perhaps as a result of this debacle, no Western academics have even considered returning to Harran. For their own reasons, Turkish academics have similarly ignored the site. It seems unlikely, then, that we shall ever see the temples exposed and studied.

The pagans of Harran are known to history as "Sabians." How this appellation came about is described in a story that has survived.[13] In 830 CE, while the caliph of Baghdad paused in Harran on his campaign against the Byzantine armies, he noticed some curiously dressed people among the crowds that came out to receive him. As they were obviously not Muslims, he asked who they were and to which of the peoples protected by Qur'anic law they belonged. All Muslims tolerate "peoples of a book," that is, members of other religions founded upon sacred writings attributed to any of the ancient figures whom the Muslims recognize as prophets. These strangely dressed inhabitants replied that they were Harranians. The caliph, dissatisfied with this response, pressed them further, asking whether they were Jews, Christians, or Magi. Their answer evaded the question. Irritated by this, the caliph then declared that they were infidels, and, as such, he was permitted by the law to execute them all. He added that if they had not either become Muslims or one of the recognized "peoples of a book" by the time he returned from his military campaign, then he would carry out his threat and kill them.

Worried by this, a number immediately converted to Islam or Christianity. Others, however, consulted an expert on Islamic law, who advised them to say that they were Sabians because they were a people recognized in the Qur'an. Although the caliph died before he could return, the Harranian pagans continued to call themselves Sabians and thus received recognition and toleration from the Islamic authorities.

However, in order to complete their new status it was required that they should name the book that they considered to be holy scripture. According to an Islamic writer, they gave as their sacred book an example of *Hermetica,* a collection of writings attributed to Hermes Trismegistus.[14]

During the first and second centuries CE an important change occurred in the intellectual world of the Roman Empire. Rather than use philosophy for the exploration of logical argument and discussion, certain philosophers became more concerned with using philosophy to seek immediate and experiential knowledge of the divine. The origins of this movement are not precisely known, but it seems most likely that this strand of philosophy was always there, lingering beneath the official repertoire of philosophical schools. Certainly a revival of Pythagorean thought was integral—falling later under the umbrella of Neoplatonism—as was, perhaps, the influence of the Indian yogis, called "gymnosophists," who taught in the Hellenistic cities of the

Middle East. Additionally, there was also a strong influence from Egypt, the temples of which were still in operation. Finally, there is an affinity with the Gnostics, both pagan and Christian.*

The first unequivocal reference to this new philosophical literature, now termed "Hermeticism," comes in the writing of the pagan Neoplatonist Porphyry, writing in the late third century CE.[15] The writings of this movement are known as the *Hermetica;* they are presented mainly as dialogues between the master—the mythical Hermes Trismegistus—and a pupil. These dialogues generally reveal Hermetic thought as a philosophical religion within which the dialogue itself is transcended and the pupil experiences some ecstatic revelation of truth, or *gnosis.* Hermes said in one dialogue: "all things are One, and the One is all things, seeing that all things were in the Creator before he created them."[16] And in the "Poimandres" of Hermes Trismegistus is written: "'I would . . . learn,' said I, 'the things that are, and understand their nature, and get knowledge of God.' . . . He [Hermes] answered, 'I know what you wish. . . . Keep in mind all that you desire to learn, and I will teach you.' After this introduction the pupil had an experience of a vast, endless vista which then transmuted itself into pure light and, the pupil reported, '. . . from the light there came forth a holy Word. . . . This Word was the voice of the Light.' And the teacher spoke, saying, 'Now fix your thought upon the Light . . . and learn to know it.'"[17]

That these Hermetic works enjoyed a wide currency was shown during the 1970s: a collection of ancient Coptic texts were found in the Egyptian desert near Nag Hammadi, after which they were named. While the majority of these texts were Gnostic, the collection also contained Hermetic tracts including two sections of the *Asclepius,* written in Coptic.†

---

*For a discussion of the origins of Hermetic thought, see Yates, *Giordano Bruno and the Hermetic Tradition,* pages 4–7.

†This library also contained part of Plato's *Republic* and another tract mentioning Hermes Trismegistus, *The Discourse on the Eighth and Ninth,* which was followed by the Hermetic prayer, *The Prayer of Thanksgiving.* See Robinson, *Nag Hammadi Library in English,* pages 300–307.

It is, given the affinity between the two traditions, curious that the other classical Neoplatonists, from Plotinus onward, did not mention the Hermetic texts. They clearly shared a common interest in the mystical, and furthermore, while they were both concerned with a "gnostic" experience, they differed in the same way from Gnosticism itself. The Gnostics held that the world was evil, the creation of a fallen deity, and thus had to be transcended. The Neoplatonists and Hermeticists regarded the world as an expression of divine creation, every part of it being infused with this divinity. They loved the world; the Gnostics hated it.

These Hermetic texts enjoyed a certain currency until around 550 CE, when they appear to drop out of sight so far as the Greek and Latin scholars were concerned. They next appear, in Arabic or Syriac, in the hands of the Sabians of Harran. Professor Green comments that despite the difficulties over documentation, "Harran most probably served as one of the entry points of Hermeticism into Islam."[18]

The Sabians in Harran, while maintaining the *Hermetica* as their sacred text, did not forgo all the other teachings of their stellar religion. In fact they added Hermetic thought to their repertoire along with Neoplatonism, astrology, and magical thought, which was already there.* This was easy, because Hermetic thought had a strong magical component that was in accord with the talismanic magic already practiced in

---

*In Professor David Pingree's important work tracing the sources (Mesopotamian, Egyptian, Iranian, Indian) of a medieval Spanish magical text, the writer of which had access to much material from Harran, Pingree states his belief that the confrontation between the Sabians of Harran and the Caliph al-Ma'mun around 830 CE was crucial and introduced a change in the writings emanating from Harran. Thereafter, he argues, there was a need to persuade the Islamic authorities that the magic used in Harran did not involve evil powers but rather worked by means of the powers of good. As a result, the Sabians began producing "a host of pseudo-Hermetic works" that placed the practice of magic into this more spiritual and positive framework. See Pingree, "Some of the Sources of the *Ghayat al-hakim*," page 15.

Whether his argument is correct or not, the *Picatrix* is certainly an example of a work that puts the art of magic firmly into the service of the spiritual.

Harran. And out of this milieu came a magical work called the *Picatrix,* which was perhaps written in Harran. Whatever the actual site of its composition, it betrays extensive Sabian influence: it puts all the magic and astrology from the ancient world into a Neoplatonic and Hermetic framework.[19]

This work first established that the practice of magic involves infusing material objects with divine power and explained that the best way to do this is to create magical talismans. The magician needed to mediate and control all the stellar influences. The *Picatrix* is the magician's textbook.[†]

While Babylonian astrology was never deterministic, that of the Greeks—especially under the influence of the Stoics—was. Magic provided a means of slipping out from under these apparently fated predictions and allowed the opportunity of turning the stellar influences to the magicians' advantage. This, of course, is just what the Babylonian Namburbi rituals were supposed to do with regard to evil. The Babylonians had other magical rituals that they used in all parts of their lives—in childbirth and love, for example.

Yates, *Giordano Bruno,* page 54. See Green, *City of the Moon God,* 179, and Hartner, "Notes on *Picatrix,*" who notes (page 438) that a close relationship exists between the prayers to the planets in the *Picatrix* and those of the Sabians in Harran. He also points out that the entire work is founded upon a Neoplatonic perspective accommodating much material from other cultures, the ancient Mesopotamian component coming via Harran (page 440).

Professor Garin, on the other hand, in his *Astrology in the Renaissance* (page 48), suggests that the *Picatrix* was a compilation from many other earlier works but written in Arab Spain. In 1256 King Alfonso X of Castile had it translated into Spanish from Arabic. From this Spanish translation came the Latin version, which was available to scholars in the fifteenth century. All the above scholars agree on its importance. Garin states, "In reality the Latin version of the *Picatrix* is as indispensible as the *Corpus Hermeticum* or the writings of Albumasar for understanding a conspicuous part of the production of the Renaissance, including the figurative arts." See Garin, *Astrology in the Renaissance,* page 47.

[†]For a discussion of the *Picatrix,* see Yates, *Giordano Bruno,* pages 49–55. A German translation of this work exists: *"Picatrix": Das Ziel des Weisen von Pseudo-Magriti,* translated by Hellmut Ritter and Martin Plessner.

Furthermore, the use of these talismans is similar to the Babylonian concept of the immanence of the gods in their statues. By means of a daily ritual the god's presence was maintained in the cult image, hence the reason behind the meals served to it. That this Babylonian practice lay behind at least part of the concepts expressed in the *Hermetica* is demonstrated by one of the dialogues, which explains that the ancients "invoked the souls" of divine beings and "implanted them in the statues by means of certain holy and sacred rites."[20] The student, Asclepius, asks Hermes Trismegistus exactly how these gods are persuaded to inhabit these statues. Hermes replies as a Babylonian or Assyrian priest would have done a thousand years before:

> They are induced . . . by means of herbs and stones and scents which have in them something divine. And would you know why frequent sacrifices are offered to do them pleasure, with hymns and praises and concord of sweet sounds that imitate heaven's harmony? These things are done to the end that, gladdened by oft-repeated worship, the heavenly beings who have been enticed into the images may continue through long ages to acquiesce in the companionship of men. Thus it is that man makes gods.[21]

The Sabians in Harran created talismans to influence daily life and were very concerned with establishing the best arrangement of factors to facilitate this. It is this arrangement that concerns the *Picatrix*. As this text explains, in order to work effectively the talisman must be used in harmony with the requisite celestial events. This necessitates the magician being well versed in astrology. Similar astrological knowledge is necessary during the construction of the talismans: depending upon the use that will be made of them there are specific times—chosen from the movements of the planets—for them to be constructed and certain times for them to be used.

But the *Picatrix* goes further than this: it moves from the magical, the mechanical, to the transcendent—it compares the true use of the magical talisman with that of the alchemical elixir, that is, it can transmute the magician in the same way that the end of alchemical procedures transmutes the alchemist. The correctly constructed talisman can evoke the transcendent experience with which the Hermetic dialogues are concerned. The correctly constructed temple is not just a house of divine *worship* but a house of divine *experience*. But how successful they were in Harran we perhaps will never know.

The *Hermetica* was the name given to the complete corpus of writings attributed to Hermes Trismegistus. These writings were the works of many different authors over a number of centuries. They are not even all internally consistent. Nevertheless, they hold more in common than they differ. Due to the wide range of manuscripts, it is unlikely that many of the "collections" of *Hermetica* held identical dialogues. This was to change: the edition of texts that we have today has the form of a canonical collection. Its modern form dates from the original manuscript of the collection that came to Europe in the early fifteenth century. But this form was derived from an even earlier compilation that was put together in Constantinople. Most scholars are agreed that the most probable compiler of this collection was the famous medieval scholar Michael Psellus.[22]

Psellus held a very prominent position in eleventh-century Constantinople: he was both secretary of state and professor of philosophy. He initiated a revival of Neoplatonic studies and boasted that his fame was such that both Arabs and Celts came to study under him.[23] In about 1050 CE he either discovered or received a damaged manuscript of Hermetic texts. It may be significant that this was not long after the destruction of a major moon temple in Harran, perhaps the temple of Sin.

From this time the Hermetic works enjoyed an increasingly significant currency. They became part of the intellectual milieu of the Neoplatonists—which they had not been during the era of the Platonic Academy in Athens.

Constantinople became a thriving center of Neoplatonic and Hermetic studies until its capture by the Arabs at dawn on Tuesday, May 29, 1453. Around seven years later a manuscript of the *Hermetica* arrived in Florence for the library of Cosimo de' Medici. In Florence, under Cosimo's patronage, there had been a revival of Platonic thought. Cosimo's protégé, the scholar Marsilio Ficino, was already at work compiling a collection of all Plato's books prior to translating them. Yet, in 1463 Cosimo insisted that Ficino drop all his other activities to translate the *Hermetica*. Only months before Cosimo's death, Ficino was able to give him the completed translation. As Dr. Frances Yates comments: "This is an extraordinary situation. There are the complete works of Plato, waiting, and they must wait whilst Ficino quickly translates Hermes, probably because Cosimo wants to read him before he dies. What a testimony this is to the mysterious reputation of the Thrice Great One."[24]

Ficino's translation of the *Hermetica*—from what was believed to have been Michael Psellus's personal copy—was to affect European culture profoundly. One of Italy's leading experts on the period, Professor Eugenio Garin of Florence, states categorically that "one cannot say enough about the enormous importance and influence of Ficino's hermetic translation."[25] Simply, it was to prove one of the catalysts of the Renaissance.

18

FROM BABYLON
TO BOTTICELLI

In the fifteenth century the Christian Church was in disarray. This temporal expression of God's will was split by argument. The unity of Christendom, a farce even when it was first implicitly established by Pope Leo I, who made the bishop of Rome preeminent, had been finally rent asunder in 1054 when the Eastern Church split from the West. Each excommunicated the other (a move that was not repealed until 1965).

Henceforth Rome ceased talking to Constantinople—at least until the fifteenth century, when Constantinople, facing military pressure from the Turks, decided to seek aid from Western kings. The price would be an accommodation with Rome. This meant, in effect, recognizing the pope.

In 1438 the emperor of the Eastern Empire and the patriarch of the Eastern Church came to Italy for a Church council, which aimed to investigate the joining together of the two halves of the Church. The council was initiated in Ferrara, but shortly after it began, plague struck, and so the proceedings were transferred to Florence, the home of the pope's banker, Cosimo de' Medici, whose prestige, already great, was thereby augmented.

Pope's Banker

Cosimo was not to know that, for reasons wholly unconnected with the split in the Church, this council was to be of inestimable value to Florence, to Italy, and to himself.

The council began in Ferrara on October 8, 1438, and ended in Florence with the departure of the emperor on August 26, 1439. A declaration of union was proclaimed on July 6, but the emperor was too afraid to tell his people of this treaty. It was kept a secret until 1452, the year before Constantinople fell to the Turks. During the council the patriarch of Constantinople died, as did the empress, who had remained in Constantinople. It would seem to have been a complete waste of time.

While the council itself might have been so, its presence in Italy was far from it. To argue the case for the Eastern Church, the emperor had been accompanied to Italy by a large group of scholars—more than 650, including ecclesiastics. As the scholars expected to have to quote from original texts of biblical writings as well as those of the early Church fathers, they had brought a large number of original Greek manuscripts with them. Not all of these manuscripts concerned purely Christian subjects; there were a number of other works previously unknown in the West, in particular those of Plato, who had hitherto been represented only by a few parts of the *Timaeus* that had managed to cross the Adriatic.

Among these scholars with the emperor was George Gemistos, who adopted the name "Plethon" during the council. He was a teacher of philosophy at his school at Mistra in the Peloponnese. An anti-Christian Neoplatonist and a committed opponent of Aristotle, he had long harbored an ambitious plan to restore to vitality the pagan religion that existed before Justinian's suppression of the cult and the Platonic Academy in Athens; in short, he was, in everything but name, a pagan philosopher.

Due to the law in Constantinople demanding the death penalty for any Christian who reverted to pagan practices, Plethon had kept his true thoughts private. They were revealed, perhaps, only to the select group of inner "initiates" among those attending his school in Mistra.[1] His experience in Florence was to change all this.

Florence proved as momentous for Plethon as he was to prove for Florence. It was a very special city, and Plethon found that he had the time to explore the intellectual freedom it offered. While he was among the advisers who had accompanied the Greek ecclesiastics to Italy, it transpired that he was not required to attend the actual conference frequently. In consequence, he was able to spend a considerable amount of his time in the company of learned Florentine humanists.

Florence was a center of humanist studies, and this tradition provided very fertile soil for the ideas that Plethon was to express, for the particular intellectual milieu of Florence was the result of a generation or two of secular learning, unfettered by ecclesiastical concerns and constraints. In this environment, freed from the guilt engendered by the Church's teaching, the dignity of humanity was given emphasis. While the Church was able to act as "cultural censor" elsewhere in Europe, its writ did not run far in Florence. The term *studia humanitatis* was adopted to describe the range of interests from which came the term *humanists.*

Hitherto Aristotle had dominated Western scholarship, but the humanists, inspired by their increasing knowledge of and facility with Greek, quickly began to emphasize Plato instead, even though they had access to only a minute part of his work. This began to change in the fourteenth century, when Petrarch, the "father of Italian humanism," studied Greek and, for probably the first time in the West since the demise of the Roman Empire, managed to obtain a Greek manuscript of a more substantial portion of Plato's works.

Such was the enthusiasm in Florence for this secular Platonic learning that by the time of the Council of Florence the leading men in the city were not just patrons of humanist scholars but were active humanists themselves. The political and economic situation in Florence also recommended itself to such an independent philosophy: Florence was a republic and the fifth largest city in Europe at the time. It also held Europe's largest bank, that of the Medici.

Plethon found life in the city very congenial; in fact, his stay there marked a turning point in his life. Following his experience in Florence he abandoned all pretense and openly embraced paganism. Something happened to him in Florence that gave him such enthusiasm for the future, such enthusiasm for a resurgence of paganism, that he is on record as proclaiming while there that "within a few years the whole world would have one and the same religion."[2] Not one of the faith of Christ or Muhammad, he explains, but "another faith which is not so different from that of the Gentiles,"[3] meaning a resurrection of the ancient Greek pagan mystery tradition. It is clear that he wanted a cult of Jupiter, of the sun, and of the stars. Plethon's Platonism reminds us of the religion of both Harran and the Emperor Julian, who in 360 CE had rejected Christianity for paganism. Before Plethon died he publicly proclaimed that "Mohammed and Christ would be forgotten, and that absolute truth would flower again throughout the whole universe."[4]

While in Florence, Plethon delivered a series of lectures to his audience of humanist scholars. He spoke on the differences between Aristotle, whom he hated, and Plato. He spoke of his belief in a universal Neoplatonic religion—"one mind, one soul, one sermon."[5] And he inspired something akin to a yearning or a hunger for more knowledge in his listeners. Especially so in the case of one of his audience: Cosimo de' Medici.

Cosimo de' Medici resolved to bring Platonic studies to Florence. It seemed that this meant more to him than simply the satisfaction to be gained by supporting a new and apparently fresh intellectual current. Rather, Cosimo had a deeply personal interest: he had responded in a direct manner to the talks of Plethon, and he had discovered in himself a yearning for truth that had not been satisfied by the Church but that he now considered to be found within the works of Plato. But this was before he discovered the works of Hermes Trismegistus. Despite Plethon's Platonism and apparent adherence to the tradition of Psellus,

Plethon is never known to have referred to the works of Hermes. Of course he might have saved that for his "initiates," but we cannot be certain.

Cosimo, after discussions with Plethon, initiated a plan that was to occupy his thoughts for the rest of his life: to create a Platonic academy in the tradition of that of antiquity. But first he had to gather teachers and texts. Unfortunately, in the summer of 1439, Plethon returned to the East and was never to return before his death. Perhaps for this reason Cosimo's idea lay moribund for a number of years. In the meantime, he had his agents seeking Greek manuscripts for his library, which eventually comprised some ten thousand manuscripts. Then, in 1453, Constantinople fell to the Turks, and dozens of manuscripts began to appear, carried west by fleeing churchmen and scholars.

Four years later a Greek philosopher, John Argiropoulos, encouraged by Cosimo de' Medici, traveled to Florence, where he established himself as a lecturer on Aristotle and Plato. While he was not the man Cosimo had in mind to run his resurrection of the ancient Platonic Academy, his presence helped constellate the idea. Two years later, in 1459, Cosimo summoned the son of his doctor from the University of Bologna, where he was studying. The boy, Marsilio Ficino, was chosen to head Cosimo's Platonic academy.

Marsilio Ficino, who had been only five years old at the time of the Council of Florence, had since received a thorough education in the humanities. Apart from the standard subjects, he had also studied Greek philosophy and language as well as music. He initially saw his career lying within the Church, until his faith was so shaken that he found it impossible to continue.

The lectures given by John Argiropoulos so affected Ficino that the archbishop of Florence forbade him to attend any more. But this restriction did not seem to quiet Ficino, who was soon accused by the archbishop of heresy—a dangerous charge in any city other than Florence. Ficino, though, left Florence and began his studies in

Bologna, which were terminally interrupted by the summons from Cosimo.

At the age of twenty-six, Ficino was established in the Medici Villa at Careggi. This became the site of Cosimo's academy and was from that time frequented by scholars, artists, bankers, lawyers, merchants, politicians, and churchmen. Cosimo had also obtained a Greek manuscript of the complete works of Plato, and he passed it over to Ficino with instructions to translate it. This Ficino proceeded to do, until he was suddenly asked to stop and concentrate all his energies upon a translation of the *Hermetica,* Michael Psellus's own copy having fallen into Cosimo's hands sometime around 1460. The translation was completed shortly before Cosimo's death in 1464.

Exposure to the ideas in Plato's dialogues and especially to those in the *Hermetica* were to affect Ficino in much the same way as the former had Plethon: Ficino began, in effect, to revive the ancient pagan religion. He saw Platonism as a species of theology, and during 1467–69 he wrote a commentary upon Plato entitled "The Platonic Theology." By this time he was deeply involved in pagan practice and ritual. He had decorated the villa at Careggi with astrological images, the contemplation of which he felt to be beneficial. He was also an advocate of the regular singing of Orphic Hymns.

But the cornerstone of his worldview was influenced by two books: the *Hermetica,* especially the dialogue called *Asclepius,* and the *Picatrix.* Ficino had become a convert to talismanic magic, the very art that had been developed so extensively in Harran, the art that ultimately owed so much to the Babylonians and their astrology.

Ficino and his contemporaries believed that Hermes Trismegistus was an ancient Egyptian sage immeasurably older and wiser than Plato or Pythagoras, both of whom, they thought, derived their theology from the earlier teacher. They believed that philosophy was purer in the past, closer to the original gnostic experience, and that since that time it had simply grown progressively more corrupt. Truth, then, was to be sought in ancient writings, especially Egyptian, for that country was believed to be the fount of wisdom; within the Hermetic texts, they believed, shone "a light of divine illumination."*

With the Renaissance discovery of the *Hermetica* came the *Asclepius,* the consequent acceptance of which, according to Dr. Francés Yates, was "one of the chief factors in the Renaissance revival of magic."[6] As she explains, magic sits well with a Gnostic approach to the world. Evil material might be removed and divine powers might be drawn down, by virtue of the employment of magical rituals and accoutrements. The magician created images, talismans, that "were held to capture the spirit or power of the star and to hold or store it for use."[7] This, of course, was the very subject covered by the *Picatrix.*

Ficino was very practical about the magic he taught and practiced, and one of his colleagues described the procedure. Should one, for example, desire the power conferred by the sun, it was necessary to wear a mantle of gold—the sun's color—then conduct a ritual in front of an altar upon which stood an image of the sun, all the while burning an incense made from those plants sacred to the sun. Then, anointed with solar oils, one would sing an Orphic Hymn to the sun.[8]

> Hearken, O blessed one, whose eternal eye sees all. . . . Yours the golden lyre and the harmony of cosmic motion, and you command noble deeds and nurture the seasons. Piping lord of the world, a fiery circle of light is your course. . . . Your light gives life and fruit. . . . Eye of justice and light of life . . . hear my words and show life's sweetness to the initiates.[9]

Ficino himself wrote a manual for all who wished to bring their lives into harmony through adherence to Hermetic principles. This was his *Liber De Vita (Book of Life),* which was first published in

Ref.

*See Yates, *Giordano Bruno,* page 16. For a discussion of the Renaissance attitude toward the antiquity of the *Hermetica,* see pages 1–19.

1489○ The third section deals extensively with the techniques by which planetary powers might be attracted and concentrated for an individual's use. For example: "If you want your body and spirit to receive power . . . from the Sun, learn which are the Solar things among metals and stones, even more among plants, but among the animal world most of all."[10] Ficino gives lists of all that each planet rules.[11] For someone who wished to draw into himself or herself the power of the sun, Ficino advises that "you put on Solar things to wear, if you live in Solar places, look Solar, hear Solar, smell Solar, imagine Solar, think Solar, and even desire Solar."[12] In general, Ficino preferred to attract the influences of a star or planet by combining the elements to make not a talisman but rather a medicine—to be drunk or applied to the body as a cream or oil.[13] Nevertheless, he still knew the rules for producing such talismans, which would take the form either of a ring or a pendant to be first hung from the neck during a time when the planetary movements were beneficial.

In such manner a talisman could be created for the moon, for Venus, for Mars, and for any of the other planets. And it would be used, in conjunction with music and the Orphic Hymns, to change the fate of the wearer. In particular it could be used to combat the unwelcome influences of Saturn, the cause of melancholy. Because Saturn ruled over the long hours of study necessary to the philosopher, the latter became even more prone to restriction and melancholy. It was thus even more important for a philosopher to take active steps to combat this through the use of the power of Jupiter. Thus, all philosophers and scholars were enjoined to surround their lives with scents, music, color, and images of Jupiter. In this manner, so Ficino writes, drawing his authority from the earlier Babylonians, Egyptians, and Platonists, "one could avoid the malignity of fate."[14]

Ficino was not ignorant of his Babylonian predecessors; indeed, he clearly knew of their magic and ritual. But he regarded their art as

---

○Also known as *De Vita Triplici*.

somewhat lesser than his own because they were trying to attract down "daemons," that is, created emissaries of the divine powers, rather than the divine, the numinous itself: "The Chaldaeans, I say, were masters of religion, for we suspect that the astrologers of the Chaldeans, far more than those of the Egyptians, tried to draw daemons through the celestial harmony into earthen statues."[15] His knowledge of this process is presumably derived from the *Asclepius,* which explains, at length, the means by which the divine emissaries, the daemons, are not only attracted into the statues but also how they are maintained there. It is worth repeating the dialogue with Hermes Trismegistus that we have already noted:

> They are induced . . . by means of herbs and stones and scents which have in them something divine. And would you know why frequent sacrifices are offered to do them pleasure, with hymns and praises and concord of sweet sounds that imitate heaven's harmony? These things are done to the end that, gladdened by oft-repeated worship, the heavenly beings who have been enticed into the images may continue through long ages to acquiesce in the companionship of men. Thus it is that man makes gods.[16]

The change that has occurred is that the aspect of the god that inhabits the statue—in other words, that is immanent in the image—has become personified; thus theology has moved toward magic.

The Babylonians sought to instill the divine power in their statues. The Sabians in Harran sought to entice it down to reside in their temples. The Renaissance "magi" sought to encapsulate the divine within their art such that each piece might become a pure crystal of divinity, a talisman able to change those who gazed upon it. And, when confronted with the extraordinary and compelling power of their creations, can we not say that they succeeded?

When, for example, Botticelli painted the *Primavera,* he was working within the Hermetic and magical world as expressed by Ficino. Dr. Frances Yates sees this painting as having a specific purpose in mind: "I want only to suggest that in the context of the study of Ficino's magic the picture begins to be seen as a practical application of that magic, as a complex talisman . . . arranged so as to transmit only health-ful, rejuvenating, anti-Saturnian influences to the beholder."[17] Frances Yates sees at least some of Botticelli's other paintings in the same light: speaking of his *Birth of Venus,* she explains, "Her function is the same, to draw down the Venereal spirit from the star, and to transmit it to the wearer or beholder of her lovely image."[18]

Botticelli's painting is a talisman designed to draw down, and to serve as a repository for, the divine power of Venus. The goddess is immanent within her image. Ishtar-shumu-eresh would have approved.

NOTES

Introduction

1. Roux, *Ancient Iraq,* 381.
2. Saggs, *Greatness That Was Babylon,* 489.
3. Parpola, *Letters from Assyrian Scholars to the Kings Esarhaddon and Assurbanipal,* 2:xxi.

Chapter 1. The Amateur Archaeologists

1. Wallis-Budge, *Rise and Progress of Assyriology,* 34.
2. Layard, *Nineveh and Its Remains,* 2:340.
3. 2 Kings 18–19.

Chapter 2. The Scramble for Antiquities

1. Rawlinson, *Memoir of Major-General Sir Henry Creswicke Rawlinson,* 180.

Chapter 3. The Land of the Twin Rivers

1. Genesis 2:10–14.
2. Herodotus, *Histories,* 1:119.
3. See Bibby, *Looking for Dilmun,* 188–200.
4. Ibid., 66–68.
5. Heyerdahl, *Tigris Expedition,* 208ff.
6. Robinson, ed., "The Hypostasis of the Archons," 89–90, in *The Nag Hammadi Library in English,* 154–55.

Chapter 4. The Royal Library of Nineveh

1. Waterman, *Royal Correspondence of the Assyrian Empire*, Supplementary Letters 6, 4:213.

2. Parpola, *Letters from Assyrian Scholars*, 34, 1:25. See also Oppenheim, "Divination and Celestial Observation in the Last Assyrian Empire," 114–19.

3. Roux, *Ancient Iraq*, 325.

4. Rochberg-Halton, *Aspects of Babylonian Celestial Divination*, 271.

5. Parpola, *Letters from Assyrian Scholars*, 43, 1:31.

6. Weidner, "Die astrologische Serie *Enuma Anu Enlil*," 14:177.

7. Rochberg-Halton, *Aspects of Babylonian Celestial Divination*, 216.

8. Parpola, "Assyrian Library Records," 11.

9. Wiseman, "Assyrian Writing-Boards," 7–8.

10. Parpola, "Assyrian Library Records," 8.

11. Parpola, *Letters from Assryrian Scholars*, 2:xvi.

12. Ibid., 1:vii.

13. Ibid., 2:xii–xiv.

14. Ibid., 2:xiv.

15. Oppenheim, "A Babylonian Diviner's Manual," 203 (line 24). See also Rochberg-Halton, *Aspects of Babylonian Celestial Divination*, 8–9.

16. Lambert and Millard, *Atra-Hasis*, 59.

17. Ibid., 57.

18. Starr, *Queries to the Sun God*, xxxiv.

19. Daniel 1:7.

20. Ibid., 2:1–12.

21. Parpola, *Letters from Assyrian Scholars*, 2:xiv.

22. Ibid., xvii–xix.

23. Ibid., 120, 1:89; 121, 1:89–91. See also 2:103 and 2:105.

24. Ibid., 2:xvii.

25. Oppenheim, "The Position of the Intellectual in Mesopotamian Society," 43.

26. Oppenheim, "Divination and Celestial Observation," 114–19.

27. Pausanius, 1:xvi (1:81).

28. Neugebauer, *Astronomical Cuneiform Texts*, 1:115.

29. Ibid., 1:10, n. 44.

Chapter 5. Letters from Assyrian Scholars

1. Parpola, *Letters from Assyrian Scholars,* 15, 1:13. See also 2:22–23, for discussion.
2. Ibid., 277, 1:223.
3. Ibid., 13, 1:9–11.
4. One partial list is supplied in ibid., 332, 1:285.
5. Ibid., 65, 1:43. The date of March 26, 669 BCE, is given in ibid., 2:70.
6. Thompson, *The Reports of the Magicians and Astrologers of Nineveh and Babylon in the British Museum,* 183, 2:lxiv–lxv. This is from tablet K-188; the writer's correct name is in Parpola, *Letters from Assyrian Scholars,* 2:501.
7. Thompson, *Reports of the Magicians and Astrologers,* 162:lxi.
8. Ibid., 17:xxxiv–xxxv.
9. Parpola, *Letters from Assyrian Scholars,* 51, 1:35.
10. Ibid., 41, 1:29.
11. Thompson, *Reports of the Magicians and Astrologers,* 154:lx.
12. Ibid., 73:xlvi.
13. Waterman, *Royal Correspondence,* 659, 1:457.
14. Thompson, *Reports of the Magicians and Astrologers,* 170:lxii.
15. Waterman, *Royal Correspondence,* 477, 1:337.
16. Thompson, *Reports of the Magicians and Astrologers,* 235:lxxv. This section is not translated in his work. See discussion in Oppenheim, "Divination and Celestial Observation," 118, and Starr, *Queries to the Sun God,* xxxii.
17. Parpola, *Letters from Assyrian Scholars,* 12, 1:9.
18. Ibid., 65, 1:43.
19. Ibid., 66, 1:43.
20. Ibid., 2:15, discussing tablet published in Thompson, *Reports of the Magicians and Astrologers,* 55:xliii (note that Thompson's translation is faulty).
21. Parpola, *Letters from Assyrian Scholars,* 12, 1:9.
22. Ibid., 13, 1:11.
23. Ibid.
24. Ibid., 110, 1:75.
25. Ibid., 2:50 (referring to ABL 1216).
26. Waterman, *Royal Correspondence,* 356, 1:247–49.
27. Ibid., 352, 1:245.

Chapter 6. The Great Omen Series

1. Reiner, *The Venus Tablet of Ammisaduqa,* 9, 21–23.
2. Ibid., 9, 21, 33.
3. Ibid., 29.
4. Weidner, "Historisches Material in der babylonischen Omina-Literatur, 231.
5. Ibid., 236.
6. Kramer, *Sumerians,* 147.
7. Ibid., 122.
8. Ibid., 138.
9. Weidner, "Die astrologische Serie," 14:175, n. 21.
10. Scheil, "Notules," 139ff.
11. Virolleaud, "The Syrian Town of Katna," 312ff.
12. Weidner, "Die astrologische Serie," 14:176.
13. Ibid., referring to Thompson, *Reports of the Magicians and Astrologers,* 200:lxviii.
14. Weidner, "Die astrologische Serie," 14:176.
15. For details, see Hunger and Pingree, *MUL.APIN*; Van der Waerden, "Babylonian Astronomy II," 13–26; Van der Waerden, *Science Awakening II,* 70–86; Reiner, *Enuma Anu Enlil,* 6–9.
16. Reiner, *Enuma Anu Enlil,* 6.
17. Ibid., 181.
18. Parpola, *Letters from Assyrian Scholars,* 13, 1:11.
19. Weidner, "Die astrologische Serie," 14:184ff.
20. Ibid., 189.
21. Sayce, "Astronomy and Astrology of the Babylonians," 3:150.
22. Rochberg-Halton, *Aspects of Babylonian Celestial Divination,* 10, n. 9; Reiner, *Enuma Anu Enlil,* 10, 14.

Chapter 7. The Numinous and the Mesopotamian Religion

1. Jacobsen, *Treasures of Darkness,* 3.
2. Oppenheim, *Ancient Mesopotamia,* 183.
3. Apuleius, *Golden Ass,* 241.
4. Scott, *Hermetica,* 117 (Corpus Hermeticum, 1:7).
5. Heidel, *Gilgamesh Epic and Old Testament Parallels,* X, i, 13–15 (p. 69).
6. Apuleius, *Golden Ass,* 241.

7. Jacobsen, *Treasures of Darkness,* 3–4.

8. Oppenheim, *Ancient Mesopotamia,* 183.

9. Jacobsen, *Treasures of Darkness,* 6.

10. Frankfort, *Kingship and the Gods,* 237–39.

11. Kramer, *Sumerians,* 328.

12. Heidel, *Gilgamesh Epic,* IX, ii, 18 (p. 66).

13. Jacobsen, *Treasures of Darkness,* 152–57.

14. Kramer, in Pritchard, ed., *Ancient Near East,* 2:139.

15. Ibid., 140–41.

16. Jacobsen, *Treasures of Darkness,* 160–61.

17. Oppenheim, "Perspectives on Mesopotamian Divination," 39.

18. Ibid., 164.

19. Jacobsen, *Treasures of Darkness,* 150.

20. Rochberg-Halton, *Aspects of Babylonian Celestial Divination,* 11.

21. Sachs, "Babylonian Horoscopes," 54.

22. Caplice, *Akkadian Namburbu Texts,* 8.

23. Oppenheim, *Ancient Mesopotamia,* 202.

24. Rochberg-Halton, "Fate and Divination in Mesopotamia," 363–64.

25. Ibid., 365.

26. Rochberg-Halton, *Aspects of Babylonian Celestial Divination,* 15–16.

27. Caplice, *Akkadian Namburbu Texts,* 2.

Chapter 8. Sin

1. Parpola, *Letters from Assyrian Scholars,* 117, 1:83; 2:101.

2. Thompson, *Reports of the Magicians and Astrologers,* 124, 2:lvi–lvii.

3. Ibid., 119, 2:lvi.

4. Rochberg-Halton, *Aspects of Babylonian Celestial Divination,* 38–39.

5. Langdon, *Semitic Mythology,* 153.

6. Gadd, "The Harran Inscriptions of Nabonidus," 47ff.

7. Ringgren, *Religions of the Ancient Near East,* 57, quoting Tallqvist, *Babyloniska Hymner och Böner,* 63.

8. Thompson, *Reports of the Magicians and Astrologers,* 94:lii.

9. Ibid., 106:liv.

10. Waterman, *Royal Correspondence,* 1214, 2:341.

11. Thompson, *Reports of the Magicians and Astrologers,* 30:xxxviii.

12. Ibid., 69:xlvi.

13. Rochberg-Halton, *Aspects of Babylonian Celestial Divination,* 8.

14. Ibid.
15. Waterman, *Royal Correspondence,* 1006, 2:197–99.
16. Rochberg-Halton, *Aspects of Babylonian Celestial Divination,* 19.
17. Ibid., 216.
18. Ibid.
19. Ibid., 232.
20. Ibid., 176.
21. Ibid., 104.
22. Ibid., 108.
23. Ibid., 141.
24. Ibid., 170.
25. Ibid., 108.
26. Ibid., 141.
27. Ptolemy, *Tetrabiblos,* 2:9 (pp. 191–93).
28. Rochberg-Halton, *Aspects of Babylonian Celestial Divination,* 57, quoting Neugebauer and Pingree, *The Pancasiddhantika of Varahamihira,* part 2, VI, 9–10.
29. Rochberg-Halton, *Aspects of Babylonian Celestial Divination,* 179 (14 Nisannu—month I). The same prediction is given on p. 180 (for 28/29 Kislimu—month IX) and on p. 182 (for 28 Nisannu—month I). A separate Venus omen is given on p. 205 (28 Arahsamna—month VIII).
30. Ibid., 205.
31. Ibid., 235 and n. 2 (*EAE* Tablet 21). See also p. 187 (*EAE* Tablet 20), where the prediction is lost, and p. 170 (*EAE* Tablet 19), where the same prediction is given.
32. Ibid., 189 and 191, both the same report.
33. Ibid., 214.
34. Parpola, *Letters from Assyrian Scholars,* 40, 1:29; 61, 1:39. The dating is given in ibid., 40, 2:49; 61, 2:66.

Chapter 9. Shamash

1. Parpola, *Letters from Assyrian Scholars,* 117, 1:83.
2. Diodorus Siculus, *Diodorus of Sicily,* 2:30.
3. Parpola, *Letters from Assyrian Scholars,* 326, 2:342–43.
4. Thompson, *Reports of the Magicians and Astrologers,* 178, 2:lxiii.
5. Parpola, *Letters from Assyrian Scholars,* 2:402–3.
6. Ibid., 104, 1:71; 2:89–91.
7. Saggs, *Greatness That Was Babylon,* 362.

8. Parpola, *Letters from Assyrian Scholars,* 280, 1:229; 2:270–72.
9. Ibid.
10. Ibid., 2:36.
11. Plutarch, *Lives,* II, "Alexander," 527.
12. Parpola, *Letters from Assyrian Scholars,* 2:271.
13. Lambert, "Part of the Ritual," 110–11.
14. Parpola, *Letters from Assyrian Scholars,* 2:428–29.
15. Thompson, *Reports of the Magicians and Astrologers,* 29:xxxviii.

Chapter 10. Ishtar

1. Heimpel, *Catalogue of Near Eastern Venus Deities,* 14–15.
2. Song of Songs 6:10.
3. Parpola, *Letters from Assyrian Scholars,* 2:182, n. 321.
4. Herodotus, *Histories,* 1:cxcix.
5. Tablet CT 4845, which was noted by M. Stol in a review published in *Journal of Cuneiform Studies* 25 (1973): 217.
6. Gallery, "Service Obligations of the Kezertu-Women," 335, 338.
7. Saggs, *Encounter with the Divine,* 351.
8. Ibid., 465.
9. Parpola, *Letters from Assyrian Scholars,* 2:111.
10. Ibid., 40.
11. Ibid., 407.
12. Thompson, *Reports of the Magicians and Astrologers,* 206, 2:lxix.
13. Ibid., 243B:lxxvi.

Chapter 11. Ninurta

1. Ramesey, *Astrology Restored,* 50.
2. Hone, *Modern Text-Book of Astrology,* 165.
3. Langdon, *Semitic Mythology,* 136–37.
4. Amos 5:26.
5. Diodorus Siculus, *Diodorus of Sicily,* 2:30.
6. Ibid.
7. Frankfort, *Kingship and the Gods,* 319, quoting Thureau-Dangin, *Rituels accadiens,* 138.
8. Watters, *Horary Astrology,* 49.
9. Thompson, *Reports of the Magicians and Astrologers,* 100, 2:liii.
10. Ibid., 90, 2:li; 124, 2:lvi–lvii; 175, 2:lxiii.
11. Ibid., 177, 2:lxiii.

12. Parpola, *Letters from Assyrian Scholars,* 2:343.
13. Thompson, *Reports of the Magicians and Astrologers,* 176:lxiii. See the same letter in Parpola, *Letters from Assyrian Scholars,* 326, 1:281.
14. Thompson, *Reports of the Magicians and Astrologers,* 107:liv.
15. Ibid., 103:liv.
16. Langdon, *Semitic Mythology,* 119–24.
17. Thompson, *Reports of the Magicians and Astrologers,* 216:lxxi.
18. Watters, *Horary Astrology,* 48–49.
19. Green, *Mundane or National Astrology,* 48.

Chapter 12. Nergal

1. Thompson, *Reports of the Magicians and Astrologers,* 103, 2:liv.
2. Ibid., 98, 2:liii.
3. Ibid., 146, 2:lviii.
4. Ibid., 272, 2:lxxxviii.
5. Watters, *Horary Astrology,* 45.
6. Greene, *Astrology of Fate,* 39.

Chapter 13. Marduk

1. Saggs, *Greatness That Was Babylon,* 385.
2. Livingstone, *Mystical and Mythological Explanatory Works of Assyrian and Babylonian Scholars,* 123, line 8.
3. Ibid., 125, line 1.
4. Ibid., 260.
5. See the two prayers to Marduk 55ff. in Lambert, "Three Literary Prayers of the Babylonians," 47–66.
6. Frankfort, *Kingship and the Gods,* 319.
7. Heidel, *Babylonian Genesis,* 36 (*Enuma Elish,* 4:13–14).
8. Saggs, *Greatness That Was Babylon,* 387.
9. Ramesey, *Astrology Restored,* 52.
10. Thompson, *Reports of the Magicians and Astrologers,* 268, 2:lxxxi. See also Parpola, *Letters from Assyrian Scholars,* 40, 1:29, and 61, 1:39, for further examples.
11. Parpola, *Letters from Assyrian Scholars,* 298, 1:255.
12. Thompson, *Reports of the Magicians and Astrologers,* 185:lxv.
13. Ibid., 162:lxi.
14. Ibid., 186:lxvi.
15. Ibid. See also ibid., 187:lxvi.

16. Ibid., 145:lxvi.
17. Ibid., 91:li.
18. Ibid., 92:lii.
19. For example, ibid., 192:lxvii.
20. Ibid., 96:liii.
21. Ibid., 103:liv.
22. Parpola, *Letters from Assyrian Scholars,* 289, 1:243.
23. Thompson, *Reports of the Magicians and Astrologers,* 195:lxvii–lxviii.
24. Waterman, *Royal Correspondence,* 519, 1:363–65.
25. Ramesey, *Astrology Restored,* 52.
26. Ebertin, *Combination of Stellar Influences,* 54.

Chapter 14. Nabu

1. Parpola, *Letters from Assyrian Scholars,* 2:55, n. 94.
2. Langdon, *Semitic Mythology,* 159.
3. Thompson, *Reports of the Magicians and Astrologers,* 184, 2:lxv.
4. Rawlinson, "On the Birs Nimrud," 17.
5. Ibid., 17–18.
6. Frankfort, *Kingship and the Gods,* 319.
7. Thompson, *Reports of the Magicians and Astrologers,* 218, 2:lxxi. See also ibid., 216c, 2:lxx; 217, 2:lxxi; 225, 2:lxxiii; 226, 2:lxxiii.
8. Ibid., 221, 2:lxxii. See also ibid., 200, 2:lxviii; 220, 2:lxxii; 222, 2:lxxii; 223, 2:lxxii.
9. Parpola, *Letters from Assyrian Scholars,* 70, 1:47. See also: 46, 1:31; 71, 1:47.
10. Ibid., 71, 1:47.
11. Watters, *Horary Astrology,* 44; Baigent, Campion, and Harvey, *Mundane Astrology,* 221.
12. Ibid.
13. Thompson, *Reports of the Magicians and Astrologers,* 224:lxxiii.

Chapter 15. Astronomy

1. Parpola, *Letters from Assyrian Scholars,* 100, 1:69.
2. Thompson, *Reports of the Magicians and Astrologers.* See, for example, 1, 2:xxxiii.
3. Pfeiffer, *State Letters of Assyria,* 317:214.
4. Parpola, *Letters from Assyrian Scholars,* 53, 1:35.
5. Thompson, *Reports of the Magicians and Astrologers,* 82:xxxxvii.

6. Heidel, *Babylonian Genesis,* 44 (*Enuma Elish,* 5:3–4).
7. Van der Waerden, *Science Awakening II,* 64ff. See also Weidner, *Handbuch der babylonischen Astronomie,* for a circular Babylonian planisphere, K 8538, 107ff.
8. See above, chapter 6, pp. 74–75.
9. Van der Waerden, *Science Awakening II,* 69.
10. Reiner, *Enuma Anu Enlil,* 6.
11. For a brief but comprehensive survey of the contents, see Van der Waerden, *Science Awakening II,* 70–71.
12. Van der Waerden, "History of the Zodiac," 219.
13. Ptolemy, *Almagest,* 3:7; 4:8.
14. Ibid., 8:6.
15. Sachs and Hunger, *Astronomical Diaries,* 1:12.
16. Van der Waerden, "History of the Zodiac," 96–97.
17. Sachs and Hunger, *Astronomical Diaries,* 1:43ff.
18. Sachs and Hunger, *Astronomical Diaries,* vols. 1 and 2. For the latest diary, see Sachs, "Babylonian Observational Astronomy," 47.

Chapter 16. The Invasions

1. See Daniel 5:22, 7:1, 8:1.
2. Pritchard, *Ancient Near Eastern Texts Relating to the Old Testament,* 312ff.
3. Ibid., 315.
4. Ibid.
5. Ezra 1:2–4; 2 Chronicles 36:23; Daniel 1:21, 6:29, 10:1.
6. Van der Waerden, *Science Awakening II,* 103–4.
7. Ibid., 107–8.
8. Ibid., 125.
9. Sachs and Hunger, *Astronomical Diaries,* 57, line 2.
10. Aaboe and Sachs, "Two Lunar Texts of the Achaemenid Period from Babylon," 18.
11. Van der Waerden, *Science Awakening II,* 126.
12. Ibid., 127.
13. Ibid., 144.
14. Sachs, "Babylonian Horoscopes," 54–57.
15. Ibid., 57.
16. Ibid., 60.
17. Van der Waerden, "Babylonian Astronomy II," 7.

18. See Plato, *Timaeus,* 42 (pp. 91–93).

19. Diogenes Laertius, *Lives of the Eminent Philosophers,* 2:45 (1:175).

20. Mekler, ed., *Academicorum Philosophorum Index Hercianensis,* p. 13, col. 3, 36.

21. Cumont, *Astrology and Religion among the Greeks and Romans,* 30.

22. Cicero, *De Divinatione,* 87, 2:xlii.

23. Neugebauer, *Astronomical Cuneiform Texts,* 22–23, 1:16.

24. Strabo, *Geography,* 6, 16:i (3:146).

25. Aaboe, "On Babylonian Planetary Theories," 210.

26. Neugebauer, *Astronomical Cuneiform Texts,* 1:7–8.

27. Ibid., 1:115.

28. VAT 7851 in Weidner, *Gestirn-Darstellungen auf babylonischen Tontafeln,* Tafel 1.

29. VAT 7847 in ibid., Tafeln 9 and 10. All three of these illustrations are depicted in Van der Waerden, *Science Awakening II,* 81.

30. Weidner, *Gestirn-Darstellungen auf babylonischen Tontafeln,* 22–23.

31. Pliny, *Natural History,* 7:37 (2:12).

32. Sachs, "Babylonian Horoscopes," 69.

33. Neugebauer and Van Hoesen, *Greek Horoscopes,* 76–78.

34. Proclus, *Procli Diadochi in Platonis Timaeum commentaria,* 24–29, 3:125.

35. Tardieu, "Sabiens Coraniques et 'Sabiens' de Harran," 22–23; Green, *City of the Moon God,* 167–68.

Chapter 17. Harran

1. Green, *City of the Moon God,* 100 (quoting Ibn Shaddad).

2. Tardieu, "Sabiens Coraniques," 13–18, 22–23.

3. Chwolsohn, *Die Ssabier,* 2:382–98.

4. Ibid., 381–82.

5. Stapleton, Azo, and Husain, "Chemistry in Iraq," and also Lloyd and Brice, "Harran," 97.

6. See Rice, "Studies in Medieval Harran," 44. See also Scott, *Hermetica,* 100, n. 1.

7. Rice, "Studies in Medieval Harran," 43 (quoting Dimashqi).

8. Lloyd and Brice, "Harran," 92, 94 (quoting Yaqut).

9. Ibid., 79, 102, and illustration on p. 103.

10. Ibid., 78.

11. For his report, see Rice, "Studies in Medieval Harran," 48ff

12. See "Harran," *Anatolian Studies* 10 (1960): 8.

13. See Scott, *Hermetica*, 97–99, quoting an-Nadim, who is translated in Chwolsohn, *Die Ssabier*, 2:14ff.

14. Scott, *Hermetica*, 101, n. 1.

15. Ibid., 92, quoting Porphyry's "Letter to Anebo."

16. *Asclepius*, in ibid., 289.

17. "Poimandres," in ibid., 115–17.

18. Green, *City of the Moon God*, 162.

19. Garin, *Astrology in the Renaissance*, 48, 54.

20. *Asclepius*, in Scott, *Hermetica*, 359.

21. Ibid., 361.

22. Ibid., 25.

23. Klibansky, *Continuity of the Platonic Tradition*, 19.

24. Yates, *Giordano Bruno*, 13.

25. Garin, *Astrology in the Renaissance*, 64–65.

Chapter 18. From Babylon to Botticelli

1. Woodhouse, *George Gemistos Plethon*, 8.

2. Garin, *Astrology in the Renaissance*, 58.

3. Ibid.

4. Ibid.

5. Ibid.

6. Yates, *Giordano Bruno*, 41.

7. Ibid., 45.

8. Walker, *Spiritual and Demonic Magic: From Ficino to Campanella*, 32–33. See also pp. 19 and 22–23.

9. Athanassakis, *Orphic Hymns*, no. 8, pp. 12–15.

10. Ficino, *Book of Life*, 90.

11. Ibid., 90–91 and 146–47.

12. Ibid., 131. See also Walker, *Spiritual and Demonic Magic*, 30–35.

13. Ibid., 110.

14. Ibid., 167.

15. Ibid., 181.

16. Scott, *Hermetica*, 361 (*Asclepius*, 3:38a). See also pp. 359, 339.

17. Yates, *Giordano Bruno*, 77.

18. Ibid., 77–78.

Bibliography

Aaboe, A. "On Babylonian Planetary Theories." *Centaurus* 5 (1958): 209–77.

Aaboe, A., and A. Sachs. "Two Lunar Texts of the Achaemenid Period from Babylon." *Centaurus* 14 (1969): 1–22.

Anastos, M. V. "Pletho's Calendar and Liturgy." *Dumbarton Oaks Papers* 4 (1948): 183–305.

Apuleius. *The Golden Ass.* Translated by Robert Graves. Harmondsworth, U.K.: Penguin Book, 1976.

Athanassakis, A. N. *The Orphic Hymns.* Atlanta, Ga.: Society of Biblical Literature, 1988.

Baigent, Michael, Nicholas Campion, and Charles Harvey. *Mundane Astrology: An Introduction to the Astrology of Nations and Groups.* Wellingborough, U.K.: Aquarian Press, 1984.

Bailey, L. R. "The Golden Calf." *Hebrew Union College Annual* 42 (1971): 97–115.

Begg, Ean. *The Cult of the Black Virgin.* London: Penguin Books, 1985.

Bibby, Geoffrey. *Looking for Dilmun.* London: Penguin Books, 1972.

Black, Jeremy, and Anthony Green. *Gods, Demons and Symbols of Ancient Mesopotamia.* London: British Museum Press, 1992.

Bouche-Leclercq, Auguste. *L'astrologie grecque.* Paris: Leroux, 1899.

Caplice, Richard. *The Akkadian Namburbu Texts.* Malibu, Calif.: Undena, 1974.

Chwolsohn, D. A. *Die Ssabier und der Ssabismus.* 2 vols. Saint Petersburg: Buchdruckerei der Kaiserlichen Akademie der Wissenschaften, 1856.

Cicero. *De Divinatione.* Translated by William Armistead Falconer. London: Heinemann, 1979.

Cornwall, P. B. "Two Letters from Dilmun." *Journal of Cuneiform Studies* 6, no. 4 (1952): 137–42.

Cumont, Franz. *Astrology and Religion among the Greeks and Romans.* New York and London: G. P. Putnam's Sons, 1912.

Curtis, John, ed. *Fifty Years of Mesopotamian Discovery.* London: The British School of Archaeology in Iraq, 1982.

Diodorus Siculus. *Diodorus of Sicily.* Translated by C. H. Oldfather and others. 9 vols. London: Heinemann, 1933.

Diogenes Laertius. *Lives of Eminent Philosophers.* Translated by R. D. Hicks. 2 vols. London: Heinemann, 1925.

Ebertin, Reinhold. *The Combination of Stellar Influences.* Translated by Alfred G. Roosedale and Linda Kratzsch. Reprint. Tempe, Ariz.: American Federation of Astrologers, 1981.

Fagan, Cyril. *Astrological Origins.* Saint Paul, Minn.: Llewellyn, 1971.

Ficino, Marsilio. *The Book of Life.* Translated by Charles Boer. Irving, Texas: Spring Publications, 1980.

Frankfort, Henri. *Kingship and the Gods.* Chicago: University of Chicago Press, 1978.

Frankfort, H., H. A. Frankfort, T. Jacobsen, and J. Wilson, eds. *Before Philosophy: The Intellectual Adventure of Ancient Man.* Baltimore: Penguin Books, 1971.

Gadd, C. J. "The Harran Inscriptions of Nabonidus." *Anatolian Studies* 8 (1958): 35–92.

———. *Ideas of Divine Rule in the Ancient East.* London: Oxford University Press, 1948.

Gallery, M. L. "Service Obligations of the Kezertu-Women." *Orientalia* 49 (1980): 333–38.

Garin, Eugenio. *Astrology in the Renaissance: The Zodiac of Life.* Translated by Carolyn Jackson and June Allen. London: Routledge, 1983.

Gill, Joseph. *The Council of Florence.* Cambridge: Cambridge University Press, 1959.

Gorman, Peter. *Pythagoras: A Life.* London: Routledge and Kegan Paul, 1979.

Green, H. S. *Mundane or National Astrology.* Reprint. North Hollywood: Symbols and Signs, 1977.

Green, Tamara. *City of the Moon God.* Leiden, Netherlands: Brill, 1992.

Greene, Liz. *The Astrology of Fate.* London: George Allen and Unwin, 1984.

Hartner, W. "Notes on *Picatrix*." *Isis* 56 (1965): 438–51.

Heidel, Alexander. *The Babylonian Genesis: The Story of Creation.* Chicago: University of Chicago Press, 1942.

———. *The Gilgamesh Epic and Old Testament Parallels.* Chicago: University of Chicago Press, 1963.

Heimpel, W. *A Catalogue of Near Eastern Venus Deities.* Malibu, Calif.: Undena, 1982.

Herodotus. *The Histories.* Translated by William Beloe. 2 vols. London, 1825.

Hesiod. *The Homeric Hymns and Homerica.* Translated by Hugh G. Evelyn-White. Reprint. London: Heinemann, 1977.

Heyerdahl, Thor. *The Tigris Expedition: In Search of Our Beginnings.* London: Allen and Unwin, 1980.

Hodson, F. R., ed. *The Place of Astronomy in the Ancient World.* London: Oxford University Press, 1974.

Hone, Margaret. *The Modern Text-Book of Astrology.* 2nd ed. London: L. N. Fowler, 1962.

Hooke, S. H. *Babylonian and Assyrian Religion.* London: Hutchinson's University Library, 1953.

Howard, M. "Technical Description of the Ivory Writing-Boards from Nimrud." *Iraq* 17 (1955): 14–20.

Huber, Peter J. *Astronomical Dating of Babylon I and Ur III.* Malibu, Calif.: Undena, 1982.

Hunger, H., and D. Pingree. *MUL.APIN: An Astronomical Compendium in Cuneiform.* Horn, Austria: F. Berger, 1989.

Jacobsen, Thorkild. "Mesopotamia." In *Before Philosophy,* edited by H. Frankfort, H. A. Frankfort, T. Jacobsen, and J. Wilson. Baltimore: Penguin Books, 1971.

———. *The Sumerian King List.* Chicago: University of Chicago Press, 1939.

———. *The Treasures of Darkness.* New Haven, Conn.: Yale University Press, 1976.

Jung, C. G. *Aion.* Translated by R. F. C. Hull. 2nd ed. London: Routledge and Kegan Paul, 1978.

———. *Memories, Dreams, Reflections.* London, 1979.

Klibansky, Raymond. *The Continuity of the Platonic Tradition during the Middle Ages.* London: London Warburg Institute, 1939.

Kollerstrom, N. "The Star Temples of Harran." In *History and Astrology,* edited by Annabella Kitson, 47–60. London: Unwin Paperbacks, 1989.

Kramer, Samuel Noah. *History Begins at Sumer: Thirty-nine Firsts in Recorded History.* London: Thames and Hudson, 1958.

————. *The Sumerians.* Chicago: University of Chicago Press, 1963.

Kristeller, Paul Oskar. *Renaissance Concepts of Man.* New York: Harper and Row, 1972.

Labat, R. *Manuel d'épigraphic akkadienne.* Paris: Librarie Orientaliste Paul Geuthner, 1952.

Lambert, W. G. "A Part of the Ritual for the Substitute King." *Archiv für Orientforschung* 18 (1957–58): 109–12.

————. "The Ritual for the Substitute King: A New Fragment." *Archiv für Orientjorschung* 19 (1959–60): 119.

————. "Three Literary Prayers of the Babylonians." *Archiv für Orientforschung* 19 (1959–60): 47–66.

————. "Two Texts from the Early Part of the Reign of Ashurbanipal." *Archiv für Orientjorschung* 18 (1957–58): 382–87.

Lambert, W. G., and A. R. Millard. *Atra-Hasis: The Babylonian Story of the Flood.* Oxford, UK: Clarendon, 1969.

Landsberger, B., and J. V. Kinner Wilson. "The Fifth Tablet of the *Enuma Elis.*" *Journal of Near Eastern Studies* 20 (1961): 154–69.

Langdon, Steven H. *The Babylonian Epic of Creation.* Oxford, UK: Clarendon, 1923.

————. *Semitic Mythology.* New York: Cooper Square, 1964.

————. *The Venus Tablets of Ammizaduqa.* London: Oxford University Press, 1928.

Laroche, E. "Catalogue des textes hittites." *Revue hittite et asianique* 14 (1956): 32–38, 69–116; 15 (1957): 30–89; 16 (1958): 18–64.

Layard, Austen Henry. *Discoveries in the Ruins of Nineveh and Babylon.* London: John Murray, 1853.

————. *Nineveh and Its Remains.* 2 vols. London: John Murray, 1849.

Lilly, William. *Christian Astrology.* London: John Partridge, 1647.

Livingstone, Alasdair. *Mystical and Mythological Explanatory Works of Assyrian and Babylonian Scholars.* Oxford, U.K.: Clarendon, 1986.

Lloyd, Seton. *The Archaeology of Mesopotamia.* London: Thames and Hudson, 1978.

————. *Foundations in the Dust.* Rev. ed. London: Thames and Hudson, 1980.

Lloyd, S., and W. Brice. "Harran." *Anatolian Studies* 1 (1951): 77–111.

Mallowan, Max Edgar Lucien. *Nimrud and Its Remains.* London: Collins, 1966.

Mayo, Jeff. *The Planets and Human Behavior.* Romford, U.K.: Fowler, 1973.

Meissner, B. "Über Genethlialogie bei den Babylonieren." *Klio* 19 (1925): 432–34.

Mekler, S., ed. *Academicorum Philosophorum Index Hercianensis.* Berlin: Weidmann, 1902.

Mellaart, James. *Earliest Civilisations of the Near East.* London: Thames and Hudson, 1978.

Neugebauer, O. *Astronomical Cuneiform Texts.* 3 vols. London: Lund Humphries, 1955.

———. *The Exact Sciences in Antiquity.* Providence, R.I.: Brown University Press, 1957.

———. "The Water Clock in Babylonian Astronomy." *Isis* 37 (1947): 37–43.

Neugebauer, O., and Pingree, D. *The Pancasiddhantika of Varahamihira.* 2 vols. Copenhagen: Munksgaard, 1970–71.

Neugebauer, O., and H. B. Van Hoesen. *Greek Horoscopes.* Philadelphia: American Philosophical Society, 1959.

Oates, Joan. *Babylon.* London: Thames and Hudson, 1979.

Oppenheim, A. Leo. "A Babylonian Diviner's Manual." *Journal of Near Eastern Studies* 33 (1974): 197–210.

———. *Ancient Mesopotamia.* Rev. ed. Chicago: University of Chicago Press, 1977.

———. "Divination and Celestial Observation in the Last Assyrian Empire." *Centaurus* 14 (1969): 97–135.

———. "Perspectives on Mesopotamian Divination." In *La divination en Mésopotamie ancienne.* Rencontre Assyriologique Internationale. Paris: Presses Universitaires de France, 1966.

———. "The Position of the Intellectual in Mesopotamian Society." *Daedalus* (Spring 1975): 37–46.

Pallis, Svend Aage. *The Babylonian Akitu Festival.* Copenhagen: Bianco Lunos Bogtrykkeri, 1926.

———. *Early Explorations in Mesopotamia.* Copenhagen: I kommission hos Munksgaard, 1954.

Parpola, S. "Assyrian Library Records." *Journal of Near Eastern Studies* 42 (1983): 1–29.

———. *Letters from Assyrian Scholars to the Kings Esarhaddon and Assurbanipal.* 2 vols. Neukirchen-Vluyn, Germany: Butzon & Bercker / Neukirchener Verlag, 1970–83.

Parrot, Andre. *The Tower of Babel.* Translated by Edwin Hudson. London: SCM Press, 1955.

Pausanias. *Description of Greece.* Translated by W. H. S. Jones. 5 vols. London: Heinemann, 1918–35.

Pearce, Alfred. *The Text-Book of Astrology.* London: Mackie, 1911.

Pfeiffer, Robert Henry. *State Letters of Assyria.* New Haven, Conn.: American Oriental Society, 1935.

Pingree, D. "Mesopotamian Astronomy and Astral Omens in Other Civilizations." In *Mesopotamien und seine Nachbarn,* edited by Hans-Jörg Nissen and Johannes Renger, 613–31. Berlin: Reimer, 1982.

———. "Some of the Sources of the *Ghayat al-hakim.*" *Journal of the Warburg and Courtauld Institutes* 43 (1980): 1–15.

Pingree, D., and E. Reiner. "A Neo-Babylonian Report on Seasonal Hours." *Archiv für Orientjorschung* 25 (1974–77): 50–55.

Place, Victor. *Ninive et l'Assyrie.* 3 vols. Paris: Imprimerie impériale, 1867–70.

Plato. *Timaeus.* Translated by R. G. Bury. London: Heinemann, 1981.

Pliny. *The Natural History.* Translated by John Bostock and H. T. Riley. 6 vols. London: Bohn's Classical Library, 1855–57.

Pomponio. *Nabu.* Rome: Istituto di Studi del Vicino Oriente, 1978.

Pritchard, James B. *Ancient Near Eastern Texts Relating to the Old Testament.* 2nd ed. Princeton, N.J.: Princeton University Press, 1955.

———, ed. *The Ancient Near East.* Vol. 2. Princeton, N.J.: Princeton University Press, 1975.

Proclus. *Procli Diadochi in Platonis Timaeum commentaria.* Edited by Ernestus Diehl. Leipzig, Germany: Teubner, 1903.

Ptolemy. *Tetrabiblos.* Translated by F. E. Robbins. Cambridge, Mass.: Harvard University Press/London: Heinemann, 1971.

Ramesey, William. *Astrology Restored.* London: R. White, 1653–55.

Raphael. *Mundane Astrology.* London: Foulsham, circa 1910.

Rassam, Hormuzd. *Asshur and the Land of Nimrod.* New York: Eston and Mains, 1897.

Rawlinson, George. *A Memoir of Major-General Sir Henry Creswicke Rawlinson.* London: Longmans, Green, and Co., 1898.

Rawlinson, H. C. "On the Birs Nimrud, or the Great Temple of Borsippa." *Journal of the Royal Asiatic Society* 18 (1861): 1–33.

Reiner, E. *Enuma Anu Enlil, Tablets 50–51.* Malibu, Calif.: Undena, 1981.

———. *The Venus Tablet of Ammisaduqa.* Malibu, Calif.: Undena, 1975.

Rice, O. S. "Studies in Medieval Harran." *Anatolian Studies* 2 (1952): 36–83.

Ringgren, H. *Religions of the Ancient Near East.* Translated by John Sturdy. London: SPCK, 1973.

Ritter, H., and M. Plessner, trans. *"Picatrix": Das Ziel des Weisen von Pseudo-Magriti.* Studies of the Warburg Institute 27. London: Warburg Institute, 1962.

Roberts, J. J. M. *The Earliest Semitic Pantheon*. Baltimore: Johns Hopkins University Press, 1972.

Robinson, James M., ed. *The Nag Hammadi Library in English*. Leiden, Netherlands: Brill, 1977.

Rochberg-Halton, Francesca. *Aspects of Babylonian Celestial Divination: The Lunar Eclipse Tablets of Enuma Anu Enlil*. Horn, Austria: F. Berger, 1988.

———. "Babylonian Cosmology." In *The Encyclopedia of Cosmology: Historical, Philosophical, and Scientific Foundations of Modern Cosmology*, edited by N. Hetherington. New York: Garland, 1993.

———. "Fate and Divination in Mesopotamia." *Archiv für Orientforschung* 19 (1982): 363–71.

Roux, Georges. *Ancient Iraq*. Reprint. Harmondsworth, UK: Penguin Books, 1977.

Sachs, A. "Babylonian Horoscopes." *Journal of Cuneiform Studies* 6 (1952): 49–75.

———. "Babylonian Observational Astronomy." *Philosophical Transactions of the Royal Society* 276 (1974): 43–50.

———. "A Late Babylonian Star Catalogue." *Journal of Cuneiform Studies* 6 (1952): 146–50.

Sachs, A., and H. Hunger. *Astronomical Diaries and Related Texts from Babylonia*. 2 vols. Vienna: Austrian Academy of Sciences, 1988–89.

Saggs, H. W. F. *The Encounter with the Divine in Mesopotamia and Israel*. London: Athlone Press, 1978.

———. *The Greatness That Was Babylon*. London: Sidgwick and Jackson, 1962.

Sayce, A. H. "The Astronomy and Astrology of the Babylonians." *Transactions of the Society of Biblical Archaeology* 3 (1974): 145–339.

Scheil, V. "Notules." *Revue d'assyriologie et d'archiologie orientale* 14, no. 3 (1917): 135–44.

Scott, W., ed. *Hermetica*. Reprint, Boulder, Colo.: Hermes House, 1982. Originally published in Oxford, U.K.: Clarendon, 1924–36.

Sileico, V. "Mondlaufprognosen aus der Zeit der ersten babylonischen Dynastie." *Zeitschrift für Assyriologie,* new series, 9, no. 43 (1936): 308–14.

Stapleton, H. E. "The Antiquity of Alchemy." *Ambix* 5 (1953): 1–43.

Stapleton, H. E., R. F. Azo, and M. H. Husain. "Chemistry in Iraq and Persia in the Tenth Century AD." *Memoirs of the Asiatic Society of Bengal* 8 (1927): 340–43, 398–404.

Starr, Ivan. *Queries to the Sun God*. Helsinki: Helsinki University Press, 1990.

———. *The Rituals of the Diviner.* Malibu, Calif.: Undena, 1983.

Strabo. *Geography.* Translated by H. C. Hamilton and W. Falconer. 3 vols. London: Henry G. Bohn, 1854–57.

Tallqvist, Knut. *Babyloniska Hymner och Böner.* Helsinki: Finska orient-sällskapet, 1953.

Tardieu, M. "Sabiens Coraniques et 'Sabiens' de Harran." *Journal Asiatique* 274 (1986): 1–44.

Thompson, R. Campbell. *The Reports of the Magicians and Astrologers of Nineveh and Babylon in the British Museum.* 2 vols. London: Luzac, 1900.

Thureau-Dangin, François. *Rituels accadiens.* Paris: Leroux, 1921.

Toulmin, Stephen, and June Goodfield. *The Fabric of the Heavens.* London: Hutchinson, 1961.

Van der Waerden, B. L. "Babylonian Astronomy II: The Thirty Six Stars." *Journal of Near Eastern Studies* 8 (1949): 6–26.

———. "Babylonian Astronomy III: The Earliest Astronomical Computations." *Journal of Near Eastern Studies* 10 (1951): 20–34.

———. "History of the Zodiac." *Archiv für Orientforschung* 16 (1953): 216–30.

———. *Science Awakening II: The Birth of Astronomy.* Leiden, Netherlands: Noordhoff International Publishing, 1974.

Virolleaud, C. "The Syrian Town of Katna." *Antiquity* 3 (1929): 312–17.

Walker, D. P. *Spiritual and Demonic Magic: From Ficino to Campanella.* Notre Dame, Ind.: University of Notre Dame Press, 1975.

Wallis-Budge, E. A. *By Nile and Tigris.* 2 vols. London: John Murray, 1920.

———. *The Rise and Progress of Assyriology.* London: Martin Hopkinson, 1925.

Waterman, Leroy. *Royal Correspondence of the Assyrian Empire.* 4 vols. Ann Arbor: University of Michigan Press, 1930.

Watters, Barbara H. *Horary Astrology and the Judgment of Events.* Redmond, Washington: Valhalla, 1973.

Weidner, E. F. "Die astrologische Serie *Enuma Anu Enlil.*" *Archiv für Orientforschung* 14 (1941–44): 172–95, 308–18.

———. "Die astrologische Serie *Enuma Anu Enlil.*" *Archiv für Orientforschung* 17 (1954–56): 71–89.

———. "Die astrologische Serie *Enuma Anu Enlil.*" *Archiv für Orientforschung* 22 (1968–69): 65–75.

———. "Ein Hauskalender aus dem alten Babylonien." *Rivista degli Studi Orientali* 32 (1957): 185–96.

———. *Gestirn-Darstellungen auf babylonischen Tontafeln. Sitzungsberichte*

(Österreichische Akademie der Wissenschaften), 254, Band 2. Vienna: Hermann Böhlaus, 1967.

———. *Handbuch der babylonischen Astronomie*. Leipzig, Germany: J. C. Hinrichs, 1915.

———. "Historisches Material in der babylonischen Omina-Literatur." *Altorientalische Studien*. Edited by Bruno Meissner. Leipzig, Germany: Harrassowitz, 1928–29.

Wiseman, D. J. "Assyrian Writing-Boards." *Iraq* 17 (1955): 3–13.

Woodhouse, Christopher M. *George Gemistos Plethon: The Last of the Hellenes*. Oxford, UK: Clarendon, 1986.

Woolley, Charles L. *The Sumerians*. New York: Norton, 1965.

Yates, Frances. *Giordano Bruno and the Hermetic Tradition*. London: Routledge and Kegan Paul, 1978.

Zafran, E. "Saturn and the Jews." *Journal of the Warburg and Courtauld Institutes* 42 (1979): 16–27.

Zosimus. *The History of Count Zosimus*. London: J. Davis, 1814.

INDEX

Books of Related Interest

Secrets of Ancient America
Archaeoastronomy and the Legacy of the Phoenicians,
Celts, and Other Forgotten Explorers
by Carl Lehrburger

Ancient Giants Who Ruled America
The Missing Skeletons and the Great Smithsonian Cover-Up
by Richard J. Dewhurst

Land of the Fallen Star Gods
The Celestial Origins of Ancient Egypt
by J. S. Gordon

Göbekli Tepe: Genesis of the Gods
The Temple of the Watchers and the Discovery of Eden
by Andrew Collins
Introduction by Graham Hancock

Slave Species of the Gods
The Secret History of the Anunnaki and Their Mission on Earth
by Michael Tellinger

The Voynich Manuscript
The Mysterious Code That Has Defied Interpretation for Centuries
by Gerry Kennedy and Rob Churchill

The Suppressed History of America
The Murder of Meriwether Lewis and the
Mysterious Discoveries of the Lewis and Clark Expedition
by Paul Schrag and Xaviant Haze

The Lost Book of Enki
Memoirs and Prophecies of an Extraterrestrial God
by Zecharia Sitchin

INNER TRADITIONS • BEAR & COMPANY
P.O. Box 388
Rochester, VT 05767
1-800-246-8648
www.InnerTraditions.com

Or contact your local bookseller